*Hilkhot Avelut*

Understanding the Laws of Mourning

RCA

מגיד

MAGGID

Rabbi David Brofsky

# HILKHOT AVELUT

## UNDERSTANDING THE LAWS OF MOURNING

Rabbinical Council of America

Maggid Books

*Hilkhot Avelut*
*Understanding the Laws of Mourning*

First Edition, 2019

*Maggid Books*
*An imprint of Koren Publishers Jerusalem Ltd.*

POB 8531, New Milford, CT 06776-8531, USA
& POB 4044, Jerusalem 9104001, Israel
www.maggidbooks.com



The publication of this book was made possible
through the generous support of *Torah Education in Israel.*



ISBN 978-1-59264-461-2, *hardcover*

A CIP catalogue record for this title is
available from the British Library

Printed and bound in the United States

*This book is dedicated by the Smilowitz family in loving memory of*

*Herbert Smilowitz z"l*
חיים בן משה הלוי ז״ל

*whose gentle wisdom, quiet dignity, and humble generosity touched all who had the good fortune to know him.*

*In memory of Yonatan Adler z"l,*
*whose memory will always be with us.*
*Yonatan's character and principles will always inspire us to be more committed, idealistic, principled, and thoughtful people.*

*To Mali*
*For your encouragement, support, partnership, friendship and love.*

*To Yehuda, Shira, Yonatan and Hadar*
*May it be His will that you will continue to follow the ways of God through Torah study, mitzvot, and concern for others.*

Rabbi Mordechai Willig
4499 Henry Hudson Parkway
Riverdale, New York 10471
718.796.8208

מרדכי ווילִיג
ריווערדיל, נוא יארק

ד׳ אייר תשע״ח

דיני אבילות רבים הם, החל ממקורות
הגמרא שבכתב ותורה שבעל פה, המבוארים
ע״י הראשונים וגדולי האחרונים עד לפוסקי זמננו.
אבל, כמו שהדגיש מו״ר הגרי״ד סולובייצ׳יק זצ״ל,
עיקר קיומם בלב. ולכן לימוד ההלכות למעשה
ביחד עם היסודות והטעמים נחוץ ביותר במקצוע זה.

ספרו של ידידי הרב דוד ברופסקי שליט״א,
כקודמיו על הלכות תפלה והלכות מועדים, הוא
מיזוג נפלא של הדינים בקיצור עם היסודות באריכות
ובעומק, בבהירות ובפשטות. רישומם של רבותיו הגדולים
ניכר בסגנון הרצאתו, ומסירותו לפסק הלכה למעשה
בולטת מבאוריו הברורים בדברי גדולי הפוסקים.

יהי רצון שהמחבר שליט״א ימשיך לזכות עם ישראל ע״י
ספריו ושיעוריו מתוך בריאות נחת והרחבה ממש

בברכת התורה המוקירו
מרדכי ווילִיג

**Rabbi Mordechai Willig**
4499 Henry Hudson Parkway
Riverdale, New York 10471

מרדכי ווילig
ריווערדיל, נוא יארק

10 Iyyar 5778

There are many laws relevant to mourning with sources in both the Written and Oral Torah, which have been illuminated by the *Rishonim* and *Aḥaronim* through contemporary *posekim*. However, as Rav Soloveitchik *zt"l* emphasized, the primary observance of mourning occurs in the heart. And for this reason, particularly in this area of halakha, it is vitally important to learn the practical laws together with their conceptual foundations.

This volume, authored by Rav David Brofsky *shlit"a* – like his earlier works on the laws of prayer and the laws of the festivals – marks a masterful blend of concise halakhot and elaborate, in-depth discussion of their underlying principles, presented in a clear, comprehensive fashion. The influence of his outstanding mentors is clearly discernible in his style of presentation, and his devotion to practical halakhic ruling is expressed in his analysis of the writings of leading *posekim*.

May the author continue to bring glory to the Almighty through his lectures and written works amid good health and prosperity, *ad me'ah ve'esrim shana*.

Fondly,
Mordechai Willig

# יוסף צבי רימון

רבה של אלון שבות דרום
ראש בתי המדרש ורב המרכז האקדמי לב
ראש מרכז הלכה והוראה

רחוב קבוצת אברהם 10
אלון שבות 9043300

משרד: 02-9933644
נייד: 052-5456060
פקס: 153-2-9933644

rimonim613@gmail.com


בס"ד, אסרו חג שבועות ה'תשע"ח

מכתב ברכה

הלכות אבלות מיוחדים הם בכך שפרט לידיעת הדינים בגמרא ובראשונים ופרט לידיעת השולחן ערוך והפוסקים, יש צורך לדעת היטב גם את מנהגי האבלות המקובלים בדורנו. אמר לי פעם מו"ר הרב אהרן ליכטנשטיין זצ"ל, שלעתים הוא מתוסכל מכך שלמרות שהוא יודע את הגמרא והראשונים והפוסקים בנושא מסוים בהלכות אבלות, הרי שהוא לא יכול לפסוק למעשה מבלי להסתכל בגשר החיים, בכדי לדעת את המנהג המקובל כיום.

הרב דוד ברופסקי שליט"א, תושב קהילתנו אלון שבות, זכה להוציא כמה ספרי הלכה מאירים, המביאים את יסודות הגמרא והראשונים ומגיעים עד להלכה למעשה. ספרים הכתובים בצורה ידידותית ונעימה.

בספר זה, ניתן לראות פרט לדרכו בלימוד ובהלכה גם את הרגישות האנושית שלו. בכמה מקומות באה לידי ביטוי הרגישות לאבל או לסביבתו, בניסוח ההלכות מחד, וביישומם למעשה מאידך.

דוגמה לכך ניתן לראות בדבריו על ילדים מאומצים. ישנם פוסקים שכתבו שאין שום עניין באבלות במקרה זה. הרב ברופסקי נוקט כדברי הפוסקים הסבורים שיש מקום לאבלות גם במקרה זה, אולם, ברגישות רבה, הוא דואג לתת מקום לאבל להתגמש במקרה זה בדיני האבלות בהתאם למצבו הרגיש, ומתוך הבנה שאין זו חובה ממשית כמו כל אבל. פרט לכך, שם לב לדקדק בפרטי הדברים בכך שאמנם יכול הילד המאומץ לקבל עליו דיני אבלות, אך לא יהיה פטור ממצוות ואין עליו את הפטורים של האנינות. כמו כן, גם ביחס לקדיש, לא תהיה כיום בעיה לילד מאומץ לומר קדיש, שהרי כל האבלים אומרים כיום את הקדיש כאחד, אולם, ביחס לתפילה לפני העמוד, הרי שלאנשים אחרים האבלים על אב ואם ביולוגים תהיה קדימות. בכך הוא משרטט בקצרה את המורכבות של הילד המאומץ, שמצד אחד איננו חייב בדיני אבילות באופן רגיל, ומצד שני ראוי מאוד שינהג באבילות מדין הכרת הטוב.

נאחל לרב ברופסקי שליט"א, שיזכה להוסיף לזכות את עם ישראל בכתיבת ספרי הלכה נוספים, ללמוד וללמד, לשמור ולעשות ולקיים.

בברכת התורה והמצווה,

יוסף צבי רימון

יוסף צבי רימו

רבה של אלון שבות דרום
ראש בתי המדרש ורב המרכז האקדמי ל
ראש מרכז הלכה והוראה

רחוב קבוצת אברהם 10
אלון שבות 9043300

משרד: 02-9933644
נ"יד: 052-5456060
פקס: 153-2-9933644

rimonim613@gmail.com


BS"D, Issru Ḥag Shavuot, 5778

A Letter of Recommendation

The laws of mourning are unique in that aside from knowledge of the laws as they appear in the Gemara and Rishonim, and aside from knowledge of the *Shulḥan Arukh* and the *posekim*, it is necessary to be familiar with the accepted customs of our generation. My teacher, Rav Lichtenstein, *zt"l*, once told me that he was often frustrated because despite his knowledge of the Gemara, Rishonim, and *posekim* regarding a certain topic of *avelut*, he was unable to offer a practical halakhic ruling without looking at the *Gesher Haḥaim*, in order to know the currently accepted custom.

Rav David Brofsky, *shlit"a*, a resident of Alon Shevut, has published a number of enlightening halakha books, which present the foundations of the law as they appear in the Gemara and Rishonim, and concluding with the practical halakha. These books are written in a friendly, pleasant manner.

In this book, in addition to his method in learning and halakha, one can perceive his sensitivity as well. In a number of places his concern for the mourner or his surroundings is evident, in his formulation of the laws and in their practical application.

We see an example of this in his treatment of adopted children. There are *posekim* who write that there is no reason to mourn in this case (i.e., for adoptive parents). Rav Brofsky, however, adopts the position of those *posekim* who maintain that there is room for *avelut* even in this situation, however, with great sensitivity, he makes sure to leave room for the mourner to be flexible in accordance with his situation, understanding that there is no formal obligation, as there is with other mourners. In addition, Rav Brofsky pays attention to the details, and writes that although an adopted child may accept upon himself laws of mourning, he is not exempt from the performance of mitzvot and he is not subject to the laws of *aninut*. Similarly, regarding the Kaddish, while there is no problem for an adopted child to recite Kaddish, as nowadays all of the mourners recite the Kaddish in unison, those mourning their biological parents still have precedence in leading the prayers. In this manner he briefly outlines the complexity of being an adopted child, who on the one hand, is not formally obligated in the laws of mourning, yet on the other, it is appropriate that he should mourn out of a sense of *hakarat hatov* (gratitude).

Let us wish Rav Brofsky, *shlit"a*, that he should continue to benefit the public by writing additional halakhic works, and to learn and teach, fulfill, act and perform.

With Torah blessings,

Yosef Zvi Rimon

# Contents

*Foreword*

# Two Faces of Halakha

When my father, Herbert Smilowitz *z"l*, suddenly collapsed and passed away on *Taanit Esther* 5774, I felt like my world fell apart. Then, halakha put it back together.

I had just put down the phone in my Beit Shemesh home after learning from my sister that my father had died in America. My father was a foundational figure in our family, and grasping that his life was over seemed impossible. I was not prepared for the shock, and it is difficult to describe in words how I felt at that moment, but I feel an obligation to try, if only to give testimony to how halakhic commitment can impact a person's inner world.

I hung up the phone and sat down, but inside I felt a sense of falling, like I were tumbling down a bottomless black hole, even though I knew in the back of my mind that I was sitting on my couch. Although I was obviously in no physical danger, I was gripped by an increasing sense of terror. What was I scared of? Perhaps I felt trapped in an unfamiliar world of swirling negative emotion, and I could see no path by which to emerge. Suddenly I noticed from the corner of my eye that my wife was holding a book on the halakhot of mourning. I asked Michelle for the book, and as I scanned the pages, reviewing the laws of *keria* (tearing the garments) and *kevura* (burial), I felt a certain calm come over me. Order and meaning started to return to my world. The terror dissipated and I felt that although there was still much sorrow and grief to go through, this brief brush with insanity – for it felt like insanity – was over.

How did this happen? How did halakha rescue me from my descent? My reflections have led me to conclude that halakha presents two faces that complement each other, and that the two in combination can offer redemption for the halakhic devotee even in the most trying of times.

Halakha is law, and law is stability. When the vicissitudes of life leave one dizzy and disoriented, the human spirit yearns for stability and reliability. The first face of halakha is the rock of law that stabilizes and redeems the storm-tossed soul.

Most systems of law are not capable of doing this. But being a communication of God's will, halakhic laws are rooted in eternity. To study and keep halakha is to join hands with God, so to speak. I recall that just before the circumcision of one of my sons, I was asked by a relative if I was afraid. I said no, because I knew that at that moment I was doing exactly what God wanted me to do. Halakha connects a person to the permanent and the eternal, and in so doing, brings serenity and tranquility and dissolves fear and doubt.

To say that halakha provides a sense of permanence and stability is not to say that it is stagnant, as if there is no movement or innovation in it. As the pages of this book show, halakha is an ongoing discourse, as sages throughout the generations seek to clarify areas that remain undefined or to grapple with new situations. Nevertheless, there always remains a firm halakhic bedrock of immutable laws. Newly adopted rules and customs can achieve an air of permanence if accepted by the Jewish people at large, as R. Yosef Dov Soloveitchik has shown us in his Hebrew essay, "Two Types of Tradition."[1] And even while our sages demonstrate the highest levels of ingenuity and creativity in their halakhic discourse, they are guided by rules of legal discourse that themselves are timeless and immutable.

This, then, is the first face of halakha, the firmly anchored permanence of law. At times this face of the law can appear friendly, but at other times it can make inconvenient demands. As consoling as the customs of *shiva* may be, there are times where *shiva* is canceled due to a higher halakhic priority, and the mourner has to manage without the usual support. At such times we are reminded that halakha is not just a kind of religious therapy,

1. R. Yosef Dov Soloveitchik, "*Shnei Sugei Masoret*," in *Shiurim LeZekher Abba Mari* (Jerusalem, 1983), vol. 1, pp. 220–39.

but an expression of service and sacrifice in response to the Almighty's communication to us of His will. Even then, despite the emotional and personal challenges involved, there is something profoundly redemptive and dignifying in expressing such commitment and devotion, in obeying God's higher will with humility.

The mood of today's general society, despite its openness to multiple cultures, remains suspicious of the idea of halakhic living, recoiling from what people perceive as a robot-like conformity. But this, of course, would be a poor caricature of halakhic life. As I have said, obedience to God's will can in itself be redemptive because it allows us to reach up to the eternal and the permanent, but halakha also presents a second face that adds a new dimension, in which it reaches down from above and penetrates deep into our inner experience. Halakhic living involves a rich and vibrant subjective experience stimulated by thoughtful reflection on the specific content of the laws and their meanings. More than just a collection of laws, halakha is also a thought system reflecting a worldview. Each rule connects to other rules in a sophisticated network of meaningful interaction; behind every regulation stands an intricately and expertly woven conceptual and historical tapestry full of life, color, and beauty.

The ideas, meanings, and messages undergirding the interrelated laws of halakha are not usually spelled out explicitly, and can be easily overlooked. Much has been said about how halakha and *hashkafa* (Jewish worldview or philosophy) are separate disciplines. This distinction is important, because what if my *hashkafa* leads me to conclusions that contradict the codified law? The Orthodox halakhic community has always held that the rock of law takes priority over the philosophy of law. As R. Soloveitchik explains in *The Halakhic Mind*, Jewish philosophy properly done emerges from the halakha, and is not a decider of halakha. In cases where philosophy and halakha clash, such a conflict may be a signal to revise the philosophical conclusions.

Nevertheless, a philosophy of Judaism can emerge through halakhic study, a philosophy that addresses our deepest thoughts and feelings. Thus, halakha is not only a rigorous master; it is also a nurturing teacher. As R. Soloveitchik describes in *And From There You Shall Seek*, through intellectual mastery of halakha, fear of God blossoms into love of God, and servile obedience turns into *dveikut*, cleaving to Him. If the first face of halakha invites me to join hands with God through action, the second face summons me to join minds with God, as it were, through understanding.

This second face of halakha, not a rock of stability but a springboard of thought, also helped to save me on that unfortunate night. The book my wife handed me merely listed the laws and did not provide background, but I was fortunate that my previous study in yeshiva of the laws of mourning provided enough context to help me remember and intuit the meanings, feelings, and concepts associated with the details of the various laws.

During *avelut* for my father *z"l*, members of my family and I felt we wanted a book that presented the laws as such but also provided the conceptual and historical framework of those various customs and laws, a framework that would help stimulate philosophical and hashkafic reflection as well as clarify practice. We wanted to see *both* faces of halakha. Knowing Rabbi David Brofsky for many years, having studied together with him in yeshiva and having seen his excellent work in his earlier books on the laws of prayer and the laws of the festivals, I knew he was an ideal author for this undertaking. One advantage of this work is that by differentiating between biblical obligations, rabbinic requirements, and that which resides in the realm of custom, it allows us to discover more easily the fundamental principles and structures that give rise to the various details of the law. This book is also of great value because it considers opinions cited in the halakhic literature that are not necessarily practiced; nevertheless, such opinions can often illuminate hidden meanings behind the laws. And the style of the book, which tells the story of the give-and-take found in responsa and other halakhic writings, also provides glimpses into the world of thought behind the law.

While Judaism has always advanced the cause of educating the layman in halakha, in many cases a rabbinic authority will need to be consulted. Expert opinion is necessary not only to avoid error, but to sustain community standards. While Judaism has always honored and valued various forms of individualism – one life is worth the world (Mishna Sanhedrin 4:5) – it is also communitarian, preferring consensus over "every man doing what is right in his eyes" (Deut. 12:8; Judges 17:6, 21:25). Still, even when one consults an authority, a book of this kind can help the layman formulate the appropriate questions, participate in the discussion, and appreciate the answer. Furthermore, there may be times when the halakhic authority concludes that there is no fixed law in the matter at hand, and he may leave the matter to the preference of the questioner; in such cases, the rigid face of strict halakhic law may open a path for the more creative and flexible face of halakhic thought to guide the practitioner. The knowledge acquired from this book will be very useful then as well.

As I reflect on my father's memory I see both faces of halakha. Halakha provided him a steadiness and dependability, demonstrated in many ways, perhaps primarily through his devotion to attending daily *minyan,* as well as through the respect and deference he showed to rabbinic authorities. Halakha also provided him with a worldview, especially in the way his particular style of halakhic living emphasized human dignity, humility, and community. This volume is a fitting tribute to his memory, and I hope that many will find it useful and meaningful in their own halakhic observance.

Rabbi Mark Smilowitz
Beit Shemesh, Nisan 5778

# *Introduction*

In his masterful and popular work, *The Jewish Way in Death and Mourning,* the late Rabbi Maurice Lamm wrote about the dilemma in producing a work on mourning. He noted, "The futility can be expressed in a paradox simply stated: People do not wish to learn about how to deal with death until they are confronted with death, and when they are confronted with death, they are not inclined to study how religion approaches it."

Although this is certainly true, a rabbi is asked more questions in *Hilkhot Avelut* than in any other area of halakha. The questions posed often include when and if to say *Viduy* with the dying patient, and how to treat the dying during the state of *gesisa*. Further issues arise in deciding when to declare death and how to treat the body once death has been established.

These are the immediate questions that one confronts. As soon as death occurs more issues must be addressed, including the handling of the body, the *tahara,* the preparations for the funeral, as well as the role of the eulogy. The unique period of *aninut* also requires special attention and halakhic responses.

From burial through the *shiva* period, halakhic issues arise and immediate answers are required. After *shiva* and through the *sheloshim* new realities surface, while the twelve months of mourning for a parent create their own questions of what is permitted and what is prohibited.

This work addresses all these issues and many more, focusing on the halakhic debate and analysis while sharing the halakhic consensus and allowing for practical reference. A special feature of this work is a compendium of practical decisions that can be referred to for immediate use.

Rabbi Brofsky's brilliant ability to clarify the most complicated halakhic problems in a coherent and user-friendly fashion will make this work a must-have *sefer* that deserves to be found in every Torah library in the English-speaking world.

The Rabbinical Council of America is honored and delighted to partner with Maggid Books in presenting this work to the public. Rabbi Brofsky is a highly regarded member of the RCA who has earned the respect of his colleagues as a master halakhic writer and a brilliant exponent of Torah.

Until the prophetic vision of Isaiah is fulfilled, "and death is wiped from the face of the earth," may this work guide all its readers in appreciating the halakhic rulings in *Hilkhot Avelut.*

Rabbi Elazar Muskin
President, RCA

# *Preface*

When I was first approached regarding the possibility of writing a halakhic compendium on the laws of mourning, I was not only honored, but also intrigued and intimidated. The laws of *avelut* are particularly interesting, but writing an in-depth yet practical treatise seemed daunting, for a number of reasons.

First, I am fervent believer in exploring both the conceptual and philosophical aspects of Torah. The laws of *avelut* are especially intriguing, as the study of these halakhot reveals the interplay between the halakhic categories and the emotional, psychological, and sociological experiences. Although R. Yosef Dov Soloveitchik often related to the action (*maase*) and fulfillment (*kiyum*) of the mitzvot, his description of the relationship between the mourning practices and inner grieving (*avelut shebalev*) is particularly powerful. The laws and customs of *avelut* simultaneously reflect and create the mourning experience; the structure of the *avelut* categories and their details guide the mourner through the various stages of grieving.

Second, I felt a great burden and heavy responsibility to present the mourner with the fundamental principles, the development of and rationale behind different halakhot (laws) and *minhagim* (customs), the spectrum of accepted practices, and clear and concise practical guidance.

While my previous halakhic works were not necessarily instructive, it was clear that the mourner cannot be left with conceptual halakhic queries. For that reason, a practical summary of the laws of *avelut*, devoid of sources, footnotes, and diversity of opinions and practices, precedes the main text of the book.[1]

I believe that the methodology used in recent halakhic literature, as described below, enables this author to write a book that can, God willing, fulfill these goals.

* * *

R. Yehoshua Hutner,[2] in his introduction to R. Shlomo Yosef Zevin's (1888–1978) *Ishim VeShitot*,[3] discusses a recent change in the style and nature of halakhic literature. In this fascinating essay, he asserts that R. Zevin, founder and chief editor of the *Encyclopedia Talmudit* and author of other important works, including *HaMo'adim BeHalakha* and *LeOr HaHalakha*, opened a new era of halakhic literature.

> It seems that we would not be exaggerating if we were to say that the *gaon* R. Shlomo Yosef Zevin not only created a new style of writing, characterized by compilation [of halakhic opinions] and clarity, but he was also the one who revealed and developed a philosophy of Jewish law in a clear and radiating light.

R. Hutner explains that this new methodology is characterized by:

> Collecting, sorting, and attaching the many various topics of the Oral Law... and molding them into one unit. From the books and *ḥiddushim*, views and opinions, from the beginning [of halakhic literature] until the later scholars of our generation, he made the words of the scholars of all the generations into one organic unit.

1. Although in this section and throughout the book male pronouns are used to refer to the mourner, the same halakhot generally apply to female mourners as well, except where otherwise noted.
2. R. Yehoshua Hutner (1920–2009) served as director of the *Encyclopedia Talmudit* project for over fifty years.
3. R. Shlomo Yosef Zevin, *Ishim VeShitot* (Kol Mevasser, 2007).

Most importantly, R. Hutner insists that R. Zevin "did not do this in Rambam's way of [halakhic] rulings and decisions, but rather, in the Talmud's way, gathering and sorting the entire assembly of opinion and debates in one collection." In other words, presenting the scope and spectrum of halakhic views, with proper analysis, in a clear and organized manner, enhances and enriches the halakhic process. Furthermore, R. Hutner writes:

> What emerges is that even the practical halakhic rulings that each and every generation needs are also enriched and made possible due to the breadth of the Torah's philosophy and scope of its insights...To the extent that the field of [Torah] *ḥiddushim* is expanded and enriched, upon the foundations of the *Rishonim* and insights of the *Aḥaronim*, so too, the rulings of the recognized halakhic authorities are further based in [the Torah's] depth and breadth, and they are unified and merged into one organic entirety of Torah and halakha.

He concludes by asserting that "one who claims that the halakha is 'frozen and fossilized' is mistaken and deceives others, and it seems that [this person] has not tasted the flavor of deep and uplifting new Torah and halakhic insights all of his days."

Although R. Hutner's analysis relates to the *Encyclopedia Talmudit* and its contribution to halakhic literature, R. Zevin himself displayed this style in his earlier works, including the aforementioned *HaMo'adim BeHalakha, LeOr HaHalakha, Ishim VeShitot,* and in his many published articles.

Over the past seventy years we have seen the proliferation of halakhic treatises, in English and Hebrew, which focus upon all areas of Jewish law, including the laws of Shabbat, Yom Tov, *kashrut,* family purity, *berakhot, ribbit,* and even *shiluaḥ haken.* These books provide a great service to the observant community, in that they make the details of Jewish law accessible to all. One who wishes to observe the laws of Shabbat or *kashrut,* for example, can simply purchase a halakhic guidebook, and study. However, these books often do not present the origins or development of a specific practice. They do not provide the reader with an opportunity to learn a topic in depth. When disagreement arises, the author often chooses which position to present as authoritative, and dissenting opinions, even those which are practiced by some, are relegated to the footnotes, and at times not even mentioned.

In recent years, in the spirit of R. Zevin's literary contribution, numerous Torah scholars have written clear, comprehensive, and accessible halakhic works, practically redefining the style of modern halakhic literature. While decades ago one might have noted the writings of R. Shimon Eider (English) and R. Chaim David Halevi (Hebrew), today, R. Yosef Zvi Rimon (Rav of southern Alon Shevut and head of Merkaz Halakha VeHoraa) in his *Halakha MiMekora* series, and R. Eliezer Melamed (Rav of Har Berakha and Rosh Yeshiva of Yeshivat Har Berakha) in his *Peninei Halakha* series, may currently best represent this genre, each in his own way.

This volume, which focuses upon the laws of *avelut*,[4] begins each topic with its primary sources, be it a talmudic passage, a comment of the *Geonim*, or a practice instituted by the *Rishonim* or *Aḥaronim*. Each section traces the halakha through the *Rishonim* and *Aḥaronim*, including relevant debates among the *posekim* regarding contemporary applications. At times, historical and philosophical sources, as well as traditional "*lomdus*," are woven into the chapter.

Without any presumption of halakhic authority, this book attempts to present a clear and comprehensive narrative, based upon the classic and contemporary halakhic literature, to the student studying *Hilkhot Avelut*, and to the mourner who, *raḥmana litzlan*, is observing its laws. Although at times the simplicity of direct instruction is sacrificed, a deeper, richer, and more accurate understanding is gained. This book, however, is still committed to presenting the "bottom-line" practical halakha. For that reason, as mentioned above, a practical summary of the laws of *avelut* precedes the main text of the book.

I sincerely hope that this volume will succeed in clearly presenting the scope, depth, complexity, and nuance of the laws of *avelut* in particular and of the halakha in general.

* * *

Over the course of writing this book, our extended family suffered a tragic loss. I would like to take this opportunity to mention our cousin Yonatan

4. I employed a similar methodology in my previous books, *Hilchot Tefilla: A Comprehensive Guide to the Laws of Daily Prayer* (Ktav/Yeshivat Har Etzion, 2010) and *Hilkhot Mo'adim: Understanding the Festivals* (Maggid/Yeshivat Har Etzion, 2013).

Adler *z"l,* whose memory will always be with us. Yonatan's character and principles will always inspire us to be more committed, idealistic, and thoughtful people.

* * *

I have been blessed in that I had the opportunity to study at Yeshiva University, and to learn from R. Michael Rosensweig. In addition, I spent close to eight years studying, and later teaching, in Yeshivat Har Etzion, primarily under the guidance of R. Aharon Lichtenstein *z"l.* I have also spent almost twenty years writing weekly halakha *shiurim* for Yeshivat Har Etzion's Israel Koschitzky Virtual Beit Midrash (VBM); I am grateful to R. Ezra Bick, R. Reuven Ziegler, and Mrs. Debra Berkowitz for this opportunity. Yeshivat Har Etzion remains my spiritual home, and its *Roshei Yeshiva,* R. Aharon Lichtenstein *z"l* and R. Yehuda Amital *z"l,* who have since passed away, are still my guiding lights. I feel forever indebted to the Yeshiva for its contribution to my growth. The Jewish people have benefited from the many graduates of the Yeshiva, and Judaism is a richer religion due to its teachings.

Throughout my research I consulted with the many modern halakhic compendiums and treatises written on the laws of *avelut,* as well as numerous articles and *shiurim* published in halakhic journals and available on the internet. R. Yechiel Michel Tukachinsky, author of the *Gesher HaḤayim* and the "*mara de'atra*" of the laws of *avelut,* continuously provided structure, insights, direction, and even inspiration. Other well-known works, such as the *Penei Barukh, Nitei Gavriel,* and R. Maurice Lamm's *The Jewish Way in Death and Mourning,* each written for a different audience, demonstrate halakhic depth and sensitivity. I sincerely hope that I duly cited all those who provided sources, ideas, or references, in fulfillment of the words of our sages, "Whoever says a thing in the name of he who [originally] said it brings redemption to the world" (Avot 6:6). If I unintentionally omitted an author, journal, or *sefer,* I express my sincere apologies.

Over the course of my research, a number of *posekim, talmidei ḥakhamim,* scholars, and friends offered their halakhic guidance and insights. I especially wish to mention R. Mordechai Willig, R. Yosef Zvi Rimon, and R. Yehoshua Reich, who were always available to discuss halakhic issues related to *avelut,* and R. Avishai David, who generously reviewed parts of this book and offered invaluable insights. I also appreciate the diligent work of R. Yehoshua Schreier, who read and meticulously edited the first draft of this book.

I would like to acknowledge and thank Mr. Matthew Miller, Publisher at Maggid Books, R. Reuven Ziegler, Chairman of the Editorial Board, and Mrs. Shira Finson, assistant editor at Maggid, for their efforts in printing this volume. I appreciate the diligent work of Mrs. Oritt Sinclair and Mrs. Ilana Sobel, who so assiduously attended to the editing of this book, and Mrs. Ita Olesker, who brought it to press.

I would like to thank the Smilowitz family, especially my friend and former *ḥevruta* R. Mark Smilowitz, for generously supporting the publication of this book. R. Smilowitz identified the need for this book, and his vision and assistance greatly contributed to the content and style of the *sefer*. I sincerely hope that this volume will succeed in providing guidance and comfort for mourners, and Torah insights for those studying the laws of *avelut*, and I pray that it will be a worthy memorial to Mr. Herbert Smilowitz, of blessed memory.

I also thank my parents, Jarrett and Arlene Brofsky, and my in-laws, Dr. Mark and Leah Adler, who have been a constant source of support and encouragement.

Finally, I am indebted to my wife, Mali, who not only encouraged me in this and all my endeavors, but is also a constant source of personal and spiritual support and inspiration. I pray for many more years of partnership and companionship, and that our children, Yehuda, Shira, Yonatan, and Hadar, will continue to learn, fulfill, and live the words of the Torah.

David Brofsky
Alon Shevut, Elul 5778

# A Practical Summary of the Laws of *Avelut*

One of the unique and profound characteristics of the laws of *avelut* is the division into different stages of mourning. The mourner first experiences the period between the death and the burial [*aninut*], and then observes the seven-day mourning period [*shiva*]. After the conclusion of the seven-day mourning period, he continues to observe certain mourning practices for thirty days [*sheloshim*], and for the loss of a parent, for twelve months [*yud-bet ḥodesh*]. These different periods of mourning are not just quantitatively different; they reflect and correspond to different stages of bereavement, and gradually ease the mourner back into his daily routine.

In this short compendium, we will summarize the fundamental laws of each stage of mourning. These issues are treated in greater depth in their corresponding chapters.

### *ANINUT*

Following the death of a close relative, i.e., a parent (father or mother), sibling (brother or sister, half-brother or half-sister), child (son or daughter), or spouse, one becomes an *onen*, and observes the laws of *aninut*, until the burial. The term *onen* connotes a deep, inner sadness.

A person who has lost a relative should not act frivolously; rather, he should conduct himself as one who is preoccupied and overwhelmed by the death and burial. The *onen* may not eat meat or drink wine, as this is inappropriate during this time of intense sorrow, and may distract him from dedicating himself to the funeral preparations. Furthermore, the *onen* must not eat in the presence of the deceased.

An *onen* is exempt and prohibited from fulfilling all positive commandments, including reciting blessings and daily prayers. Some sources suggest that this exemption enables the *onen* to single-mindedly attend to the burial of his relative. Other sources explain that out of respect for the deceased, he is not to be distracted by the performance of mitzvot. There is much discussion regarding whether the *onen* remains exempt from fulfilling mitzvot after the deceased has been entrusted to the *ḥevra kadisha,* or in a case where the mourner must travel to a different city to attend the funeral. Although some *Aḥaronim* rule that in these cases, if the *onen* is not engaged in any funeral preparations, he may perform mitzvot, it is customary to observe *aninut* in all situations, from the time of the relative's death until the burial.

The *onen* should wash *netilat yadayim* in the morning, as well as before eating bread, without reciting the blessing. He may also wear his *tzitzit.* The *onen* is not counted in a *minyan* or a *zimun,* and should not answer "Amen." An *onen* may recite psalms for the protection of the deceased [*shemirat hamet*].

The *onen* does not don *tefillin* on the day of the death, on the day of the burial, or, in a case of delay, on any days in between them. Some maintain that if the deceased is buried on a day other than the day of death, the mourner should don *tefillin* in private after the burial, without reciting the blessings; this is not the common custom.

The *onen* must also observe the laws of mourning that do not interfere with the preparations for the burial, i.e., one should refrain from washing, anointing, participating in joyful occasions, greeting, haircuts and shaving, marital relations, work, and Torah study. He may wear leather shoes if necessary. Although technically an *onen* may not bathe, if the need arises, he may shower briefly in lukewarm water, thereby limiting the degree of pleasure. He may also apply deodorant. The *onen* may change his clothing before the burial if he wishes to rend a shirt other than the one he is wearing. The *onen* does not sit on the ground, or on a low chair; he does not do so until he becomes a mourner, after the burial.

There are different customs regarding whether an *onen* may, or should, recite the Mourner's Kaddish before the burial. While Ashkenazim do not recite Kaddish before the burial, some Sephardim recite it.

On Shabbat and Yom Tov most of the restrictions of *aninut* are lifted: An *onen* may eat meat and drink wine, participate in a *zimun*, recite *Shema* and the *Shemoneh Esreh*, and perform all of the mitzvot. The *onen* may not engage in marital relations on Shabbat, nor may he study or read the Torah, and he is not called to the Torah for an *aliya*. An *onen* who is a Kohen should leave the sanctuary before being called for *Birkat Kohanim*, and should not ascend to recite *Birkat Kohanim* even if called. In some Sephardic communities the Kohen participates in the *Birkat Kohanim* on Shabbat.

After Shabbat, the *onen* does not recite Havdala, although he may eat, and perform *melakha*, after reciting: *Barukh hamavdil bein kodesh leḥol*. Havdala should be recited, without the spices and candle, after the burial.

During this time, if the *onen* is a business owner or partner, he should consult with a halakhic authority regarding the proper manner in which his business should be conducted.

## BURIAL

The mitzva of burying the dead [*kevurat hamet*] appears in various places throughout the Torah and rabbinic literature. The Talmud notes that burial was apparently an ancient Jewish custom. Burial is such an important commandment that the Torah commands a Kohen to become impure to bury a relative (Lev. 21:1–3).

The Talmud suggests that burial may be part of the process of atonement [*kappara*]. Alternatively, the Gemara explains that burial may be for the purpose of preserving the dignity of the deceased. Some explain that the Gemara is concerned with preventing the embarrassment of the family. The wishes of one who requests not to be buried are not honored.

The Torah prohibits leaving the corpse unburied overnight. However, the Mishna teaches: "If he kept him overnight for the sake of his honor, to procure for him a coffin or a shroud, he does not transgress [the prohibition]." Therefore, one may delay burial to enable relatives to come from another place, even from overseas. One should make certain not to delay the burial unnecessarily.

Halakhic authorities oppose cremation and prohibit even the interment of ashes in Jewish cemeteries. The *Aḥaronim* raise numerous objections to the practice of cremation. Some suggest that cremation is a violation of the Torah obligation to bury the dead and is a form of mutilating the corpse [*nivul hamet*]. R. Avraham Yitzchak HaKohen Kook suggests that cremation may even be a form of *ḥukkat akum* (imitating the ways of the gentiles). Others add that just as burial is an affirmation of the belief in the resurrection of the dead [*teḥiyat hametim*], destroying the body through cremation may demonstrate a rejection of this fundamental principle. After millions of Jews were murdered and then cremated by the Nazis during the Holocaust, cremation seems even more distasteful. Some insist that one should not observe the laws of mourning for one who chooses to be cremated. Most authorities maintain that the Mourner's Kaddish is recited in any case. One should discuss these complicated and sensitive issues with a halakhic authority.

There are numerous laws that relate to and protect the human body even after death. For example, there is a prohibition to derive benefit [*issur hanaa*] from or to mistreat or mutilate a corpse [*nivul hamet*]. The *Aḥaronim* consider whether one is permitted to perform forensic, clinical, or academic autopsies.

The Talmud likens the human body to a *sefer Torah*. The body is the vessel that contains the soul, similar to the *sefer Torah*, which contains the names of God. The body of the deceased is treated with the utmost respect; one must behave appropriately in its presence. It is carefully guarded, and meticulously prepared for burial. The Talmud teaches that one should not eat or drink in the presence of the deceased. Furthermore, the Gemara even expresses concern that certain behavior may be viewed as mocking the deceased.

It is proper to appoint a guard [*shomer*] to protect the body until it is entrusted to the *ḥevra kadisha*. The Talmud mentions protecting the deceased from a weasel or from mice. In addition, other sources indicate that watching the body is an act of respect so that the deceased should not appear to be "an unwanted vessel" (Jer. 22:28). It is proper for those guarding the deceased to recite psalms and other prayers, and to refrain from idle conversation.

There is an ancient Jewish custom to wash and prepare the body for burial. The *ḥevra kadisha* is entrusted with this task, known as *tahara*, during which its members wash and dress the body in burial shrouds [*takhrikhin*]. Just as when the body enters this world it is washed and cleaned, the same is done to it when a person leaves this world. The body is washed, and then nine *kavim* (20 L) of water are poured over it, after which the body is dressed in *takhrikhin*. The *tahara* is performed with the utmost modesty and sensitivity; those engaged in preparing the body for burial recite biblical verses relating to the *tahara*. The details of the *tahara* differ from community to community. There are circumstances where a *tahara* is not performed, e.g., if the deceased was killed by gentiles or if much blood was discharged from the body before death, such as in the case of a fatal accident, and according to some, even if a person dies by natural causes in a manner involving significant bleeding, such as a woman in childbirth; in those cases the body is simply dressed in burial shrouds.

The human body is buried in the ground, in accordance with the verse: "And to dust you shall return" (Gen. 3:19). Although in Israel it is customary to bury the body directly in the ground, in many countries it is customary to bury in wooden coffins. If possible, in accordance with the law of the land, and with the custom of each community, holes should be made in the coffin. Although halakhic authorities prohibit interment in a mausoleum, in recent years, multi-tier burial structures have been built in numerous cemeteries in Israel, including Jerusalem's Har HaMenuḥot, according to the strict requirements of Jewish law.

There is an ancient tradition, tracing back to biblical times, to make every effort to be buried in the Land of Israel. Indeed, the Book of Genesis concludes as both Jacob (Gen. 47:29) and Joseph (ibid., 50:25) request that their bodies be brought from Egypt to Eretz Yisrael for burial. The Talmud relates different reasons for burial in Eretz Yisrael. One source indicates that burial in Eretz Yisrael may atone for one's sins. Others indicate that burial in Eretz Yisrael may be auspicious during the resurrection of the dead [*teḥiyat hametim*]. Many pious individuals instruct their children to bury them in Eretz Yisrael. Interestingly, R. Yosef Eliyahu Henkin sharply criticized the practice of ordinary people spending large sums of money on funeral arrangements, including burial in Israel, and recommended instead to give money to charity or to support Torah study.

## RENDING ONE'S GARMENTS [*KERIA*]

Rending one's garments is one of the earliest expressions of mourning (Gen. 37:29, 34; II Sam. 13:31; Job 1:20). The commentaries offer numerous insights into this practice. While tearing one's garment may be viewed as an expression of outrage and intense grief, Rambam explains that tearing one's garment ultimately assuages one's anger and calms one's soul. Rending the article of clothing that covers the heart, in response to the death of a parent, may symbolize a broken heart, as the prophet Joel says: "And rend your heart, and not your garments" (Joel 2:13).

One performs *keria* upon the death of a parent, spouse, child, or sibling, i.e., anyone for whom one is obligated to mourn. Although an adopted child, adoptive parent, and adoptive sibling are not obligated to mourn, they may perform *keria,* and may recite the *Dayan HaEmet* blessing as well. Regarding a child under the age of bar or bat mitzva, the Talmud teaches: "[The relatives] rend the garment of a child to arouse grief." One rends the garment of a small child only slightly, while the garment of a child who has reached the age of *ḥinukh* is rent in accordance with the laws of *keria.*

In most communities, it is customary to perform *keria* at the funeral service. It is also customary to recite: *Barukh ... dayan ha'emet* when rending one's garment. If one did not rend his garment upon hearing of the death, or at the burial, he may perform *keria* during the *shiva.*

Before the funeral, a mourner may change his shirt, putting on one that he would prefer to rend. He should be aware that this is the shirt that he will likely wear the entire week. During the week, one mourning the death of a parent should not change his shirt; if he does, he must rend the other shirt. One mourning other relatives may change into a different shirt, although it is customary to wear a torn shirt for the entire week of mourning.

*Keria* is performed while standing. The custom is that another person begins cutting the garment, and the mourner then completes the *keria;* a man cuts the garment for a man and a woman cuts the garment for a woman. For one's parents, he rips all except for his innermost garments that absorb perspiration, his overcoat, and a sweater worn for warmth. He rends the garments on the left side, with his hand, reflecting a more intense bitterness. He rends the garment until he reveals his heart. For other relatives, one rends only the outer garment, on the right side, and he should rend at least one handbreadth [*tefaḥ*] (8–10 cm), with either a knife or his hand.

One should begin the tear at the edge of the garment, at the neck, and continue along the length of the garment vertically, not horizontally. A woman should perform *keria* in a modest manner, rending only the outer layer, and should either close the tear with a safety pin or wear a shirt under the outer garment.

### *LEVAYAT HAMET* AND THE FUNERAL SERVICE

Attending to the dead and escorting them to their burial, is perceived as a selfless act, for which one is rewarded in this world and in the World to Come. Rambam teaches that participation in the accompanying of the deceased and in the burial service is a fulfillment of a positive commandment: "You shall love your neighbor as yourself" (Lev. 19:18).

It is a great mitzva to properly eulogize the deceased, just as Abraham eulogized his wife, Sarah (Gen. 23:2). Since the eulogy [*hesped*] is intended primarily to honor the deceased, if a person explicitly requests that a *hesped* not be said for him, one honors his wishes.

Eulogies, in their fullest sense, are not delivered on festivals (i.e., Ḥol HaMo'ed), Rosh Ḥodesh, Ḥanukka, Purim (fourteenth and fifteenth of Adar), or Purim Katan (fourteenth and fifteenth of I Adar). Likewise, they are not delivered during the entire month of Nissan, or on Tu BiShevat, Lag BaOmer, or other days on which *Taḥanun* is not recited.

After lowering the body into the grave, it is customary and appropriate for the mourner, and those attending the funeral, to participate in covering the open grave with dirt. The shovel should not be handed directly from one person to another, so as to avoid the appearance of transferring tragedy to another. The final *tziduk hadin* prayer is recited, and the mourners say the unique burial Kaddish, known as *Kaddish HaGadol.* This Kaddish is unique in that it expresses hope for the redemption and *teḥiyat hametim.* The *El Maleh Raḥamim* prayer is recited, and a representative of the *ḥevra kadisha* then asks forgiveness from the deceased, lest they did not treat the body with proper respect.

After the interment, the seven-day period of mourning [*shiva*] begins. The first act of mourning is usually performed at the cemetery, when those attending the funeral line up in two rows (this is called *shura*), and the mourner walks between them as they offer their condolences. In many communities, separate rows are formed for comforting male and female mourners.

As one leaves the cemetery it is customary to wash his hands before returning home. Some write that one should wash each hand three times, alternating between the right and the left, in the manner that one washes his hands after awakening in the morning. It is customary not to dry one's hands after washing them, and not to pass the cup directly to another person.

### AFTER THE BURIAL

After the burial, *shiva* begins, and the mourner is once again obligated to perform mitzvot. If the mourner did not hear Havdala, and the funeral took place before Tuesday night, he should recite Havdala, without the candle and spices. The mourner does not compensate for missed prayers [*tefillat tashlumin*].

However, he should recite the morning blessings [*birkot hashaḥar* and *birkot haTorah*] discreetly. Some don their *tefillin* discreetly, without a blessing, after the burial; this is not the widespread practice.

### SEUDAT HAVRAA

The first meal after the funeral is known as the *seudat havraa*. The mourner should not eat his own food at this meal. Some *Rishonim* indicate that the neighbors are obligated to provide the *seudat havraa* as an expression of concern for the mourner. Other sources indicate that the *seudat havraa* may be for the purpose of comforting the mourners [*niḥum avelim*]. The mourner may drink coffee or tea before the *seudat havraa*. The meal often begins with foods symbolic of mourning, after which the mourner eats a regular meal.

Rema rules that if the burial took place late in the day and the mourner did not eat a *seudat havraa,* he may eat his own food. There is no *seudat havraa* at night. *Shulḥan Arukh* rules that if the funeral is on Ḥol HaMo'ed, there is a *seudat havraa* with the mourners sitting on regular chairs.

### FOR WHOM DOES ONE MOURN?

As mentioned above, one is obligated to mourn for a parent (father or mother), sibling (brother or sister, half-brother or half-sister), child (son or daughter), or spouse.

Jewish law distinguishes between biological and adoptive parents in many laws. However, the Talmud does teach: Anyone who raises an orphan in his house, the verse ascribes him credit as if he fathered the child. Similarly, the Talmud teaches that in addition to the honor due to his parent, who brought him into this world, honor is due to his teacher, who taught him wisdom and brings him to life in the World to Come. Therefore, halakha recognizes the relationship between a child and his adoptive parent, and this is manifest in several laws.

Some contemporary authorities, including R. Yosef Dov Soloveitchik and R. Ovadia Yosef, rule that an adopted child may, and should, observe the laws of mourning. In addition to observing the laws of mourning, one may recite Kaddish for an adoptive parent. Although an adopted child is encouraged to observe the mourning practices, the laws of *aninut* would not apply. Therefore, unless the mourner is actively engaged in burial preparations, he is not exempt from performing mitzvot, and he should don *tefillin* discreetly. Furthermore, the adopted mourner should not refrain from learning Torah due to *avelut*. An adopted child, as well as adoptive siblings, stepparents and stepsiblings, may also perform *keria* and recite the *Dayan HaEmet* blessing. Of course, the decision to accept upon oneself some or all of the laws of mourning may be a function of the nature, extent, and depth of the relationship between the mourner and the deceased.

The Talmud teaches that one who converts to Judaism is like a newborn child. From a purely legal perspective, despite the biological connection, halakha does not ascribe significance to the pre-conversion familial relationships. Likewise, halakha does not ascribe significance to the relationship between the child of a Jewish mother and his gentile father. Of course, a convert should treat his or her gentile parents with proper respect, so that it does not appear as if the convert left a culture of greater sanctity for one of lesser sanctity, and to demonstrate gratitude for bringing him into this world. Some *Aḥaronim* suggest that not only should a convert show respect for his gentile parent, but he should even recite Kaddish after the parent's death, as failure to do so may be perceived as demeaning his parents after their deaths. Indeed, the biblical model for Kaddish: "I will be glorified and I will be sanctified and I will become known before the eyes of many nations, and they will know that I am the Lord" (Ezek. 38:29), is stated with regard to gentiles. Furthermore, some suggest that while the convert should certainly not compromise his religious observance by refraining from Torah study, he may choose to observe some mourning practices, and may rend his garments. In some cases, it may even be appropriate to observe *shiva* for a gentile parent, like in the case of an adopted child, discussed above. Of course, the convert must make certain to avoid participating in halakhically problematic burial or memorial services performed for the deceased.

In our times it is customary to mourn for almost all Jews, regardless of their religious commitment or level of observance. That said, there are cases in which the *Aḥaronim* advised against observing mourning practices, e.g., for one who arranged to be cremated, one who converted to another religion, and one who married a gentile. One should discuss the details and context with a halakhic authority as each case is unique and may warrant a ruling specific to that case.

One may choose not to mourn for an abusive parent. Similarly, one in the process of divorcing a spouse, or a victim of spousal abuse, may be exempt from mourning. These questions are complicated and should be discussed with a halakhic authority.

Tragically, there are times when, due to mental illness or the heavy burdens of life, a person chooses to take his own life. While aware of the tragedy of suicide, the sages adamantly insisted that suicide is not a religiously acceptable or halakhically valid option. However, R. Yechiel Michel Tukachinsky, in his *Gesher HaḤayim*, asserts, "In most cases that appear to be suicide, God forbid, they are not to be adjudged as suicide, as whenever it is possible to attribute his death to someone else, even if it is a far-fetched scenario, or if it is possible to attribute it to the fact that he was not sane and was confused for any of a number of reasons, or if as he was in the throes of death he regretted his actions and repented, one attributes the case in a lenient manner and we accord him the presumptive status of one who did not take his own life." Nowadays, it is customary to mourn and recite Kaddish for those who took their own lives, in accordance with the reasons mentioned above.

The laws of *avelut* are not observed after a miscarriage or a stillbirth. Furthermore, regardless of whether a child died due to illness or accident, the laws of mourning are not observed for a child who passed away within thirty days of the birth. Some *Aḥaronim* rule that one may recite the *Dayan HaEmet* blessing when hearing of a miscarriage or of the death of an infant for whom one does not observe the mourning practices. Others suggest that one should omit the name of God when reciting the blessing *Barukh Dayan HaEmet.*

## CHILDREN

Although children may technically be exempt from observing the laws of mourning, the child's clothes are rent, and a young boy recites Kaddish. Furthermore, one should demonstrate understanding and sensitivity with regard to young mourners. At times it may be appropriate for them to sit and participate in *shiva* with the other mourners, and at times it may be better for them to be away from the intensity of the *shiva.*

## THE BEGINNING OF THE SEVEN-DAY MOURNING PERIOD

The Talmud teaches that after the burial, the mourner begins a seven-day period of *avelut,* known as *shiva,* which consists of mourning practices and prohibitions. In most cases, the mourning period begins with the burial; at times, the *shiva* begins even before the burial.

When the mourner does not accompany the body for burial in a different city or country, the mourning period begins immediately after the mourner takes his leave of the deceased, often at the airport or funeral home. When one of the relatives accompanies the body to the burial, he begins *shiva* after the burial. If he returns and joins those already sitting *shiva,* he concludes *shiva* with them, even though he observed fewer than seven days of mourning. If the cemetery is near the city, those who remain behind do not begin mourning until they are informed of the burial, or until they estimate that the burial was completed.

When one hears of the death of a close relative in another city, but does not plan on attending the burial and is not involved in the funeral preparations, it is customary to begin mourning immediately.

## THE PROHIBITIONS OF THE WEEK OF MOURNING [*SHIVA*]

The laws and customs of *avelut* reflect a variety of themes, including respect and honor for the deceased [*kevod hamet*], inner sorrow and grief [*avelut shebalev*], appreciation for human life, and repentance [*teshuva*].

During the seven days after the burial, the mourner, overcome by grief, doesn't tend to his personal needs, not even to basic hygiene. He allows himself to become unkempt and disheveled. He refrains from activities that bring him joy, withdraws from his social environment, and interrupts his daily routine. The mourning practices described below reflect, express, and mold the experience of the mourner for the seven-day period of *avelut.*

### Haircuts, Shaving, and Nail Cutting

A mourner may not cut his hair during the thirty-day mourning period, which includes *shiva.* He may comb his hair even during *shiva.* A mourner may trim hair that interferes with his eating after *shiva.* Furthermore, the mourner should not cut his nails for thirty days with a nail clipper, but may remove them in an alternate manner, i.e., with his hands or teeth, even during *shiva.*

### Bathing and Anointing

A mourner must refrain from bathing and anointing for the entire *shiva.* All bathing in hot water is prohibited. The mourner may wash his face, hands, and feet in lukewarm water [*mayim poshrim*].

Only bathing or anointing for pleasure [*taanug*] is prohibited. Therefore, it is permitted to bathe or anoint to remove dirt, filth, or perspiration, or for medicinal reasons, including washing one's hair or scalp to remove lice or to alleviate the discomfort of blisters, and bathing in warm water to heal a skin rash, infestation (scabies), or hemorrhoids. Similarly, a woman who has recently given birth, and someone after surgery, may certainly bathe. Furthermore, one who is especially delicate [*istenis*], and experiences significant discomfort, may wash, preferably quickly and in cold or lukewarm water. A person who experiences two consecutive mourning periods [*tekhafuhu avelut*] may bathe his entire body in cold water after the first week.

Although anointing is prohibited, one may use medicinal lotions, moisturizers for dry skin, and deodorants. Children, who do not observe the laws of mourning, may bathe during the week of mourning.

### Laundering

A mourner is prohibited to launder clothing, and may not wear laundered clothing. Although wearing laundered clothing for pleasure is prohibited, if the mourner's clothes become stained or dirty, he may wash them, without soap, to remove the dirt, or change into laundered clothing. Clothing intended to absorb perspiration [*bigdei ze'a*], e.g., underwear and socks, may be worn. One may launder the clothes of a child who is in mourning.

On Shabbat it is customary to wear Shabbat clothing to avoid public displays of mourning.

### Wearing Leather Shoes [*Ne'ilat HaSandal*]

A mourner is not permitted to wear leather shoes during the seven days of mourning. This prohibition includes only leather shoes, or shoes made of another material but covered with leather. It is customary to wear shoes not made of leather to the funeral or to remove one's shoes immediately after the burial.

### Sexual Relations [*Tashmish HaMita*]

The mourner must refrain from marital relations during the seven days of mourning. Other forms of intimacy prohibited during the period of *nidut*, known as *harḥakot*, need not be avoided during *shiva*. Although there is no prohibition of physical contact, e.g., hugging and kissing [*ḥibuk venishuk*], some suggest that physical contact of an intimate nature should be avoided; this should be left to the discretion of the mourner and should be weighed against the value of providing emotional support and comfort.

### Prohibition of Work [*Issur Melakha*] During *Shiva*

The mourner should not work during the seven-day period of mourning. This prohibition is designed to allow the mourner to focus on his loss, and not be distracted by his mundane obligations. Just as one is not permitted to work, one is not allowed to engage in business transactions. One may perform household chores, including cooking and cleaning, during *shiva*. A business partner or owner should consult with a halakhic authority regarding how to conduct his business during the week of mourning.

### Torah Study [*Talmud Torah*]

A mourner should not engage in Torah study during the week of mourning. Some explain that *Talmud Torah* is similar to bathing, anointing, and wearing freshly laundered clothing, in the sense that it provides physical or spiritual happiness. Indeed, the verse states: "The precepts of the Lord are just, rejoicing the heart" (Ps. 19:9). Others explain that the mourner's obligation to refrain from Torah study stems from the verse: "Sigh in silence" (Ezek. 24:17).

On may study the sad portions of the Bible, e.g., the Books of Job and Lamentations, and the gloomy parts of Jeremiah, as well as the laws of mourning. One may also study works of *mussar*. It is customary to recite all of the biblical verses and rabbinic passages found in the prayer book.

### Greeting [*She'elat Shalom*]

A mourner should refrain from extending greetings during the seven-day period of mourning. After the first three days, he may respond to a greeting. Others should refrain from greeting the mourner for the entire period of mourning, i.e., twelve months for a parent and thirty days for other relatives. In practice, Rema records that it is not customary to observe this prohibition after *sheloshim* for those mourning their parents.

When parting from a mourner during the *shiva*, it is customary to say: May God comfort you among the other mouners of Zion and Jerusalem [*HaMakom yenaḥem etkhem betokh she'ar avelei tziyon viyerushalayim*]. In Sephardic communities, and in many communities in Israel, the comforters say: May you be comforted from the heavens [*min hashamayim tenuḥamu*]. In some places, it is customary to shake the mourner's hand and wish him long life.

One should refrain from sending the mourner gifts during the entire period of mourning, as sending gifts is a form of *she'elat shalom*. For that reason, one should not send *mishlo'aḥ manot* on Purim, during the period of mourning. One may, however, send *mishlo'aḥ manot* to the mourner's spouse, or to his entire family. One may also send *mishlo'aḥ manot* to a mourner as a sign of respect, e.g., to a rabbi or a parent.

### Rejoicing [*Simḥa*]

There is a broad prohibition of *simḥa* during the entire period of mourning. There are occasions when a mourner, even during *shiva*, may participate in certain festivities. For example, if a mourner's son's *Brit Mila* is during the seven-day mourning period, the parent may wear festive garments [*bigdei Shabbat*] and leather shoes. The mourner may participate in the *seudat mitzva*, which preferably should be held in the mourner's house. Some even permit the grandparents, if they are mourners, to attend the *seudat mitzva*. A mourner during the week of mourning may serve as the *mohel* or the *sandak*, wearing *bigdei Shabbat*, but should not participate in the *seudat mitzva*. Similar to the halakha in the case of a *Brit Mila*, the parents, and a Kohen, may hold a *Pidyon HaBen* during the seven days of mourning, wearing *bigdei Shabbat*, and may participate in the *seudat mitzva*.

The parents of a child whose bar mitzva occurs during the week of mourning may join the child as he is called to the Torah, but the *seudat mitzva* should be held after the *shiva*. Finally, some *Aḥaronim* permit the parents, who are mourners, to attend their child's wedding, although they should not eat with the other guests.

## THE HOUSE OF THE MOURNER [*BEIT HAAVEL*]

R. Yosef Dov Soloveitchik explains that in addition to the mourning practices observed during *shiva*, there are also laws and customs that relate to the house of the mourner [*beit haavel*].

It is customary to light a candle in the house of the mourner that will last for the seven days of mourning. This candle is known as the *ner neshama*. Even if the death occurs on Yom Tov or Ḥol HaMo'ed, one lights the candle after the funeral and it remains lit until after the seven days of mourning.

It is also customary to cover the mirrors during the seven days of mourning. R. Soloveitchik explains that as a sign of respect for the deceased, who was created in the image of God [*tzelem Elokim*], the mirrors, which reflect the image of God, should be covered. Others suggest that mirrors represent, and encourage, a focus on beauty and vanity, themes that are far from the mind of the mourner. Yet others explain that since the daily prayers are conducted in the house of the mourner, the mirrors should be covered, as it is customary to avoid praying toward mirrors. There is no need to cover mirrors on Shabbat.

In addition to the laws and customs that reflect and create the proper environment for mourning, the Talmud teaches that the mourner should remain in the *beit haavel* for the entire week. However, a mourner may leave his house and travel to join other mourners. In addition, a mourner may leave the *beit haavel* at night to sleep in a different house.

### PRAYERS IN THE *BEIT HAAVEL*

It is proper for the mourner to pray with a *minyan* in the *beit haavel*. If the community cannot gather a *minyan* in the home of the mourner, in which case he would be unable to recite Kaddish, *Kedusha*, and *Barekhu*, he may leave his home to attend the *minyan* at a local synagogue.

On Shabbat during the week of mourning, the mourner may leave his house to attend communal prayers.

There are numerous changes in the prayers recited in the house of the mourner, reflecting the uniqueness and atmosphere of the *beit haavel*. *Taḥanun* is not recited in the house of the mourner, as the days of mourning are described as having the potential to be festive days (Amos 8:10), when *Taḥanun* and *Viduy* are not recited. Furthermore, the days of mourning, and the house of a mourner, are particularly inauspicious, as they are under the influence of *midat hadin*; therefore, *Taḥanun* should be omitted. For similar reasons, many omit the *El Erekh Apayim* passage said before *keriat haTorah*, as well as *Lamenatze'aḥ* and the verse: "And for me, this is my covenant," in the *Uva LeTziyon* prayer, in addition to abridging the *Seliḥot*. *Avinu Malkeinu*, recited during the *Aseret Yemei Teshuva* and on public fast days, is recited in the house of a mourner.

Hallel is not recited in the house of the mourner on Rosh Ḥodesh. Some suggest that it is inappropriate to recite the verse: "This is the day that the Lord has made; we will rejoice and be glad in it" (Ps. 118:24), or: "The dead do not praise the Lord" (Ps. 115:17). Others note that just as Hallel is not recited on Rosh HaShana, as: Is it possible that while the King is sitting on the throne of judgment and the books of life and the books of death are open before Him, the Jewish people are reciting joyous songs of praise; so too, it would be inappropriate to recite Hallel in the house of a mourner.

In practice, there are different customs. Regarding the congregation praying in the house of the mourner, some rule that there is no need to recite Hallel upon returning home from the mourner's house, as the recitation of Hallel on Rosh Ḥodesh is a custom, and not an obligation. R. Yechezkel Landau, in his *Noda BiYehuda,* writes that the mourners should leave the room and then return after the *minyan* has concluded reciting Hallel. Others disagree and suggest that the *minyan* should move to a different room to recite Hallel. Some rule that although Hallel may be omitted in the mourner's house, one should recite it upon returning home. On Ḥanukka, when the recitation of Hallel is an obligation, some *Aḥaronim* write that the congregation should recite Hallel upon returning home, while some say that it should be recited in the *beit haavel,* with the mourner.

If Rosh Ḥodesh, Ḥanukka, or another day upon which Hallel is recited coincides with the seventh day of the *shiva,* some suggest that before Hallel, those praying with the mourner should comfort the mourner, marking the official conclusion of *shiva,* in accordance with the halakhic principle: "The legal status of part of the day is like that of the entire day" [*miktzat hayom kekhulo*], and then they may all continue and recite Hallel. Some disagree with this practice.

At the end of the morning and evening prayers, it is customary to recite Psalms 49, *Lamenatze'aḥ Livnei Koraḥ Mizmor.* On days when *Taḥanun* is omitted, Psalms 16, *Mikhtam LeDavid,* is recited instead. *Mishnayot* are also often studied after the *tefillot,* especially after Minḥa.

In most communities in Israel, *Birkat Kohanim* is recited daily. Outside of Israel, in Ashkenazic communities, *Birkat Kohanim* is recited only in the Musaf prayer on festivals. In Israel, it is customary that during the seven days of mourning a Kohen does not recite *Birkat Kohanim,* but resumes immediately after the *shiva.* In most communities, *Birkat Kohanim* is not recited at all in the house of a mourner. In some Sephardic communities, and in Jerusalem, *Birkat Kohanim* is often recited in the house of a mourner.

### *AVELUT* ON SHABBAT

Shabbat does not terminate the mourning period; however, only certain aspects of mourning are observed, discreetly, and full-fledged mourning resumes immediately after Shabbat. Shabbat apparently does not pose an inherent contradiction to mourning, as its essence is that of a day of enjoyment [*oneg*] as opposed to the joy [*simḥa*] that is the essence of Yom Tov.

The laws of *avelut* are in effect for the entire day of Erev Shabbat. One may rise from *shiva* and begin preparation for Shabbat two and a half halakhic hours before sunset [*Minḥa ketana*]. Some write that one should not rise from *shiva* until one and a quarter hours before sunset [*pelag haMinḥa*]. One should not bathe, even in the manner permitted for the mourner, nor change his clothing, until just before Shabbat.

There is an ancient custom that the mourner enters the synagogue on Friday night just before Maariv, and when he enters, the congregation comforts him with the traditional *HaMakom* greeting. This is most likely based on a beautiful passage from *Pirkei DeRabbi Eliezer*: When the Temple was destroyed, the sages instituted that the bridegrooms and mourners should go to the synagogues and to the houses of study. The men of the place see the bridegroom and rejoice with him, and they see the mourner and sit with him on the earth, so that all the Israelites may fulfill their obligation of loving-kindness. It is customary for the mourner to enter the synagogue before the congregation recites *Mizmor Shir LeYom HaShabbat*, as the congregation accepts Shabbat with the recitation of that psalm.

On Shabbat, it is customary for the mourner to wear regular Shabbat clothes. In addition, he observes inconspicuous mourning practices [*devarim shebetzina*], e.g., refraining from bathing and from engaging in sexual relations, but it is permitted for him to wear leather shoes. Torah study is also in the category of an inconspicuous mourning practice and is prohibited. Similarly, a mourner does not read from the Torah, or receive an *aliya*, unless he is the only Kohen present. One is permitted to comfort mourners on Shabbat.

It is preferable to hold the Saturday-night prayers in the mourner's house. Immediately after Shabbat, the mourner removes his leather shoes. He must also remove his Shabbat clothing and wear his mourning clothing, including the shirt with the tear in it. It is preferable to wait until after the seven days of mourning to recite *Kiddush Levana*. If it will then be too late to say *Kiddush Levana*, i.e., fifteen days after the new moon, the mourner recites the blessing of *Kiddush Levana* alone, without the verses of blessing and the traditional greetings. Some write that a mourner who recites Havdala should omit the joyful verses recited prior to the blessings of Havdala, and begin with the blessings themselves.

### THE SEVENTH DAY: THE CONCLUSION OF *SHIVA*

Although the requirement is to observe seven days of mourning, in practice, the halakhic principle is: The legal status of part of the day is like that of the entire day [*miktzat hayom kekhulo*], and the mourner ends his observance of the laws of *shiva* in the morning, after the comforters depart.

Some are accustomed to leave the house accompanied by the comforters and walk a short distance, symbolizing the mourner's reentry into society after a week of mourning. There is a custom to visit the cemetery on the seventh day of mourning to recite prayers, and, if there is a *minyan*, to recite Kaddish. Even if there is no *minyan*, the custom is to recite *El Maleh Raḥamim*.

## THE THIRTY-DAY MOURNING PERIOD [*SHELOSHIM*]

After the seven-day mourning period, the mourner continues with twenty-three additional days of mourning, known as the *sheloshim*, meaning thirty, as the period concludes thirty days after the burial. The mourner observes several mourning practices during this period.

### Haircuts and Cutting Nails during *Sheloshim*

The mourner refrains from cutting his hair until the end of the thirty-day period when mourning for relatives other than his parents. A man may trim his mustache if it interferes with eating, and a woman may trim the hair around her hair covering for reasons of modesty, and may remove other bodily hair. In Sephardic communities, the custom is that a woman may cut her hair after *shiva*.

Although one may not cut his nails for thirty days with a nail clipper, one may remove them in an alternate manner, e.g., with his hands or teeth, even during *shiva*. If one's nails are particularly long one may cut them before Shabbat.

### Freshly Laundered and New Clothing

While Sephardim observe the prohibition of laundering for only seven days, the original Ashkenazic custom was to refrain from wearing freshly laundered clothing for the entire month, unless others wear the mourner's clothing briefly before he wears them. Many modern authorities note that this custom does not apply to undergarments or clothing worn to absorb perspiration. In addition, as some observe, many people are disgusted by the notion of wearing a shirt worn by others. Therefore, while one may launder clothing, and wear laundered clothing, it is preferable to avoid wearing starched or freshly dry-cleaned clothing, e.g., suits and dress pants. If necessary, they should first be worn by another, or placed on the ground.

A mourner should not wear new clothing during the thirty days of mourning. One may buy and wear undergarments and clothes that are not worn for one's dignity [*kavod*].

## *SIMḤA*, MARRIAGE, AND ATTENDING SOCIAL AND FESTIVE GATHERINGS

### *Simḥa*

The Talmud, in several contexts, discourages a mourner from engaging in excessive *simḥa* during the entire mourning period. This explains why the Yerushalmi prohibits joining a caravan of merchants, as the traveling was conspicuous, and was perceived as especially social and festive. Nowadays, while one may travel for business purposes, a mourner should refrain from recreational outings and vacations. He may, however, take a family vacation, or travel for medical reasons, or to rest. In other words, the mourner should avoid public, overtly festive activities, and choose a quieter form of recreation, if necessary, during the mourning period.

Due to the general prohibition of *simḥa*, many authorities prohibit listening to live music. Although some completely refrain from listening to music during the entire period of mourning, only music that moves one to dance is prohibited. Listening to music while driving, in order to remain awake, as well as hearing background music, is certainly not prohibited. The mourner's family certainly need not refrain from listening to music during the mourning period, although they should be considerate regarding the type and volume of the music that is played.

### Attending Social Gatherings and *Semaḥot* during *Sheloshim*

One of the defining characteristics, as well as one of the most challenging, of the post-*shiva* mourning practices, is the obligation to refrain from participating in social gatherings and festive celebrations. On the one hand, the mourner often wishes to avoid socializing or celebrating, and may also feel a sense of duty to the deceased to refrain from excessive socializing and festivities. On the other hand, the mourner may feel pressure, and at times even an obligation, to attend and participate in the *semaḥot* of close friends and relatives. We will present the basic halakhic principles, and based on this the mourner should decide when and how to participate in a social or festive event, if necessary.

There are different types of social participation to consider.

1. ***Simḥat Mere'ut***: The Talmud prohibits participating in *simḥat mere'ut*, which is some form of social engagement. There is no clear definition of *simḥat mere'ut*. It appears that one should take the size and nature of the interaction into account. While basic social interaction is certainly permitted, one should avoid public, festive events. Quantity and quality both play a role, and therefore attending a charity dinner, while avoiding music and dancing, or a conference or awards ceremony, may be permitted, while going out with friends for a dinner that is accompanied by a recreational activity should be avoided. As R. Maurice Lamm writes "Fellowship is fine, but festivities are not appropriate."

   On Shabbat, there is room to be lenient, as one is supposed to avoid public displays of mourning. Nevertheless, while one is not expected to eat alone for the entire period of mourning, large and festive meals may be inappropriate. It is important to note the distinction between hosting those in need of a meal or of companionship [*hakhnasat orḥim*], business meetings, hosting students or teachers, and hosting purely for social reasons. Some Sephardim refrain from attending only festive meals [*seudat simḥa*], not social meals.

2. **Weddings:** A wedding and its festive meal are perceived as one of the most joyous occasions. Therefore, a mourner should not attend or participate in a wedding, including both the ceremony and the meal that follows.

   There is room to permit a mourner to attend the wedding ceremony and to hear the wedding blessings. Therefore, while a mourner after the *sheloshim* (when mourning for a parent) and a mourner after the *shiva* (when mourning for another relative) should not attend the reception or enter the wedding hall, they may attend the ceremony itself when there is a need. Whether or not a mourner chooses to attend the ceremony should be determined based upon several factors, including the mourner's relationship with the *ḥatan* and *kalla*.

   In certain circumstances, the mourner may participate even in the wedding ceremony and the festive wedding meal.

   Regarding the ceremony itself, the mourner, after the thirty-day mourning period, may escort the *ḥatan* or *kalla* to the *ḥuppa*, and recite the wedding blessings.

As for the festive meal, many authorities permit parents, grandparents, and even siblings to participate in the festive meal during the period of mourning. The mourner may attend if his absence will cause the bride or groom distress [*mitzaarin*]. The mourner should try to minimize his participation, limiting it to rejoicing with the *ḥatan* and *kalla,* all the while conscious of the fact that he is in mourning.

R. Moshe Feinstein permits a parent to attend a child's wedding even during the *shiva,* and explains that it is extremely painful for a parent not to attend the wedding of a child. He adds, however, that the mourner should not partake in the festive meal like the other guests.

3. ***Brit Mila, Pidyon HaBen,* Bar/Bat Mitzva, and *Ḥanukkat HaBayit*:** A mourner may participate in a *seudat mitzva* that is less joyful than a wedding, e.g., a *Brit Mila* or *Pidyon HaBen.* It is customary not to participate in the meal for the entire thirty-day or twelve-month mourning period. Therefore, the mourner may attend, and even eat and drink a bit, but should not participate in the meal. He should also refrain from participating in the festive dancing.

Some permit one who is mourning a parent, after the thirty-day mourning period, to participate in the festive meal celebrating the completion of a tractate of the Talmud [*siyum*]. Some insist that only if the mourner himself finished the tractate may he partake of the meal. Others insist that the mourner may not participate in any festive meal.

As mentioned above, a parent, sibling, or grandparent may participate in a child's bar mitzva or bat mitzva. Other family members, or even close friends, who feel that they must attend a bar mitzva celebration, should not partake of the festive meal nor participate in the dancing.

To summarize, a mourner may not participate in festive, social gatherings [*simḥat mere'ut*]. One mourning for a parent may not attend a wedding celebration, which includes the meal, but he may attend the wedding ceremony, preferably only after the thirty-day mourning period, as long as the music is meant to honor the *ḥatan* and *kalla* and not to stir the participants to dance. He may also attend a *seudat mitzva,* such as a *Brit Mila,* a festive meal on the occasion of finishing a tractate of the Talmud, or a bar mitzva, as long as there is no instrumental music. Although one may attend a *seudat mitzva*, e.g., a *Brit Mila* or *Pidyon HaBen*, it is customary not to eat at those events for the entire twelve-month mourning period, for one mourning a parent.

### *SHINUI MAKOM*: MOVING ONE'S SEAT IN SYNAGOGUE

Rema relates: It is customary [for mourners] not to sit in their regular places for thirty days, and [when mourning for one's father or mother] for twelve months.

There are different customs regarding whether a mourner should change his place on Shabbat as well. *Gesher HaḤayim* suggests, as a compromise, that during the thirty-day mourning period the mourner should change his seat; afterward, for those mourning the loss of a parent, there is no need to change one's seat. A rabbi or others with assigned seats or pews, as well as one who will pray with greater fervor [*kavana*] in his regular location, need not change their place in synagogue during the mourning period; they may also agree to exchange seats with their neighbors for the period of mourning.

### THE CONLUSION OF THE *SHELOSHIM*

The halakhic principle: "The legal status of part of the day is like that of the entire day" [*miktzat hayom kekhulo*] applies on the thirtieth day, and the mourner for relatives other than his parents may cut his hair or shave any time after sunrise on the thirtieth day. If the thirtieth day falls out on Shabbat, the mourner may not cut his hair on Friday.

### THE TWELVE-MONTH PERIOD OF MOURNING

The Talmud teaches that in addition to the seven-day and thirty-day mourning periods, a child observes certain mourning practices for the entire twelve months following a parent's death. Some explain that continuing to observe mourning practices for twelve months somehow atones for the sins of the deceased. Others view these mourning practices as an expression of respect for the mourner's parent, i.e., a fulfillment of *kibbud av va'em*.

During the twelve-month mourning period, the mourner does not cut his hair or attend festive meals, and in general, restricts his participation in joyous activities. In addition, he recites the Mourner's Kaddish, and if possible, leads the prayer service. He refrains from purchasing and wearing new, elegant clothing. Some mourners also refrain from participating in other festive rituals, such as *Hoshanot* on Sukkot, and dancing with the Torah on Simḥat Torah.

### Haircuts [*Tisporet*]

One mourning a parent may not cut his hair until, in the words of the Talmud: His colleagues have rebuked him for his hair being unkempt. This is known as *ge'ara*. Although technically, if a mourner is rebuked immediately after *sheloshim*, he may cut his hair, several *Rishonim* establish a minimum period after which a mourner may cut his hair even without being rebuked. Rema rules in accordance with those *Rishonim* who maintain that a mourner should not cut his hair until at least three months have passed. R. Moshe Feinstein explains that one should wait an interval twice the time he usually waits between haircuts. Therefore, if this mourner generally cuts his hair every month, he should wait two months before his next haircut. Clearly, this interval is much shorter for beards, especially for one who is generally clean shaven. He may shave immediately after the thirty days of mourning.

The *Aḥaronim* discuss whether the prohibition of cutting one's hair is in effect throughout the entire twelve months, i.e., all of the mourner's haircuts may be carried out only after he is rebuked or after two or three months have passed, as described above, or whether this prohibition applies only to the first haircut. R. Moshe Feinstein rules that the accepted practice is in accordance with those who maintain that after the mourner's first haircut, subsequent haircuts do not require *ge'ara*.

## *AVELUT* ON YOM TOV AND ḤOL HAMO'ED

If a close relative is buried even one hour before a festival, the festival abrogates the seven-day mourning period. This applies to Pesaḥ, Shavuot, and Sukkot, as well as Rosh HaShana and Yom Kippur. In these cases, the *shiva* should be observed until close to nightfall, preferably after Minḥa, at which time one may bathe, and even launder clothing. On Erev Yom Kippur it is permitted to wash even before Minḥa, and the mourner may attend the Minḥa service and eat the *seuda mafseket* while sitting on a chair. On the day before Pesaḥ, restrictions are lifted at midday.

During a festival (i.e., on Ḥol HaMo'ed), one observes the laws of *sheloshim*; therefore, in addition to refraining from cutting one's hair and from doing laundry, which are already prohibited on Ḥol HaMo'ed, the mourner may not cut his nails, and should refrain from attending and participating in festive social gatherings [*simḥat mere'ut*].

If the burial occurred eight days before the festival, the thirty-day mourning period is abrogated. If the burial occurred seven days before the festival, the principle of *miktzat hayom kekhulo* takes effect on the morning of the seventh day, the afternoon counts as the eighth day, the first day of *sheloshim,* and the remaining days of mourning are abrogated. If the eighth day after the burial coincides with a Shabbat that immediately precedes a festival, one may launder his garments and cut his hair on Erev Shabbat. However, if the seventh day coincides with the Shabbat before a festival, the mourner may not cut his hair on Friday; but he may cut his hair during Ḥol HaMo'ed, as he was unable to cut his hair before the festival.

What is the halakha if the burial occurred on any of the six days before the festival? If the burial occurred before Pesaḥ, the days before Pesaḥ count as seven days of mourning, and Pesaḥ counts as another seven, or eight outside of Israel, so the mourner observes an additional sixteen days of *sheloshim* after the festival, or fifteen days outside of Israel. Similarly, if the burial occurred before Shavuot, the festival counts as seven days, or eight days outside of Israel, and the mourner observes an additional sixteen days of *sheloshim,* or fifteen days outside of Israel. If the burial occurs before Sukkot, the first day of Sukkot abrogates the *shiva* and counts as seven days, the festival itself counts as seven days, and Shemini Atzeret counts as seven additional days, totaling twenty-one days, or twenty-two days outside of Israel.

If the burial occurred before Rosh HaShana, the days before Rosh HaShana count as seven days and Rosh HaShana counts as an additional seven days, totaling fourteen days, and the mourner observes an additional sixteen days. If the burial occurs before Yom Kippur, Yom Kippur abrogates the *shiva* and Sukkot abrogates the *sheloshim,* and the mourner may cut his hair before Sukkot.

If the burial occurs on Ḥol HaMo'ed, the *shiva* begins after Yom Tov. Outside of Israel, *shiva* begins after Yom Tov Sheni, but Yom Tov Sheni counts as the first day of *shiva,* and therefore, six days are observed after Yom Tov Sheni. In this case, inconspicuous mourning practices [*devarim shebetzina*] are practiced on Ḥol HaMo'ed; therefore, the mourner may not engage in sexual relations or bathe in hot water for pleasure. It is customary not to refrain from Torah study during Ḥol HaMo'ed, although the mourner should not be called to the Torah for an *aliya.* He may bathe as usual before Yom Tov Aḥaron.

Although the mourner serves as the *sheliaḥ tzibbur* whenever possible on weekdays, he may not lead the services on Rosh HaShana or Yom Kippur, unless there is no one better qualified to do so. Similarly, some write that he should not sound the shofar on Rosh HaShana during the period of mourning.

There are different opinions regarding whether a mourner wears the white outer garment [*kittel*] worn by some during prayers on Rosh HaShana and Yom Kippur and at the Pesaḥ Seder. This may depend upon whether the *kittel* is worn in order to emulate the angels, or to subdue and humble a person's heart.

### SUKKOT

In Ashkenazic communities a mourner does not participate in the *Hoshanot,* i.e., circling the *bima* with the lulav. Some suggest that circling the *bima* evokes the circling of the altar in the Temple, which a mourner may not do. Others explain that just as a mourner does not serve as *sheliaḥ tzibbur,* so too, he does not circle the *bima* during the *Hoshanot.* R. Yechiel Michel Tukachinsky, in his *Gesher HaḤayim,* concludes that the *Hoshanot* are a manifestation of rejoicing [*simḥa*], from which a mourner should refrain. Some suggest that the mourner may participate in the *Hoshanot* on the first day of Yom Tov, and on Ḥol HaMo'ed. One should follow the local custom. In most communities, mourners are asked to hold *sifrei Torah* and stand on the *bima* during the *Hoshanot,* to avoid a public display of their state of mourning.

On Simḥat Torah, mourners refrain from the festive dancing that accompanies the *hakafot.* The rabbi, and other individuals whose absence would constitute a public display of mourning, may participate in the *hakafot.* In Sephardic communities, the custom is that mourners after *shiva* participate fully in the Simḥat Torah festivities.

### *AVELUT* ON PURIM

Rema rules that one does not observe *avelut* on Purim, or on the next day, Shushan Purim. The mourner observes *devarim shebetzina,* refraining from bathing and marital relations. The mourner is obligated to hear the Megilla at night and again during the day, to give *mishlo'aḥ manot* and *matanot la'evyonim,* and to eat a *seudat Purim.* The mourner may wear regular garments, as well as leather shoes, but should keep festive conduct to a minimum. If the burial occurs on Purim, the mourner should rend his shirt and then change his clothes. He eats the *seudat havraa* upon returning home from the burial, although some write that he should not eat hard-boiled eggs.

## THE MOURNER'S KADDISH [*KADDISH YATOM*]

Despite being a relatively recent custom, i.e., approximately eight hundred years old, the Mourner's Kaddish undoubtedly plays a central role in personal mourning and communal prayer. The recitation of Kaddish is perceived as helping the deceased and spiritually benefiting and religiously uplifting the mourner.

Some suggest that the recitation of Kaddish fulfills the talmudic principle: "The son may cause merit for the father" [*bera mezakei abba*] (Sanhedrin 104a). The child is an extension of the parent, and the parent is partially responsible and subsequently rewarded for his good deeds. In that manner, the merit of reciting the Kaddish and publicly sanctifying the name of God greatly benefits the deceased. Others view the recitation of Kaddish as a form of acceptance and justification of God's judgment [*tziduk hadin*]. R. Yechiel Michel Tukachinsky explains that the mourner may be inclined to question God's ways, and Kaddish is an affirmation of his belief that all of God's ways are true and just. R. Soloveitchik viewed the Mourner's Kaddish as the mourner's declaration: "No matter how powerful death is… we declare and profess publicly and solemnly that we are not giving up, that we are not surrendering, that we will carry on the work of our ancestors as though nothing has happened, that we will not be satisfied with less than the full realization of the ultimate goal – the establishment of God's kingdom, the resurrection of the dead, and eternal life for man."

Although according to the original custom, one person would recite each Kaddish, this practice led to disputes, communal strife, and at times, even violence. Nowadays, it is customary in almost all congregations for all mourners to recite Kaddish together. It is proper for the mourners to stand together and recite Kaddish in unison, at the same pace.

Although many authorities prohibited women from reciting Kaddish, others permit women to express their mourning through the public recitation of Kaddish. In communities where it is customary for women to recite the Mourner's Kaddish it is advisable to ensure that there is always at least one man reciting Kaddish at the same time, so that female mourners, and other members of the congregation, will not feel any discomfort. It is customary in many communities for women not to recite Kaddish, and it is paramount to avoid causing communal strife; this question must be handled with the greatest care and sensitivity. Of course, those women who do not recite Kaddish should, like other mourners, dedicate the period of mourning to other means of sanctifying God's name, through Torah study, charitable acts, and good deeds, as we shall see.

It is customary to recite Kaddish for only eleven months. There are some who continue to recite *Kaddish DeRabbanan* for the entire twelve months, as even one whose parents are alive, theoretically, may recite this Kaddish. When someone other than the child of the deceased is reciting Kaddish, they should recite it for the entire twelve months of mourning.

At times, there may be no one with the capability of reciting Kaddish for the deceased, or the mourner may be unable to consistently commit to the daily demands of *minyan* attendance. The *Aḥaronim* discuss whether, and under what circumstances, one may pay someone to say Kaddish on his behalf. One should consider whether there would be greater honor accorded the deceased through giving charity and studying Torah, rather than appointing another person to recite Kaddish.

Nowadays, it is customary, whenever possible, for the mourner to lead the prayer services during the entire mourning period. It is customary for the mourner not to lead the services on Shabbat or Yom Tov. On Rosh Ḥodesh, the mourner may lead the service until Hallel is recited; a non-mourner leads the congregation in Hallel and Musaf. When there is no one else better qualified to serve as the *sheliaḥ tzibbur*, a mourner may lead the services. This is especially relevant on Rosh HaShana and Yom Kippur. In some communities, the mourner does not lead the services on days when *Lamenatze'aḥ* is omitted, i.e., Rosh Ḥodesh, Ḥanukka, Purim, and Erev Pesaḥ; this custom is especially prevalent among Hasidim.

Some emphasize the fact that reciting Kaddish is not the only means of properly commemorating and praying for the soul of the departed, and as R. Joseph Yospa Hahn, in his *Yosef Ometz*, writes: "Torah study, however, is seventy times more effective than any prayer, and through this one brings the deceased into *Gan Eden*; and if the child can produce Torah novellae, there is no estimating the honor the parent receives in the world above."

While Kaddish is often perceived as the primary form of both commemorating and elevating the soul of the deceased, one should view the entire mourning period as an opportunity to strengthen one's faith and commitment to mitzvot, to study Torah, and to engage in acts of charity and kindness, which are all appropriate and effective means of commemorating the death of a loved one.

## THE *YAHRZEIT*

It is customary to commemorate the death of a parent each year. The day of commemoration is commonly known as the *yahrzeit*. Some suggest that observing the *yahrzeit* benefits the soul of the deceased; others insist that the *yahrzeit* benefits the relatives. The *yahrzeit* is most certainly a proper occasion to remember, express appreciation, and learn from the qualities and attributes of the deceased. The *yahrzeit* is observed on the anniversary of the death of a parent. One may observe the *yahrzeit* of other relatives as well.

### Fasting

A custom to fast on the *yahrzeit* of a parent developed during the Middle Ages. R. Mordekhai Yoffe, in his commentary to the *Shulḥan Arukh*, suggests that since the day upon which one's father or mother dies is apparently not a fortuitous day [*re'a mazlei*], one should repent on those days. The *Kitzur Shulḥan Arukh* writes: "It is a meritorious practice to fast on the anniversary of the death of one's father or mother as an inducement to repentance and to self-introspection. By doing this one obtains divine grace for one's father and mother in heaven."

If the *yahrzeit* coincides with a day on which *Taḥanun* is omitted, one does not fast. Furthermore, the main participants in a *Brit Mila*, i.e., the father, *mohel*, and *sandak*; or a *Pidyon HaBen*, i.e., the father and the Kohen; and a bride or groom during the seven festive days following their wedding, should not fast.

The day before the fast, at Minḥa, one should accept upon oneself to fast the next day, as one does for every individual fast [*taanit yaḥid*]. This should preferably be done after the *Shemoneh Esreh*, before or during the concluding paragraph, *Elokai Netzor*. One should say: I intend to fast tomorrow [*hareini betaanit maḥar*], or at least have this in mind. If he forgot to mention this during the Minḥa prayer, it may be said any time during the afternoon. This is unnecessary if he fasts every year.

### *Yahrzeit* Candle

It is customary to light a candle that will burn for the entire *shiva* period, in the place where the deceased passed away, or where the relatives are observing *shiva*. It is also customary to light a candle on Yom Kippur eve that will burn for one day. Some have the custom to light a candle on the last day of Pesaḥ, on Shavuot, and on Shemini Atzeret, i.e., days when the *Yizkor* prayer is recited, as well as on the anniversaries of the days on which one's mother and father died.

Ostensibly, this practice is related to the verses: "The soul of man is the candle of the Lord" (Prov. 20:27), and "For the commandment is a lamp, and the teaching is light" (Prov. 6:23). The soul is likened to a candle, which also evokes both God and the Torah. The eternity and sanctity of the soul are a source of comfort for the mourner.

The candle generally burns for more than twenty-four hours. If one does not have a candle or is unable to light a candle, one should light an electric lamp designated for this purpose. While on Yom Kippur it is customary to light one *ner neshama* for both parents, some suggest that one who observes *yahrzeit* for both parents on one day should kindle two lights.

**Visiting the Gravesite on the *Yahrzeit***

Some are accustomed to visit the graves of their parents at the conclusion of the *shiva, sheloshim,* and twelve-month mourning period, as well as on subsequent *yahrzeits.* In addition, there are different customs regarding the prayers said at the cemetery. Some recite psalms (33, 16, 17, 72, 91, 104, and 130), as well as the passages corresponding to the name of the deceased from Psalms 119. If there is a *minyan,* one recites the Mourner's Kaddish, and the service concludes with the *El Maleh Raḥamim* prayer.

# Chapter 1

# Aninut

The laws of mourning, or *avelut,* as prescribed by the Talmud, are complex, intricate, and multifaceted. Mourning is divided into different stages, reflecting different stages of bereavement. As mentioned previously, the mourner first experiences the period between the death and the burial, called *aninut,* and then observes the seven-day mourning period, known as *shiva.* After the conclusion of the *shiva,* he continues to observe certain mourning practices for thirty days, known as the *sheloshim,* or for twelve months for the loss of a parent. This chapter focuses on *aninut,* during which the mourner is occupied with the burial of a close relative while experiencing the raw and unadulterated feelings of loss.

Following the death of a close relative, i.e., a parent (father or mother), sibling (brother or sister, half-brother or half-sister), child (son or daughter), or spouse, one becomes an *onen,*[1] and observes the

1. Rosh (Berakhot 3:3) writes that anyone who is obligated in the laws of mourning [*avelut*] is subject to the laws of *aninut. Avelut* and *aninut* apply to all of the relatives listed above (Mo'ed Katan 20b). Although technically, one is not obligated to mourn the loss of an adopted relative or a stepparent, one may certainly volunteer to observe the laws of mourning and one is often encouraged to do so (R. Akiva Eiger, *Yoreh De'ah* 341:1; see also *Shulḥan Arukh, Yoreh De'ah* 374:6). Similarly, a convert is not obligated to mourn those related to him before his conversion, even

laws of *aninut*, until the burial. The term *onen* connotes a deep, inner sadness.[2]

There are two types of *aninut*: By Torah law and by rabbinic law.

### *ANINUT* BY TORAH LAW

The Torah relates to the status of *aninut* twice, once regarding the eating of offerings [*korbanot*], and again regarding second tithe [*maaser sheni*] (the tithe separated in the first, second, fourth and fifth years, which must be eaten in a state of ritual purity, in Jerusalem). A careful analysis of these sources may offer insights into the nature of *aninut*.

In one place, after the death of his sons Nadav and Avihu, Aaron explains that, due to his loss, he did not partake of the sin offering [*ḥatat*], which was brought on that day, Rosh Ḥodesh.

> Aaron spoke to Moses: Indeed, today they offered their sin offering and their burnt offering before the Lord, and these have befallen me; had I eaten the sin offering today, would it have been satisfactory in the eyes of the Lord? (Lev. 10:19)

Elsewhere, the Torah (Deut. 26:13–14) describes the "confession of the tithe" [*viduy maaser*], recited after each three-year *maaser* cycle (on Pesaḥ of the fourth and seventh years). The individual declares that he has treated the tithes properly, that he did not eat them while in a state of mourning [*oni*], and that he removed them from his house in a timely fashion.[3]

> You shall say before the Lord your God: I have disposed of the consecrated from my house, and also I gave them to the Levite, and to the stranger, to the orphan, and to the widow, in accordance with all

---

if they have since converted. One is not obligated to mourn for an aborted fetus, a stillborn, or a child who dies within thirty full calendar days of birth (ibid., 374:8). In these cases, the laws of *aninut* also do not apply, although one actively involved in funeral preparations may be exempt from mitzvot due to the principle of *osek bemitzva patur min hamitzva* (*Shulḥan Arukh, Yoreh De'ah* 341:6). Finally, a child under the age of bar or bat mitzva does not observe *aninut* (*Kol Bo* 2:3:19). These issues will be discussed in greater depth in chapter 4.

2. Gen. 35:18. See also Sanhedrin 6:6.
3. See Rambam, *Hilkhot Maaser Sheni* 11.

> Your commandment that You commanded me; I did not violate any of Your commandments, and I did not forget. I did not eat from it in my mourning, and I did not dispose of it in a state of impurity, and I did not give from it for the dead; I heeded the voice of the Lord my God; I have acted in accordance with everything that You commanded me.

These two verses teach that after the death of a close relative, one is not permitted to eat consecrated foods, e.g., offerings and *maaser sheni*.[4] The mishna[5] teaches that it is also prohibited for an *onen* to eat *bikkurim*.[6] This form of *aninut* applies on the day of the death of the relative, even after the burial,[7] through the first night.[8]

Why is it prohibited for an *onen* to eat these sacred foods? The two sources cited above point to two different reasons. The first passage relates to the Kohen himself: An *onen* may not partake of *korbanot*, as this festive and joyous activity contradicts and undermines his state of inner sorrow. The second source relates to the *maaser* and the obligation to treat tithes appropriately; eating it in a state of *aninut* violates the sanctity of *maaser sheni*, which is supposed to be consumed in an appropriate state of mind.[9]

---

4. Interestingly, Rambam (*Hilkhot Maaser Sheni* 3:5) understands that although: "I did not eat from it in my mourning," is not written as an imperative, it is still considered to be a negative commandment, for which one receives *malkot* (lashes). See also *Sefer HaMitzvot, shoresh* 8. Ramban, in his comments to the *Sefer HaMitzvot*, maintains that this verse should not be enumerated as a negative commandment and therefore a mourner who ate *maaser sheni* would not receive *malkot*. Due to this difficulty, *Semag* (Negative Commandments 259–64) suggests an alternative source for the prohibition (see Num. 18:8).
5. Bikkurim 2:2.
6. Rash (ibid.) explains that this is derived from the juxtaposition [*hekesh*] between *maaser sheni* and *bikkurim*. Rambam, in his Commentary on the Mishna (ibid.), explains that since *bikkurim* must be eaten in a state of joy, as the verse says: "And you shall rejoice in all the good that the Lord your God has given to you" (Deut. 26:11), the *onen* may not eat *bikkurim*.
7. Zevaḥim 100a–100b. The Yerushalmi (Pesaḥim 8:8 and Sanhedrin 2:1) and the *Rishonim* (see Rashi, Pesaḥim 90b, s.v. *vehaonen*; see also *Taz, Yoreh De'ah* 398:2) cite a dispute regarding whether *aninut* continues after the burial by Torah law or by rabbinic law.
8. The Talmud (Zevaḥim 100b) cites a dispute regarding whether the biblical status of *aninut* continues after the death of one's relative through the first night, or only during the day.
9. *Semag* (Negative Commandments 259–64) explains that although the verse does not explicitly prohibit eating *maaser sheni* in a state of *aninut*, the prohibition is

In other words, while the verse: "Had I eaten the sin offering today, would it have been satisfactory in the eyes of the Lord," indicates that partaking of *kodashim* violates the state of mourning of the *onen*, the verse: "I did not eat from it in my mourning," indicates that eating it in a state of *aninut* violates the sanctity of *maaser sheni* and *kodashim*.[10] *Aninut* by Torah law appears to be rooted in these two themes: The anguish of the mourner, and upholding the sanctity of sacred foods.

### *ANINUT* BY RABBINIC LAW: *MI SHEMETO MUTAL LEFANAV*[11]

The Talmud[12] teaches that in addition to the Torah prohibitions listed above, the Rabbis instituted other expressions of *aninut*.

> One whose deceased relative is laid out before him...he does not recline while he eats. Furthermore, he neither eats meat nor drinks wine, and does not recite a blessing before eating, and does not recite the formula to invite the participants in the meal to join together in the Grace after Meals (*zimun*), [i.e., he is exempt from the obligation of Grace after Meals]. He is exempt from the recitation of *Shema*, from the *Shemoneh Esreh* prayer, and from phylacteries, and from all mitzvot mentioned in the Torah.

The Talmud refers to two prohibitions: Reclining while eating, and eating meat and wine, as well as one exemption: From all the [positive] mitzvot

---

derived from the verse that describes how offerings should be eaten: "The Lord spoke to Aaron: Behold, I have given you the commission of My *terumot*, with regard to all the consecrated items [*kodshei*] of the children of Israel I have given them to you for prominence [*lemashḥa*], and to your sons, as an eternal allotment" (Num. 18:8). Based on this verse, the Talmud (Zevaḥim 91a) teaches: "The text states: '*lemashḥa*' - i.e., for prominence, in the same manner that kings take their food." *Maaser sheni* and *kodashim* must be eaten in the same manner that kings take their food. Therefore, it would be inappropriate for an *onen*, who is in a state of sadness, to eat these foods.

10. We will see a similar idea regarding donning *tefillin* on the first day of mourning.
11. R. Soloveitchik would often remark that although the *Shulḥan Arukh* (*Yoreh De'ah* 341) refers to these laws as *Hilkhot Onen*, the term *onen* refers to the Torah laws, while when describing the rabbinic laws, the Talmud uses the phrase: One whose deceased is laid out before him [*mi shemeto mutal lefanav*].
12. Berakhot 17b; Mo'ed Katan 23b.

mentioned in the Torah. In addition, an *onen* does not don *tefillin,* and according to some is obligated to observe many of the laws of *shiva.* We will discuss the practical applications of these categories below.

Many view the exemption from mitzvot as the most jarring expression of *aninut.* Why is an *onen* exempt from fulfilling mitzvot? The Talmud and its commentaries suggest two broad approaches to this question.

Some suggest that the *onen* must focus his thoughts and energy on tending to the proper burial of the deceased. The halakha exempts the *onen* from performing positive mitzvot to enable the *onen* to tend to the burial of his relative. Some[13] even understand this exemption in light of other cases in which one who is engaged in the performance of one mitzva is exempt from fulfilling another [*osek bemitzva patur min hamitzva*].[14]

Others suggest that as an expression of respect for his deceased relative he must devote all of his thoughts and actions to the deceased and is not to be distracted by the performance of mitzvot. Tosafot[15] cite a passage from the Yerushalmi indicating that one's behavior before the burial must differ from his typical behavior.

> Said R. Bun: "It is written: 'So that you will remember the day of your exodus from the land of Egypt all the days of your life' [Deut. 16:3]. On days when you are caring for the living [you must recite *Shema* and remember the Exodus], but not on days when you are caring for the dead."

13. Rashi, Berakhot 17b, s.v. *mi shemeto;* Rambam, *Hilkhot Keriat Shema* 4:3.
14. R. Soloveitchik (cited in R. Eliakim Koenigsberg, *Shiurei HaRav al Inyanei Avelut VeTisha B'Av* [1999], pp. 1–2) notes that some texts of the mishna (see Rabbeinu Yona, Berakhot 10b, s.v. *patur;* see also MS Kaufmann, Berakhot 3:1) read: One whose deceased is laid out before him is exempt from reciting *Shema,* from reciting *Shemoneh Esreh,* and from donning *tefillin,* omitting the phrase: And from all mitzvot mentioned in the Torah. He explains that in addition to the broader exemption based upon the principle of *osek bemitzva,* an *onen* may be exempt from these three mitzvot, as they require a unique level of intent [*kavana*]. An *onen,* who is distressed by the loss of his relative, cannot achieve the minimum level of intent required for *Keriat Shema* (Berakhot 13a–b), *Shemoneh Esreh* (ibid., 34b), and *tefillin* (Sukka 42a). R. Soloveitchik concludes that even in a case where the *onen* is no longer actively involved in burial preparations, he may still be exempt from these three mitzvot.
15. Berakhot 17b, s.v. *patur.*

R. Bun contrasts one's normative behavior, when "caring for the living," to one's behavior when "caring for the dead."

R. Yosef Dov Soloveitchik[16] cites this passage and relates it to the natural, human experience of mourning. He writes:

> Judaism does not want man to rationalize evil or theologize it away. It challenges him to defy evil and, in case of defeat, to give vent to his distress. Both rationalizing and theologizing harden the human heart and make it insensitive to disaster. Man, Judaism says, must act like a human being. He must cry, weep, despair, grieve and mourn as if he could change the cosmic laws by exhibiting these emotions. In times of distress and sorrow, these emotions are noble even though they express the human protest against iniquity in nature and also pose an unanswerable question regarding justice in the world. The Book of Job was not written in vain. Judaism does not tolerate hypocrisy and unnatural behavior which is contrary to human sensitivity...I want the sufferer to act as a human being, God says. Let him not suppress his humanity in order to please Me. Let him tear his clothes in frustrating anger and stop observing mitzvot because his whole personality in enveloped by dark despair and finds itself in a trance of the senses and of the faculties.

After citing the Yerushalmi mentioned above, he explains:

> That means that the mourner is relieved of his obligation in mitzvot because he is incapable of performing them. He has simply lost his own sense of dignity; the focus on his personality has been lost... that is what Tosafot and all the *Rishonim* [medieval halakhic authorities] mean when they say that it is completely forbidden to perform a mitzva during this first stage of mourning: the mourner is incapable of performing mitzvot...Of course, emotions, like the tide, reach a high mark, make an about face, and begin to recede. The Torah has therefore recommended to man not only to submit himself to the emotional onslaught, but to gradually and slowly redeem himself from its impact. Therefore the Halakhah divided mourning into various stages.

16. *Out of the Whirlwind: Essays on Mourning, Suffering and the Human Condition* (2003), pp. 12–13; see also pp. 1–3.

According to this approach, one might even suggest that refraining from fulfilling mitzvot is a positive fulfillment of the laws of mourning.[17]

Many relate this debate as to whether the exemption from mitzvot is due to the involvement of the *onen* in burial preparations or to the reason cited by Tosafot, to another question: May an *onen* choose to perform mitzvot voluntarily? Rashi[18] writes that the *onen* "need not recite the blessing of *hamotzi*," inferring that if he wishes, he *may* do so. Tosafot[19] disagree with Rashi and insist that the *onen* may not recite the blessing, or perform mitzvot. It appears that since Rashi understands the exemption to be rooted in the involvement of the *onen* in burial preparations, the *onen* may choose to perform those mitzvot which will not distract him. Tosafot view the exemption as an absolute release from the obligation of mitzvot, and therefore the *onen* may not perform the mitzvot even if he wishes to do so.

These two approaches can be traced to a dispute cited in the Yerushalmi.[20]

> It was taught: "If [a mourner] wished to be strict with himself [and recite *Shema*] they do not listen to him." Why? Is it due to respect for the dead [*kevodo shel met*] or due to [the fact] that he has no one to bear his burden [and facilitate the interment while he recites *Shema*]? What is the [practical] difference between [these two explanations]? [The difference is in a case where] there was another to bear his burden. If you say [he may not recite *Shema*] due to respect for the dead, it would be prohibited to recite [*Shema*]. But if you say it is due to [the fact] that he has no one to bear his burden, [in this case] he has someone to bear his burden [and it would be permitted to recite *Shema*].

According to one opinion, the *onen* is exempt from mitzvot because he has no one to bear his burden [*ein mi sheyisa masao*]. The other opinion understands that the exemption of the *onen* from mitzvot is an expression of *kevodo shel met*, respect for the deceased. Some explain that the mourner wishes to

17. R. Yosef Dov Soloveitchik, as cited in *Shiurei HaRav al Inyanei Avelut VeTisha B'Av*, p. 3.
18. Ibid., s.v. *ve'eino mevarekh*.
19. Ibid., s.v. *ve'eino mevarekh*.
20. Y. Berakhot 3:1.

avoid the appearance that he is acting disrespectfully toward the deceased.[21] Others suggest that the *onen* abstains from performing mitzvot "so that his heart will be free to consider the needs of the deceased and to think of them constantly."[22] The Yerushalmi suggests that while according to the first view it would be permitted for an *onen* to perform mitzvot when someone else is tending to the burial, according to the second view, even if he is not actively involved in the burial, he must still refrain from performing mitzvot.[23]

The majority of *Rishonim* accept the second approach, which views the exemption from mitzvot as rooted in *kevodo shel met,*[24] and therefore an *onen* is exempt and even prohibited from fulfilling positive mitzvot. That said, these two themes, tending to the burial and honoring the deceased, continue to impact many halakhic questions regarding the application of *aninut.*

Let us address some common scenarios with regard to which there are disputes among the *Rishonim* and *Aḥaronim* as to whether or not the laws of *aninut* are in effect.

## IN WHICH CASES DOES *ANINUT* APPLY?

*Aninut* typically begins upon hearing of the death of a relative, and ends with the burial. Are there situations in which the laws of *aninut* do not apply? On the one hand, the Talmud describes the transition from *aninut* to *avelut*[25] and does not mention any exceptions to the laws of *aninut.* On the other hand, the mishna[26] implies, as Rashi notes (see above), that the exemption of the *onen* from mitzvot is rooted in the well-known halakhic principle: "One who

---

21. *Shita Mekubetzet,* Berakhot 17b, s.v. *ha de'amrinan; Penei Moshe,* Y. Berakhot 3:1; see also *Taz, Yoreh De'ah* 341:1 and Shakh (ibid., 3).
22. See *Baḥ, Oraḥ Ḥayim* 71 and *Yoreh De'ah* 341.
23. We should note that while most *Rishonim* assume that an *onen* does not recite blessings before eating [*birkot hanehenin*], Rash (Demai 1:4, s.v. *umevarkhin alav*) explains that although the *onen* cannot recite blessings on behalf of others, he does recite a blessing before he eats. This may be understood in light of the talmudic passage that states that one may not benefit from this world without first reciting a blessing (Berakhot 35a). This passage indicates that reciting a blessing before eating should not be understood as a mitzva, but rather, it is required to avoid violating a prohibition.
24. Some explain that even the notion of *kevodo shel met* would apply only when preparing for the burial (see *Gesher HaḤayim* 18:2:21).
25. See Mo'ed Katan 27a.
26. Berakhot 17b.

is engaged in a mitzva is exempt from performing another mitzva" [*osek bemitzva patur min hamitzva*], which might lead to the conclusion that *aninut* does not apply when one is not involved in the preparations for the burial.

The mishna[27] describes *aninut* as a case in which one's deceased is laid out before him [*meto mutal lefanav*]. What is the definition of, and what are the parameters of, *mutal lefanav*? Let us begin by discussing two simpler cases, and then we will present more difficult scenarios.

### *Aninut* When There Is No Burial

If there is absolutely no possibility of burying the deceased, then the laws of *aninut* do not apply. For example, Tractate Semaḥot (2:10) teaches:

> One who drowned in the sea or was swept away by a river, or was devoured by a wild beast, one does not withhold anything from him. From when does one begin to count [the days of the mourning]? From the time they despaired of seeking [the body].

Related to this passage, Rosh[28] writes:

> It once happened in Mainz that a person was traveling in a wagon and the driver killed him. This occurred on Rosh Ḥodesh Shevat. His son searched all the roads for many days, but did not find him. On Rosh Ḥodesh Adar he approached Rabbeinu Elyakim, son of R. Yosef, and asked what he should do. [Rabbeinu Elyakim] responded that he should count *shiva* and *sheloshim* from Rosh Ḥodesh Adar onward, in accordance with that which is written in Evel Rabbati (2:13): "One who drowned in the sea."

In this case, the mourner certainly doesn't observe *aninut,* as there is no *meto mutal lefanav*.

The *Rishonim* discuss other cases in which, although there will be a burial, the deceased is not considered *mutal lefanav*. For example, Rosh[29] writes:

27. Ibid.

28. Mo'ed Katan 3:56; see also Tosafot, Berakhot 18a, s.v. *ve'eino*.

29. Mo'ed Katan 3:55; see also *Mordekhai* 899.

> R. Yitzḥak ruled, regarding a Jew who was captured by the governor and died in captivity, and the governor refuses to hand over [the body] for burial for many days, that the status of *aninut* does not take effect on the relatives, as they cannot be characterized as one whose deceased is laid out before him since it is not incumbent upon them to bury him. However, we should not equate this to a case of one who despairs of burying [his dead], who begins mourning immediately... as they have not completely despaired of burying him and they hope for divine salvation, that He will stir the spirit of the leader from above, and he will release the body for burial for a nominal price; therefore, the status of mourning does not take effect.

Rabbeinu Yona[30] explains that since the relatives are not preoccupied with the burial there is no concern that they will be remiss in respecting the deceased. The *Shulḥan Arukh*[31] rules in accordance with this view and adds that if the relatives of the deceased are in captivity, they are not subject to the laws of *aninut*.[32]

### *Aninut* When the Deceased Is Entrusted to the *Ḥevra Kadisha*

Is a person who is not actively involved in the burial preparations considered an *onen*? This possibility is raised numerous times in the Yerushalmi.

In the passage cited above, two reasons for *aninut* are suggested: Respect for the deceased [*kevodo shel met*] or: Because there is no one to bear his burden and facilitate the interment [*ein mi sheyisa masao*]. The Yerushalmi asserts that according to the second reason if there is another to bear the burden of the burial he would not become an *onen*. Most *Rishonim*

---

30. Berakhot 11a, s.v. *kol zeman*.
31. *Shulḥan Arukh, Yoreh De'ah* 341:4. Shakh (341:15) adds that if the body is withheld due to anti-Semitism, and not for financial gain, the relatives should begin mourning immediately, as most likely they will not receive the body in return.
32. Interestingly, the *Aḥaronim* discuss whether *aninut* applies when the government mandates that one delay burial for several days. R. Yechezkel Landau, in his *Noda BiYehuda* (*Mahadura Tinyana, Yoreh De'ah* 211), rules that since one may begin preparing for the burial, he becomes an *onen* during this period. R. Eliyahu Ragoler, in his *Yad Eliyahu* (16), disagrees and rules that since he cannot prepare the deceased for burial, he does not become an *onen*. See *Pitḥei Teshuva* 341:22.

rule that the primary reason for *aninut* is *kevodo shel met,* and the *Shulḥan Arukh*[33] rules: Even if he need not be involved in the needs of the deceased, he may not perform the mitzvot.

However, a different passage apparently relates to a more extreme case, where one has literally handed over the deceased to others, in which case some or all of the laws of *aninut* may not apply.

> If [the body] was handed to the public, [the *onen*] eats meat and drinks wine. If it is given to the pallbearers [*katafim*], it is as one who is handed to the public.[34]

The *Shulḥan Arukh* cites this passage and rules:

> In a place where it is customary for special pallbearers [*katafim*] to carry the deceased, after the relatives have engaged in the burial needs, they shall hand [the deceased] to them and they bury him. From when they hand [the deceased] to them it is permitted for the relatives to [eat] meat and [drink] wine even before they removed the [deceased] from the house, as it is no longer incumbent upon them [to bury the deceased].

Although the Yerushalmi and the *Shulḥan Arukh* do not address the matter of mitzvot, the *Aḥaronim*[35] assume that at that point one may perform mitzvot as well.

The *Aḥaronim* question the relevance of this ruling to modern-day burial practices. Nowadays it is customary to entrust the body to the *ḥevra kadisha,* community members or professionals responsible for preparing the body for burial and for doing the burial itself. After the deceased is given to the *ḥevra kadisha,* the mourner need not concern himself with direct preparations for the burial; rather, his concern is with other issues, including preparing a eulogy [*hesped*], traveling to the burial, informing friends and relatives, etc.

Do the laws of *aninut* apply after the body is entrusted to the *ḥevra kadisha*? Some *Aḥaronim,* among them R. Yechiel Michel Epstein (1829–1908)[36]

---

33. *Shulḥan Arukh, Yoreh De'ah* 341:1.
34. Y. Mo'ed Katan 3:5; see also Tosafot, Berakhot 18a, s.v. *ve'eino*.
35. See, for example, *Noda BiYehuda, Mahadura Tinyana, Yoreh De'ah* 211.
36. *Arukh HaShulḥan, Yoreh De'ah* 341:20.

and R. Yekutiel Yehuda Greenwald,[37] caution that if this passage is taken literally, *aninut* would almost never apply nowadays.

Indeed, R. Avraham Danzig (1748–1820), in his *Ḥokhmat Adam*, relates to this scenario:

> In a place where it is customary... that after the relatives complete the burial preparations they give the deceased to [the *ḥevra kadisha,*] who bury him... it is permitted for them to [eat] meat and [drink] wine. Similarly, it seems obvious to me that it is permitted for them to pray and recite blessings even before the deceased is removed from his house, as the [deceased] is no longer their responsibility. If so, those mourners who wait until after the burial to pray are acting improperly.[38]

R. Danzig clearly rules that entrusting the deceased to the *ḥevra kadisha* terminates the status of *aninut.*[39]

R. Yechezkel Landau, in his *Noda BiYehuda,*[40] understands the role of the *katafim* differently. He writes:

> Handed to the *katafim* refers to a case in which the deceased is taken to a distant place [for burial] and the *onen* does not accompany them to the place of burial. In that case, once the deceased is handed to the *katafim,* even though the deceased is still in the house, the *aninut* is terminated, as he no longer has any involvement with him. However, when the relatives travel with [the deceased] to the

37. *Sefer Kol Bo al Avelut,* p. 120.
38. *Ḥokhmat Adam* 153:3.
39. Interestingly, elsewhere (*Ḥokhmat Adam, Kuntres Matzevet Moshe,* p. 702, section 3) R. Danzig describes his behavior after his son, Moshe, passed away: "After I entrusted the *ḥevra kadisha* with the preparations for the burial, and I chose a spot for the burial, and they dug the grave... even though he had not yet been buried, since I gave him to the pallbearers I recited blessings, as it is stated in the *Shulḥan Arukh.* And someone asked that, still, there is the factor of *kevod hamet* regarding which Rosh writes explicitly that even after one has dealt with the details of the burial, one remains exempt [from fulfilling mitzvot]. I responded that Rosh himself cites this ruling that if one transfers full responsibility to the pallbearers, even if the deceased is still in the house it is permitted [to perform mitzvot]."
40. *Mahadura Tinyana, Yoreh De'ah* 211.

> burial, handing [the deceased to the *katafim*] is of no consequence, as since he is traveling there, [the deceased] remains laid out before him [*mutal lefanav*].

It is customary to follow the opinion of *Noda BiYehuda*.[41] Even in a case where the mourner does not accompany the deceased, one observes *aninut* until after the burial, as the mourner is often still involved in arrangements for the funeral.[42]

Although it is customary to observe *aninut* even after entrusting the deceased to the *ḥevra kadisha*, the *Aḥaronim* discuss whether the laws of *aninut* apply in several other scenarios.

**If the Deceased Is in a Different City than the Mourner**

What if the *onen* is in a different city than the deceased, is not directly involved in organizing the burial, and does not plan to attend the funeral? The *Rishonim* and *Aḥaronim* discuss this case in great depth and question whether *aninut* applies, and when to begin the period of mourning [*shiva*].

Regarding *aninut*, Tosafot[43] relate the following story:

> It occurred that the sister of Rabbeinu Tam died on Shabbat, and after Shabbat he received the news in a different city. He ate meat and drank wine, and said that since she had a husband who was obligated to see to her burial, it was not prohibited for him [Rabbeinu Tam] to [eat] meat and [drink] wine. Perhaps, even if he had been in the same city [where she died], Rabbeinu Tam would have been lenient, for the same reason.

Rabbeinu Tam ruled that since he was not involved in the burial arrangements it was permitted for him to eat meat and drink wine.

---

41. *Pitḥei Teshuva* 341:21; *Gilyon Maharsha* 341:3. *Sefer Kol Bo al Avelut* (p. 124) emphatically embraces this view, and adds that even according to this view one should not pray or recite *berakhot* until after the burial.
42. *Yalkut Yosef* 7:1; see also *MeOlam VeAd Olam*, p. 66, n. 6. The *Mishna Berura* (61:4) appears to adopt the view of the *Ḥokhmat Adam*. *Gesher HaḤayim* (18:2:22) suggests that once the *ḥevra kadisha* assumes responsibility for the deceased, and the mourner is no longer actively involved in preparations for the burial, it is permitted for him to pray.
43. Tosafot, Berakhot 18a, s.v. *ve'eino*.

There is a dispute regarding Rabbeinu Tam's conduct. Rosh[44] understood that Rabbeinu Tam maintained that since his brother-in-law was halakhically responsible for arranging the burial, he alone assumes the status of an *onen*. Rosh strongly disagrees with Rabbeinu Tam and rules that even a brother, who is not halakhically responsible for the burial arrangements, is obligated to observe the laws of *aninut*. In contrast, R. Yoel Sirkis, in his commentary to the *Tur*,[45] explains that Rabbeinu Tam ate meat and drank wine only because he was not in the same city as his sister. Had he been in the same city, the obligation to involve oneself in the burial, and the corresponding *aninut*, would have applied to him as well.

The *Shulḥan Arukh*[46] rules in accordance with the opinion of Rosh; therefore, the laws of *aninut* apply regardless of whether or not the mourner is in the same city as the deceased or plans on attending the funeral. Many *Aḥaronim*, however, dispute this ruling.[47]

The *Aḥaronim* discuss the relevance of this dispute to a more common, contemporary question: When does one who hears of the death of a relative but does not plan to attend the funeral begin sitting *shiva*? R. Naftali Tzvi Yehuda Berlin[48] rules that *shiva* begins only after the burial. His son-in-law, R. Refael Shapiro,[49] and R. Moshe Feinstein[50] maintain that *avelut* begins immediately. R. Shapiro insists that the dispute between Rabbeinu Tam and Rosh relates to a different scenario. As we shall see,[51] most communities adopt the position of R. Refael Shapiro, and mourners begin observing *avelut* immediately, with no period of *aninut*.[52]

---

44. Rosh, Berakhot 3:3.
45. *Baḥ, Yoreh De'ah* 341.
46. *Shulḥan Arukh, Yoreh De'ah* 341:1.
47. *Shulḥan Arukh HaRav* (*Oraḥ Ḥayim* 71:1) and *Arukh HaShulḥan* (*Yoreh De'ah* 341:12) rule in accordance with Rosh (*Shulḥan Arukh*), while *Peri Ḥadash* (*Oraḥ Ḥayim* 71), *Kitzur Shulḥan Arukh* (196:4), and *Gesher HaḤayim* (18:1:6) accept the lenient ruling of the *Baḥ*.
48. *Meshiv Davar* 2:72; see also R. Simḥa Bunim Sofer, *Shevet Sofer, Yoreh De'ah* 106; *Arukh HaShulḥan* 341:12.
49. *Sedei Ḥemed*, vol. 8, *Pe'at HaSadeh, Maarekhet Avelut* 14 (also cited in Maharsham 2:270); see also *Iggerot Moshe, Yoreh De'ah* 1:253.
50. *Iggerot Moshe, Yoreh De'ah* 2:354.
51. See chapter 4.
52. If the mourner continues to be involved in the burial preparations from afar, and certainly if he delivers a *hesped* (eulogy) over the telephone or via a live video call or similar, then even R. Refael Shapiro might agree that he should begin mourning

The *Aḥaronim* discuss whether and when a mourner, who plans to travel to a different city to attend the funeral, becomes an *onen*. This question may depend upon the length of time between the death and burial, as well as whether the mourner will be involved in burial preparations by telephone. R. Yechiel Michel Tukachinsky (1872–1955), in his *Gesher HaḤayim*, concludes:

> One who can assist [in the preparations] is characterized as *meto mutal lefanav* and one who is unable to assist in any way is called *ein meto mutal lefanav* and would therefore not be considered to be an *onen*.

Even those who maintain that *aninut* does not apply in this case agree that he becomes an *onen* upon arrival in the city where the relative will be buried.[53] The common practice is to observe *aninut* from the death until the burial, even when the mourner must travel to a different city to attend the funeral.

What if the mourner is currently in the same city as the deceased, but does not plan on accompanying the body to attend the burial in a different city? In this case, when the body is taken to the other city, and the mourner remains behind, *aninut* ends and the *shiva* begins after the mourners take their leave of the deceased and return home, as we will learn in chapter 6. If the burial is nearby, then the mourner remains an *onen* until the burial, at which point he begins to observe the *shiva*. If the mourner accompanies the deceased to a distant city, he observes *aninut* until the burial.[54]

What if the mourner is waiting for the deceased to be brought to his city? In this case, as the mourner is most often engaged in preparations for the funeral, notifying relatives, and preparing a eulogy, he observes *aninut*. In case of a significant delay, of more than two days, and if the mourner is no longer involved in funeral preparations, *aninut* may be suspended until the arrival of the deceased.[55]

---

after the burial. See R. Asher Bush, "*Hatḥalat Avelut LeMi SheEino Nimtza BeKevurat Aviv Umishtatef al yedei Telefon,*" *Beit Yitzḥak* 46 (5775/2015).

53. *Peri Ḥadash, Oraḥ Ḥayim* 71; *Gesher HaḤayim* 18:1:6.

54. The *Aḥaronim* discuss whether one remains an *onen* while flying on a plane. Some argue that if the *onen* is not involved in the burial preparations at all, then he should pray and recite blessings (R. Shlomo Zalman Auerbach, as cited by *Nitei Gavriel* 14:5, n. 15). It is customary to observe the laws of *aninut* even on the plane.

55. Rema, *Yoreh De'ah* 341:3.

Some of these questions remain unresolved and subject to disputes between the authorities to this day. When encountering a complicated situation, the mourner should consult a halakhic authority.

### *TEFILLIN*

As mentioned above, the mishna teaches that the *onen* is exempt from reciting *Shema,* from reciting the *Shemoneh Esreh,* from donning *tefillin,* and from all the mitzvot mentioned in the Torah.[56] It appears that the *onen* is exempt from fulfilling the mitzva of *tefillin* just as he is exempt from fulfilling all other positive commandments.

Elsewhere, the Talmud[57] teaches that a mourner is exempt from *tefillin,* for a different reason.

> R. Abba b. Zavda said that Rav said: A mourner is obligated in all the mitzvot mentioned in the Torah except for phylacteries, as "splendor" is stated, from the fact that the Merciful One said to Ezekiel: "Bind your splendor upon you" (Ezek. 24:17). You are obligated; however, everyone is exempt. This applies on the first day, as it is written: "And its end as a bitter day" (Amos 8:10).

The Talmud derives this law, and other laws of mourning, from a passage in the Book of Ezekiel, where God tells the prophet Ezekiel that his most beloved wife will be taken from him, and instructs him that he should not conduct himself as a mourner.

> Son of man, behold, I am taking from you the delight of your eyes in a plague; but you will not eulogize and you will not weep, and your tears will not come. Sigh in silence, make no mourning for the dead, bind your splendor upon you, and put your shoes upon your feet, and do not cover your upper lip, and do not eat the bread of people. (Ezek. 24:16–17)

From the fact that Ezekiel is commanded: "Bind your splendor [*pe'er*] upon you," we derive that other mourners may not don their splendor, or

56. Berakhot 17b.
57. Sukka 25b.

*tefillin,* upon their heads. Furthermore, the Talmud limits this exemption to the first day, in accordance with the verse: "And its end as a bitter day [*ve'aḥaritah keyom mar*]."

Why must a mourner refrain from donning *tefillin* on the first day of his mourning? The *Rishonim* dispute whether the reason is that in the mourner's disheveled state, it is inappropriate for him to don *tefillin,*[58] or whether donning *tefillin* contradicts the appropriate appearance of a mourner.[59] Interestingly, we encountered this same dispute earlier regarding why it is prohibited for an *onen* to eat *kodashim* and *maaser sheni.*

The *Aḥaronim* dispute whether a mourner should don *tefillin* if the death is on one day and the burial is the next day (even that evening). Most[60] rule that on the day of the burial, even after the burial, the mourner does not don *tefillin.* R. Yom Tov Tzahalon (Tzefat, 1559–1638), known as Maharitatz[61], disagrees and rules that the mourner is exempt from *tefillin* only when the death and burial are on the same day. It is customary to follow the first opinion, although some recommend donning *tefillin* privately, without a blessing, after the interment.[62] *Gesher HaḤayim* (ibid.) cites the *Sefer Eretz Ḥayim,* which records that the custom in Jerusalem [*minhag Yerushalayim*] is to don *tefillin* without a blessing.[63]

When the burial takes place more than a day after the death, if the mourner is engaged in preparations for the funeral and is therefore exempt from fulfilling mitzvot, he is exempt from the mitzva of *tefillin* as well. *Gesher HaḤayim* insists that in that case, if he interrupted his *aninut* and donned *tefillin,* then on the day of the burial he should certainly don *tefillin* after the funeral.[64]

---

58. Rashi, Berakhot 11a, s.v. *alma.*
59. Rashi, Sukka 25b, s.v. *mide'amar.*
60. *Taz* 38:3; *Eliya Rabba* 38:3; *Peri Megadim, Mishbetzot Zahav* 38:3; R. Akiva Eiger, *Yoreh De'ah* 388:1; *Dagul Merevava, Yoreh De'ah* 388; *Mishna Berura* 38:16; *Arukh HaShulḥan, Yoreh De'ah* 388:2; *Kaf HaḤayim* 38:16; *Gesher HaḤayim* 18:4:1.
61. Cited by *Be'er Heitev* 38:3.
62. *Ḥayei Adam* 14:19. R. Ovadia Yosef (*Yabia Omer, Yoreh De'ah* 2:27) discusses this topic at great length, and also concludes that while it is customary not to don *tefillin* on the day of the burial, he instructs those who ask that they should don *tefillin* privately without a blessing. R. Shlomo Zalman Auerbach (*Minḥat Shlomo Tinyana* 99:5) concurs.
63. R. Mordekhai Eliyahu, in his rulings on the laws of mourning, *Tzeror HaḤayim,* also writes that the custom in Jerusalem is to don *tefillin* privately without a blessing.
64. *Gesher HaḤayim* 18:4:5. He adds that even those who disagree would admit that one may voluntarily wear *tefillin,* as the Talmud only prohibits an *onen* from performing

If the death and burial occurred on Ḥol HaMo'ed, the mourner should don *tefillin* on the day after Yom Tov [*Isru Ḥag*], despite it being the first day that the *shiva* is observed.[65] If the burial is on Ḥol HaMo'ed, the *Aḥaronim* disagree whether one who typically dons *tefillin* on Ḥol HaMo'ed should don *tefillin* after the burial.[66]

## OBSERVING THE LAWS OF *AVELUT* DURING *ANINUT*

As mentioned above, the *onen* must maintain the appropriate disposition, must refrain from eating meat and drinking wine, is prohibited from fulfilling all the [positive] mitzvot mentioned in the Torah, and does not don *tefillin*.

Is the *onen* obligated to observe the prohibitions of mourning [*avelut*]? The *Rishonim* disagree regarding a fascinating and fundamental question: Do the laws of *avelut*, including washing and laundering, begin at the time of death, or only after the burial? Or, in other words, is *aninut* a period of mourning, during which the mourner must also ensure the proper burial of the deceased, or is it a period of deep and profound sadness, of shock, coupled with the responsibilities of burial, but not technically a period of mourning?[67]

Some *Rishonim*[68] maintain that the laws of *avelut* do not begin until after the burial, and therefore a mourner may wash, launder his clothes, study Torah, and even cut his hair. Tosafot[69] explain:

> Those [laws] that are due to the *avelut* are permitted for an *onen* and prohibited for a mourner. However, those matters that are not prohibited due to *avelut*, but rather to enable [the mourner] to concentrate on burying his deceased and not be distracted by other matters, such as [eating] meat and [drinking] wine, are prohibited to the *onen*.

---

mitzvot, but does not say that a mourner cannot adopt a stringency and don *tefillin* after the burial.

65. *Mishna Berura* 38:16.

66. *Magen Avraham* (548:5) rules that one should don *tefillin*. *Shevut Yaakov* (2:25), cited by *Shaarei Teshuva* (548:4), disagrees. The *Mishna Berura* (38:16) rules that one should don *tefillin* without a blessing (which is the custom on Ḥol HaMo'ed in any case).

67. This question will be addressed at greater length in chapter 4, in the discussion of the source and origins of *avelut*.

68. Rambam, *Hilkhot Avel* 1:2; R. Yitzchak ibn Ghiyyat (cited by Ramban, *Torat HaAdam, Inyan Mi SheMeto Mutal Lefanav*, p. 73).

69. Mo'ed Katan 23b, s.v. *ve'eino*.

They add that sexual relations are also prohibited, lest he become distracted from his duties, or because it is impertinence [*ḥutzpa*] to engage in sexual relations then. Tosafot discuss whether doing laundry and cutting one's hair should be prohibited for an *onen*.

Ramban[70] disagrees, and maintains that the *onen* observes most of the laws of *avelut*, and must refrain from sexual relations, washing, anointing, greeting [*she'elat shalom*], and participating in festivities. However, an *onen* may wear leather shoes, to ensure that there will be no obstacle to properly arranging the interment. Ramban adds that one should even sleep on the floor.

*Shulḥan Arukh*[71] rules that although an *onen* may not sit or sleep on a bed, he need not remove his shoes.[72] The *Aḥaronim* dispute whether he agrees with Ramban or Rambam.[73] Rema adds that the *onen* may not engage in marital relations (Tosafot). He then cites the view of Ramban, and rules that certain laws of *avelut*, e.g., bathing, anointing, participating in joyous occasions, greeting [*she'elat shalom*], cutting one's hair, and working, are prohibited.

In practice, *Gesher HaḤayim*[74] notes: The prevalent custom is to permit sitting on a chair, as well as sleeping on a bed, before the burial. Furthermore, the *onen* may leave his house to attend to needs that concern the deceased. He may not engage in marital relations, apply lotions or oils to himself (although deodorant is permitted),[75] participate in joyful occasions, extend greetings [*she'elat shalom*], or cut his hair or shave. He should refrain from bathing, although if he is uncomfortable, he may wash, preferably one limb at a time, in lukewarm water.[76] The *onen* should also refrain from working and from Torah study.[77]

70. Ramban, ibid.
71. *Shulḥan Arukh, Yoreh De'ah* 341:5.
72. Some suggest that nowadays, since the *onen* can just as easily wear non-leather sneakers, he should refrain from wearing leather shoes as well.
73. See Ḥatam Sofer, as cited in *Pitḥei Teshuva* 341:23; *Arukh HaShulḥan* 341:28.
74. *Gesher HaḤayim* 18:2:2. He offers different explanations for this custom.
75. *Shulḥan Arukh, Yoreh De'ah* 381:2.
76. Since this matter itself is subject to dispute, and a delicate person [*istenis*] may bathe even during *shiva*, one who must bathe may be lenient during *aninut*.
77. R. Akiva Eiger, *Yoreh De'ah* 341:1. He may study the laws of mourning, and if he is a rabbi, he may issue halakhic rulings.

The *Aharonim* disagree whether it is appropriate to recite Kaddish before the burial. R. David HaLevi Segal (1586–1667), in his commentary to the *Shulḥan Arukh, Turei Zahav (Taz)*,[78] writes that if others are tending to the deceased, the mourner should attend the synagogue and recite Kaddish, as "this is the honor of his father." R. Shabtai HaKohen (Shakh), a younger contemporary of the *Taz*, rules that it is inappropriate to recite Kaddish before the burial.[79]

As the *onen* is generally preoccupied with burial preparations and is also exempt from prayer and other mitzvot, it is customary not to recite Kaddish before the burial. Some Sephardim recite Kaddish before the burial.[80] Several authorities relate that the custom in Eretz Yisrael is to recite Kaddish before the burial.[81]

### SUMMARY OF THE LAWS OF *ANINUT*

The laws of *aninut* are complex. One who has lost a close relative has very little time, and is often too busy to review these halakhot. This section summarizes the laws discussed above and includes other important practical guidance.

A person who has lost a relative should not act in a frivolous manner; rather, he should conduct himself as one preoccupied and overwhelmed by the death and burial.[82] As we learned above, the *onen* does not don *tefillin* on the day of the death or the burial, and if there is an interval between them, then during that interval as well. He must also observe the laws of mourning that do not interfere with the burial preparations (bathing, anointing, participating in joyful occasions, *she'elat shalom*, cutting one's hair and shaving, marital relations, work, and Torah study). In addition, the *onen* may not eat

---

78. *Taz, Oraḥ Ḥayim* 71:2. Elsewhere (*Yoreh De'ah* 376:4), he writes that on Shabbat, when one is unable to bury the deceased, he should recite Kaddish. *Be'er Heitev* (*Oraḥ Ḥayim* 71:4) explains that even on a weekday, if the mourner is not involved in funeral preparations, he should recite Kaddish. *Hokhmat Adam* (153:1) concurs.

79. *Nekudot HaKesef, Yoreh De'ah* 376.

80. *Birkei Yosef, Yoreh De'ah* 341:12; *Yabia Omer, Yoreh De'ah* 6:33.

81. See *Birkei Yosef, Yoreh De'ah* 341; *Tzitz Eliezer*, vol. 5, *Ramat Raḥel* 46. R. Ovadia Yosef (*Yabia Omer*, ibid.) also supports this practice.

82. *Hokhmat Adam* 153:1.

in the vicinity of the deceased.[83] The Yerushalmi adds that one should not eat or drink his fill.[84]

The *onen* may not eat meat or drink wine.[85] Some *Rishonim* explain that eating meat and drinking wine may distract the *onen* from dedicating himself to the burial preparations.[86] Some sources indicate that eating meat and drinking wine may also be viewed as inappropriate during this time of intense sorrow.[87] Although the *onen* is permitted to wear leather shoes, some suggest that nowadays, since non-leather shoes are just as comfortable as leather shoes, he should not wear leather shoes.

An *onen* is exempt and prohibited from fulfilling all positive commandments, including reciting blessings and daily prayers.[88] However, the *onen* should wash *netilat yadayim* in the morning[89] and before eating bread.[90] Some say that he may also wear his *tzitzit*.[91] He is not counted for a *minyan* or a *zimun*. He should not answer "Amen." An *onen* may recite psalms for the protection of the deceased [*shemirat hamet*].[92]

The Talmud[93] teaches that on Shabbat and Yom Tov, the restrictions of *aninut* are lifted: one may eat meat and drink wine, participate in a *zimun*, recite *Shema* and *Shemoneh Esreh*, and perform all of the mitzvot. The *Shulḥan Arukh*[94] prohibits marital relations on Shabbat. Similarly, the *onen* may not

83. *Shulḥan Arukh, Yoreh De'ah* 341:1.

84. Y. Berakhot 3:1. Although the *Beit Yosef* insists that this ruling is not cited by the *Rishonim*, the *Gesher HaḤayim* (18:2:3) notes that it is cited by many *Aḥaronim*.

85. Berakhot 17b.

86. Rashba, Berakhot 17b. He cites Rabbeinu Tam as well, who ate meat and drank wine after hearing that his sister had passed away in a different city (see above).

87. See *Shulḥan Arukh, Yoreh De'ah* 242:27 and Rema 341:1, who cite the opinion of those who rule that a student should refrain from eating meat and drinking wine after the death of his teacher. In addition, the *Arukh HaShulḥan* writes: "And he does not eat meat or drink wine, in order to display his sadness [*tzaar*]."

88. Some *Aḥaronim* (*Minḥat Shlomo* 1:91:9; see also *Ḥazon Ovadia*, vol. 1, p. 120) suggest that he should recite *Keriat Shema* and *Birkat HaMapil* before going to sleep, as the reasons that an *onen* is exempt from mitzvot do not apply at that time.

89. *Kitzur Shulḥan Arukh* 196:2.

90. *Pitḥei Teshuva* 341:4.

91. *Minḥat Shlomo* 1:91:25:3.

92. *Tzitz Eliezer*, vol. 5, *Ramat Raḥel* 46. R. Ovadia Yosef (*Yalkut Yosef* 8:11) insists that an *onen* may not recite psalms.

93. Mo'ed Katan 23b.

94. *Shulḥan Arukh, Yoreh De'ah* 341:1.

study or read the Torah, and is not called to the Torah for an *aliya*.[95] An *onen* who is a Kohen should leave the sanctuary before being called for *Birkat Kohanim*, and should not ascend to recite *Birkat Kohanim* even if called.[96] Some suggest that if the death occurs before Shabbat and the *onen* is no longer involved in burial preparations, the laws of *aninut* are not in effect, even before Shabbat begins. Therefore, the *onen* may recite Minḥa.[97]

There are different customs regarding whether an *onen* may, or should, recite the Mourner's Kaddish before the burial. Ashkenazim generally do not recite Kaddish before the burial, whereas Sephardim do.[98]

After Shabbat,[99] the *onen* does not recite Havdala, although he may eat, and perform *melakha*,[100] after reciting the formula: *Barukh hamavdil bein kodesh leḥol*.[101]

---

95. R. Akiva Eiger, *Yoreh De'ah* 341:1.
96. *Mishna Berura* 128:158.
97. See, for example, *Shemirat Shabbat KeHilkhata* 2:64:22.
98. *Birkei Yosef*, *Yoreh De'ah* 341:12; *Yabia Omer*, ibid.
99. Some *Aḥaronim* (*Taz, Oraḥ Ḥayim* 71:4; *Shulḥan Arukh HaRav, Oraḥ Ḥayim* 71:2; *Sedei Ḥemed*, vol. 4, *Maarekhet Avelut* 175) suggest that the *onen* should recite *Keriat Shema* and Maariv after sunset, before the conclusion of Shabbat. Others (*Shevut Yaakov* 1:8) disagree. The custom is to refrain from reciting *Keriat Shema* and Maariv until after the burial (see *Nitei Gavriel* 28:1).
100. *Shulḥan Arukh, Yoreh De'ah* 341:2.
101. *Shemirat Shabbat KeHilkhata* 2:64:26.

*Chapter 2*

# Burial

The mitzva of burying the dead [*kevurat hamet*] appears in various places throughout the Torah and rabbinic literature. *Pirkei DeRabbi Eliezer*[1] traces the practice of burying one's deceased relative to the beginning of time:

> Adam and his partner were sitting, crying and mourning for him, and they did not know what to do with Abel, as they were not accustomed to burial. One raven, one of whose counterparts died, took him, dug in the earth before their eyes, and buried him. Adam said: I will do as the raven did. Immediately, he took Abel's corpse, dug [a hole in] the ground, and buried him.

The Torah recounts how Abraham acquired a plot to bury his wife, Sarah.

> I am a foreigner and resident alien with you; give me a burial portion with you, and I will bury my dead from before me. (Gen. 23:4)

Later, the Torah relates that Isaac and Ishmael buried Abraham (Gen. 25:9), Jacob buried Rachel (ibid., 35:19–20), Jacob and Esau buried Isaac

1. *Pirkei DeRabbi Eliezer* 21.

(ibid., 35:29), Jacob is buried in Maarat HaMakhpela (ibid., 49:13), and Joseph requests that after his descendants are redeemed from Egypt, his remains should be brought to and buried in Eretz Yisrael (ibid., 50:25–26; see Ex. 13:19). The Torah concludes by relating that God Himself buried Moses (Deut. 34:6). The Talmud also notes that burial was apparently an ancient Jewish custom.[2]

Burial is such an important commandment that the Torah instructs a Kohen to become impure to bury a relative (Lev. 21:1–3). The Talmud teaches that burial overrides all other mitzvot, even the *korban pesaḥ*.[3] Indeed, as we discussed in the previous chapter, a mourner involved in burial preparations is exempt from mitzvot.[4]

In this chapter, we will study the nature, scope, parameters, and contemporary challenges of the obligation of *kevura* and the prohibition of delaying the burial.

## THE OBLIGATION OF *KEVURA*

The Torah mentions an obligation to bury the deceased, and a prohibition of leaving the body unburied, in the context of one who is executed by the *beit din*.

> If there is in a man a sin with a death sentence, and he is put to death, you shall hang him on a tree. His carcass shall not remain overnight on the tree; rather, you shall bury him on that day, as one hung is a curse of God, and you shall not defile your land that the Lord your God is giving you as an inheritance. (Deut. 21:22–23)

The Mishna[5] describes how a person executed by the *beit din* was publicly hung, and then immediately lowered and buried.

> They immediately untie him [from the gallows]. If he was left overnight, [the court] violates a prohibition on his account, as it is stated: "His carcass shall not remain overnight on the tree; rather, you shall bury him on that day, as one hung is a curse of God" (Deut. 21:23).

2. Sanhedrin 46b.
3. Sukka 25b.
4. Berakhot 17b.
5. Sanhedrin 6:4.

> That is to say: For what reason was he hung? Because he blessed [i.e., cursed] God, and the name of God would be desecrated.

The mishna extends this prohibition to relate to all deceased persons:

> And not only this; rather, anyone who leaves his deceased relative overnight violates a prohibition.

The Talmud[6] derives from the verse a general obligation to bury the dead, not restricted to those executed by the *beit din*.

> R. Yoḥanan said in the name of R. Shimon b. Yoḥai: From where is it derived that one who leaves his deceased relative [unburied] overnight violates a prohibition? The verse states: "Rather, you shall bury him [*kavor tikberennu*]" (Deut. 21:23). From here it is derived that one who leaves his deceased relative [unburied] overnight violates a prohibition.
>
> There are those who say: R. Yoḥanan said in the name of R. Shimon b. Yoḥai: From where in the Torah is there an allusion to [the mitzva of] burial? The verse states: "Rather, you shall bury him [*kavor tikberennu*]." From here there is an allusion to [the mitzva of] burial in the Torah.

Interestingly, R. Avraham Hiyya de Boton, in his commentary on Rambam's *Mishneh Torah, Leḥem Mishneh*,[7] explains that the two versions cited in the Gemara disagree as to whether burial is a rabbinic obligation, with an allusion in the Torah, or a Torah obligation. Indeed, Rabbeinu Ḥananel[8] rules that burial is a rabbinic obligation. Almost all *Rishonim*, however, disagree and rule that burial is a Torah obligation and that it is prohibited by Torah law to delay the burial [*halanat hamet*].[9]

---

6. Sanhedrin 46b
7. *Leḥem Mishneh, Hilkhot Avel* 12:1.
8. Sanhedrin 47a.
9. Interestingly, Radbaz (311) asserts that in addition to the prohibition of leaving the body overnight, there is an obligation to bury those executed by the *beit din* the same day. However, this obligation applies only with regard to those executed by the *beit din*, whereas the prohibition of leaving the body overnight applies with regard to all deceased people. While in one place Rambam equates the bodies of

In addition to the obligation of burial and the prohibition of delaying interment, Ramban asserts that one who leaves a body unburied in Israel violates another prohibition: "And you shall not defile your land that the Lord your God is giving you as an inheritance."[10]

The *Aḥaronim* discuss whether one is obligated to bury limbs or smaller parts of a corpse.[11] R. Yom-Tov Lipmann Heller (1579–1654) suggests that there is an obligation to bury any part of a corpse larger than an olive-bulk [*kezayit*].[12] *Minḥat Ḥinukh* agrees, and questions whether one is required to bury even a smaller part as well.[13] R. Yehuda Rosanes (1657–1727), in his commentary to Rambam's *Mishneh Torah, Mishneh LaMelekh,* disagrees and insists that the obligation to bury applies only to *rosho verubo* (the head and the majority of the body).[14]

---

those executed by the *beit din* and the bodies of others (*Hilkhot Sanhedrin* 15:8), elsewhere, he appears to distinguish between them and states: While the mitzva of burial applies to all deceased (*Sefer HaMitzvot,* Positive Commandment 231), the prohibition of leaving the deceased overnight applies only to those executed by the *beit din* (Negative Commandment 66). Ascertaining the opinion of Rambam is further complicated by his ruling in *Hilkhot Avel* (14:1), where he writes:

> There is a positive commandment by rabbinic law to visit the sick, comfort mourners, to prepare for a funeral, prepare a bride, accompany guests, attend to all the needs of a burial, carry the deceased on one's shoulders, walk before the bier, eulogize, dig a grave, and bury the dead, and also to bring joy to a bride and groom and help them in all their needs. These are deeds of kindness that one carries out with his person that have no limit. Although all these mitzvot are by rabbinic law, they are included in the Torah commandment: "Love your neighbor as yourself" (Lev. 19:18). That mitzva instructs that whatever you would like others to perform on your behalf, you should perform for your colleague in Torah and mitzvot.

This passage, based upon the Talmud (Sota 14a), indicates that the obligation of burial might be only by rabbinic law (see Rambam, *Sefer HaMitzvot, shoresh* 1, and comments of Ramban). The *Aḥaronim* (see *Lev Same'aḥ, shoresh* 1; *Gesher HaḤayim* 2:12; *Kehilat Yaakov* 100:284, et al.) discuss this apparent contradiction at length.

10. Deut. 21:22.
11. Regarding a Kohen defiling himself [*tumat Kohanim*] to bury a close relative, and a person who has no relatives to tend to his burial [*met mitzva*], see *Shulḥan Arukh, Yoreh De'ah* 373:9, 374:1–2.
12. *Tosafot Yom Tov,* Shabbat 10:5; see also *Noda BiYehuda* (*Mahadura Kama, Yoreh De'ah* 90), who explains that the reason of *kevodo* applies to a *kezayit* of a corpse as well.
13. *Minḥat Ḥinukh* 537:1. See Rashi, Berakhot 5b, s.v. *bir,* and R. Nissim Gaon. See also Rashbam, Bava Batra 116a, s.v. *dein garma.*
14. *Mishneh LaMelekh, Hilkhot Avel* 14:21.

*Gesher HaḤayim*[15] rules that even parts as small as an olive-bulk should be buried, if not due to the obligation of burial, then due to other reasons,[16] e.g., the prohibition of benefiting from a corpse, and the concern of impurity. Furthermore, he explains that since the Talmud likens the body to the parchment of a *sefer Torah*[17] as the soul is like the divine names on the parchment, the body, like a Torah scroll, must be buried.[18] R. Moshe Feinstein adds that there is an obligation to bury all parts of the body, as an expression of respect for the deceased [*kevod hamet*].[19] The prohibition of delaying burial does not apply in this case.[20]

Is there a requirement to bury limbs and organs removed during one's lifetime? The Talmud relates that lepers would bury their limbs.[21] Most *Aḥaronim*, however, assume that there is no mitzva to bury limbs amputated during one's lifetime. Some suggest that they should be buried or sequestered so that a Kohen does not inadvertently come in contact with the limb and become impure.[22] Although nowadays hospitals dispose of amputated limbs and organs in a manner that would not pose a problem for Kohanim, some authorities continue to encourage the practice of burying limbs and organs.[23] R. Moshe Feinstein[24] rules that there is an obligation to bury an amputated limb [*ever min haḥai*] as well as a removed organ. Teeth that fall out or are extracted do not require burial.[25]

## WHO IS OBLIGATED IN THE MITZVA OF BURIAL?

Who is obligated to fulfill this mitzva of burial? R. Yechiel Michel Tukachinsky, in his *Gesher HaḤayim*,[26] suggests that there are three levels of obligation regarding burial.

15. *Gesher HaḤayim* 1:16:2.
16. See Temura 24a.
17. Shabbat 105a.
18. See also Ḥatam Sofer, *Yoreh De'ah* 353.
19. *Iggerot Moshe, Yoreh De'ah* 2:150.
20. *Gesher HaḤayim* 7:1:10.
21. Ketubot 20b.
22. See *Noda BiYehuda, Mahadura Tinyana, Yoreh De'ah* 209; *Shevut Yaakov* 2:101 (see also *Pitḥei Teshuva* 262:1). The *Gesher HaḤayim* (1:16:2:2) relates that the custom in Jerusalem is to bury amputated limbs.
23. See *Melamed LeHo'il* 118; *Sefer Kol Bo al Avelut*, p. 184; *Tzitz Eliezer* 10:25:8; *Yabia Omer, Yoreh De'ah* 3:22, 9:35.
24. *Iggerot Moshe, Yoreh De'ah* 1:231; see also *Yad HaMelekh, Hilkhot Avel* 2:14.
25. *Gesher HaḤayim* 2:16:3.
26. *Gesher HaḤayim* 2:12:3.

The primary obligation of burial, derived from the Kohen's obligation to become impure for the burial of his seven closest relatives (spouse, father, mother, son, daughter, brother, and unmarried sister),[27] is incumbent upon these relatives. He suggests that the fact that burial overrides the prohibition of becoming impure, by definition, indicates that there is an obligation to bury.[28]

The next level of obligation is that of the community (more specifically, the *beit din*), which bears responsibility to bury the deceased, especially in the case of one with no relatives to tend to his burial [*met mitzva*].[29] The Talmud teaches that a Nazirite is obligated to become impure to bury a *met mitzva*.[30] Moreover, burying a *met mitzva* overrides even the mitzvot of *korban pesaḥ* and *Brit Mila*,[31] positive commandments punishable by *karet* if they are not fulfilled.

Finally, there is a broader rabbinic obligation to attend to all the needs of burial, carry the deceased on one's shoulders, walk before him, eulogize, dig a grave, and bury the dead. These are included in the Torah commandment: "You shall love your neighbor as yourself" (Lev 19:18).[32]

## REASONS FOR BURIAL

The Talmud[33] offers two reasons for burial.

> A dilemma was raised before the sages: Is burial on account of disgrace [*bizyona*] or is it on account of atonement [*kappara*]? What is the practical difference? When one said: I do not want them to bury that man [i.e., me]. If you say on account of disgrace, it is not in his power; but if you say it is on account of atonement, didn't he say: I do not want atonement?

27. Lev. 21:1–4.
28. Interestingly, R. Soloveitchik ("*BeInyan Avelut*," in *Shiurim LeZekher Abba Mari*, vol. 2) notes that Rambam (Introduction to *Hilkhot Avel*) writes: "[The first mitzva is] to mourn one's close relatives; even a Kohen must become impure and mourn his close relatives" (see also *Hilkhot Avel* 2:6). R. Soloveitchik derives from this passage that becoming impure for a close relative is an expression and a fulfillment of the obligation to mourn.
29. In addition, R. Tukachinsky notes that technically, the first obligation may not apply if the deceased is not whole [*shalem*].
30. Nazir 47a.
31. Megilla 2b.
32. Rambam, *Hilkhot Avel* 14:1.
33. Sanhedrin 46b.

The Gemara suggests that burial may be part of the process of atonement [*kappara*]. This passage can be understood in different ways. Some attribute the atonement to the lowering of the body into the ground,[34] while other sources indicate that atonement may result from its decomposition[35] or from the person's return to the land, as it is written: "For you are dust, and to dust you shall return" (Gen. 3:19).

Alternatively, the Gemara explains that the purpose of burial may be to avoid disgrace, so that the deceased is not disgraced before everyone who sees him dead and decomposing.[36] Others[37] explain that the Gemara is concerned with the disgrace of the family. Ramban[38] insists that the Gemara is referring to the discomfort felt by everyone who sees an unburied corpse.

The Talmud explains that the practical difference between these two reasons relates to the question of whether one may say: I do not want them to bury me. Although the dilemma was not resolved in the Gemara,[39] the *Rishonim* rule that we do not respect the wishes of one who requests not to be buried.[40]

## REASONS FOR DELAYING THE BURIAL

As mentioned above, the Torah prohibits leaving a corpse unburied overnight.[41] Furthermore, the Talmud[42] teaches that it is praiseworthy to perform the burial as soon as possible. However, the mishna[43] teaches: "If he left him overnight to honor him, to bring a coffin or a shroud, he does not violate [the prohibition]." Furthermore, the Talmud[44] explains:

---

34. Rashi, ibid., s.v. *o*.
35. Sanhedrin 47b; Y. Sanhedrin 6:10; see also Eduyot 2:10.
36. Rashi, s.v. *mishum bizyona hu*.
37. Rashi, s.v. *mishum*; Tosafot, s.v. *kevura*.
38. *Torat HaAdam, Shaar HaKevura*; see also *Arukh HaShulḥan, Yoreh De'ah* 362:1.
39. Rosh, Sanhedrin 5:2.
40. Rambam, *Hilkhot Avel* 12:1 and *Hilkhot Zekhiya UMatana* 11:24; Ramban, *Torat HaAdam*; see *Shulḥan Arukh, Yoreh De'ah* 348:3.
41. Some *Aḥaronim* (*Shulḥan Arukh HaRav* 72:2; Rashash, Sanhedrin 46b; *Minḥat Ḥinukh* 537:1; see *Mishna Berura* 72:6) rule that one must bury the deceased before dark; others disagree (see *Ḥazon Ovadia*, vol. 1, p. 376).
42. Mo'ed Katan 22a.
43. Sanhedrin 46a.
44. Ibid., 47a; see also Semaḥot 11:1.

> Come and hear! If one [the relative] left him overnight to honor him, to inform the [neighboring] towns about him, or to bring him lamenters, or to bring him a coffin or a shroud, he does not violate [the prohibition], as anyone who acts does so only for the honor of the deceased.

The *Rishonim* and *Aḥaronim* discuss numerous circumstances where one may wish, or need, to delay the burial.

For example, *Shulḥan Arukh*[45] cites the Mishna,[46] which teaches that one may delay burial "so that his relatives may come from another place." The *Aḥaronim* discuss the scope of that leniency. R. Malkiel Tannenbaum (1847–1910), in his *Divrei Malkiel*,[47] rules that the burial should not be delayed so that more relatives may attend. Most *Aḥaronim* disagree, and permit delaying the burial until all of the relatives arrive,[48] and even until close acquaintances of the deceased [*mekuravim*] arrive.[49] R. Ovadia Yosef even permits delaying burial until the mourner's relatives arrive from overseas.[50] This is indeed the custom; however, one should be certain not to delay the burial unnecessarily.[51] We discussed in chapter 1 whether the mourner is an *onen* and exempt from mitzvot during an extended delay.

The Talmud teaches: "Ten matters were stated with regard to Jerusalem…one may not leave a corpse overnight in Jerusalem."[52] This indicates that even for the "sake of his honor" one does not delay burial in Jerusalem. R. David b. Solomon ibn Zimra, known as Radbaz (Egypt and Eretz Yisrael, fifteenth and sixteenth centuries), writes that this ordinance is no longer in effect, as today everyone's status is that of one impure due to impurity imparted by a corpse [*teme met*].[53] Most *Aḥaronim* disagree and assert that this strin-

45. *Yoreh De'ah* 357:1.
46. Semaḥot 11:1.
47. *Divrei Malkiel* 2:95.
48. *Taz, Yoreh De'ah* 357:1; see also *Shevet HaLevi* 4:154.
49. *Gesher HaḤayim* 7:1:2.
50. *Ḥazon Ovadia, Avelut, Dinei Kevura* 4.
51. *Iggerot Moshe, Yoreh De'ah* 3:139.
52. Bava Kama 82b.
53. Radbaz 2:733.

gency is in effect even today.[54] R. Tukachinsky[55] affirms this custom, but insists that it relates only to corpses in the Old City of Jerusalem. In other parts of Jerusalem, one may delay the burial for the sake of the honor of the deceased.

## BURIAL IN THE GROUND

R. Yechiel Michel Epstein, in his *Arukh HaShulḥan*,[56] writes that although "logic dictates and all people would agree" that a human corpse should not be left exposed, covering the body and keeping it in storage might be sufficient to resolve that issue. Judaism, however, demands that the corpse be buried in the ground, in accordance with the verse: "To dust you shall return" (Gen. 3:19).

Ramban[57] concludes based on the Talmud that the body must be buried in the ground. Despite the ancient practice of burial in coffins,[58] he insists that it is preferable to bury the corpse directly in the ground.

The Yerushalmi[59] relates that before he died, R. Yehuda HaNasi commanded: Let my bier be open to the ground. *Tur*[60] explains that he meant that they should remove the bottom of the coffin. R. Aharon HaKohen of Narbonne[61] writes that a hole in the coffin is sufficient for it to be considered burial in the ground.

*Tur* cites different customs regarding whether burial should be in a coffin or directly in the ground. *Shulḥan Arukh*[62] rules in accordance with the opinion of Ramban, that burial in the ground is proper [*yafa*]. Although in Israel it is customary to bury directly in the ground,[63] in many countries it is customary to bury in wooden coffins.[64] If it is possible according to the law of the land and the custom of the community, it is preferable to make holes in the coffin.

---

54. See, for example, *Yam Shel Shlomo* 8:44:10; *Meshekh Ḥokhma, Parashat Ki Tetzeh*; and *Pe'at HaShulḥan, Hilkhot Eretz Yisrael* 3:3.
55. *Gesher HaḤayim* 1:7:3; see also *Ḥazon Ovadia, Avelut* (vol. 1, *Dinei Kevura*, n. 4) regarding the current borders of Jerusalem.
56. *Arukh HaShulḥan, Yoreh De'ah* 362:1.
57. *Torat HaAdam, Shaar HaKevura*.
58. See, for example, Mo'ed Katan 1:6; Eduyot 5:6; Y. Pesaḥim 8:8.
59. Y. Ketubot 12:3; see also Y. Kilayim 9:3.
60. *Yoreh De'ah* 362.
61. *Orḥot Ḥayim, Hilkhot Avel* 31; see also Shakh, *Yoreh De'ah* 362:1.
62. *Yoreh De'ah* 362:1.
63. See, for example, *Har Tzvi, Yoreh De'ah* 269. It is customary to bury all soldiers in coffins.
64. R. Yehoshua Ehrenberg, in his *Devar Yehoshua* (1:32), discusses burial in a metal coffin.

Although halakhic authorities generally prohibited interment in a mausoleum,[65] in recent years, multi-tier burial structures have been built in numerous cemeteries in Israel, including Jerusalem's Har HaMenuḥot. These graves were constructed in a manner that accords them the status of burial caves, unlike the typical mausoleum outside of Israel. This method was approved by the Israeli Chief Rabbinate in 1987[66] and gained the approval of numerous halakhic authorities.[67] In Israeli cemeteries, husbands and wives are often buried one atop the other.[68]

### BURIAL NEXT TO NON-JEWS

The Talmud teaches: "One sustains poor gentiles along with poor Jews, and one visits sick gentiles along with sick Jews, and one buries dead gentiles along with dead Jews, on account of the ways of peace [*mipnei darkhei shalom*]."[69]

Rashi[70] explains that the Gemara is referring to a case where one finds the bodies of both Jews and gentiles. In that case, one tends to the burial of both the Jews and the gentiles. However, they are not buried together. Ran[71] explains that even if one finds the bodies of gentiles only, he tends to their burial.

What is the role of *darkhei shalom* in this context? Is it based on the fear that gentiles are liable to take some form of retribution for our actions? Interestingly, Rambam writes:[72]

---

65. *Iggerot Moshe, Yoreh De'ah* 3:143; *Minḥat Yitzḥak* 10:122. Although see *Ein Yitzḥak, Yoreh De'ah* 1:33.
66. See *BeMareh HaBazak* 4:114; see also *Shulḥan Arukh, Yoreh De'ah* 362:4.
67. See, for example, R. Shlomo Amar (in *Teḥumin* 27); R. Ovadia Yosef, *Yalkut Yosef*, p. 710; and see also R. Yaakov Roza, *HaMaayan*, 2014. Some authorities remain opposed to this method of burial. R. Yosef Shalom Elyashiv fundamentally accepted the validity of this method, and even notes that this was the common custom in the Diaspora, but objects to changing the burial customs in Eretz Yisrael (See *Kovetz Teshuvot* 2:64; *Tziyunei Halakha, Hilkhot Avelut*, chap. 9).
68. See *Shulḥan Arukh, Yoreh De'ah* 362:4; *Baḥ* 362; see also R. Yitzchak Elchanan Spektor (1817–1896), *Ein Yitzḥak* 1:34; R. Chaim Ozer Grodzinski (1863–1940), *Aḥiezer* 9:79. As these sources testify, this practice was widespread throughout Eastern Europe for the last five hundred years. This form of burial is often, but not always, performed with a separation of over 60 cm [six *tefaḥim*] between the two bodies. See *MeOlam VeAd Olam*, pp. 457–61.
69. Gittin 61a.
70. Rashi, ibid., s.v. *im*.
71. Ran, ibid., 28a, s.v. *kovrin*.
72. Rambam, *Hilkhot Melakhim* 10:12.

> The sages commanded to visit their [the gentiles'] sick, and to bury their dead with the Jewish dead, and to sustain their poor in the framework of the Jewish poor on account of the ways of peace. It is stated: "The Lord is good to all and His mercy extends to all of His creations" (Ps. 145:9), and it is stated: "Its ways are the ways of pleasantness and all its pathways are peace" (Prov. 3:17).

Rambam maintains that *darkhei shalom* is not based on the fear that if Jews do not tend to the burial of gentiles, gentiles will not protect the rights of Jews. Rather, burying gentiles is an expression of the broader obligation to engage in acts of kindness [*gemilut ḥasadim*].[73]

The commentaries agree that gentiles are not buried in Jewish cemeteries. Although the Talmud teaches that one buries dead gentiles along with dead Jews, it does not mean with Jews in the literal sense. What is the source of this practice?

Ran[74] invokes a Gemara that describes the burial of those who are executed by the *beit din*. The mishna[75] teaches:

> And they would not bury him [the executed] in his ancestral burial plot, but two graveyards were established for those executed by the court, one for those who were decapitated or strangled, and one for those who were stoned or burned.

The Talmud[76] questions why in addition to one's family burial tomb, the *beit din* established two other areas, i.e., one for those executed by beheading [*hereg*] and strangulation [*ḥenek*], and another for those executed by stoning [*sekila*] and burning [*serefa*].

> And why is all this necessary? Because a wicked man is not buried next to a righteous man… And just as a wicked man is not buried

---

73. The *Rishonim* discuss whether the Torah obligation to bury the dead and the prohibition of delaying the burial apply to gentiles. The *Minḥat Ḥinukh* (537, *Kometz Minḥa*) suggests that this is a dispute between Rashi (Deut. 21:23) and Ramban (ibid., 24). Furthermore, see the mishna in Avot: Beloved is man, as he was created in the image [of God] (3:14), and the comments of the *Tiferet Yisrael*.

74. Ibid. Ḥatam Sofer (*Yoreh De'ah* 141) suggests that this is a *halakha leMoshe miSinai*.

75. Sanhedrin 46a.

76. Ibid., 47a.

> next to a righteous man, so too, an extremely wicked man is not buried next to a less wicked man. If so, let them establish four graveyards? It is learned as a tradition that there are two graveyards.

According to the Talmud, one should be buried next to someone with a comparable level of religious observance.

*Shulḥan Arukh*[77] cites this ruling, and applies it to people with different levels of piety. Most communities are not particular about this matter and bury alongside one another Jews who apparently adhered to different levels of religious observance.

Ran, cited above, cites this principle as the source for the custom not to bury gentiles next to Jews.[78] Interestingly, the Aramaic translation (Targum) of the Book of Ruth interprets Ruth's declaration to Naomi: "Wherever you die I will die, and there I will be buried" (Ruth 1:15), as: "Ruth said: However you die, I will die. Naomi said: We have separate cemeteries. Ruth said: And there I will be buried." Thus the Targum traces the practice of separate Jewish burial to the days of the Judges.

Of course, one need not conclude from this that all gentiles are wicked. R. Moshe Feinstein writes that even a gentile who observed the seven Noahide laws is not buried in a Jewish cemetery, as this distinction is rooted in the sanctity of the Jewish people [*kedushat Yisrael*], and not in the piety of each individual gentile.[79]

Nevertheless, since the basis for this prohibition is the principle that a wicked person is not buried beside a righteous one, the question arises whether in certain circumstances it may be permitted to bury a gentile together with Jews.

Some cite R. Yoel Sirkis,[80] who writes that the above passage teaches that if Jewish and gentile dead are found together, they may be buried together, i.e., the corpses of gentiles may be buried with those of Jews, due to the principle of *darkhei shalom*. R. Sirkis, however, was referring to extremely rare, extenuating circumstances.

In recent years, this practice has been discussed in numerous contexts. Some authorities were asked about the burial of non-Jewish spouses

---

77. *Shulḥan Arukh, Yoreh De'ah* 362:5. Interestingly, Rambam omits this passage.
78. Some examples of recent authorities who affirmed this practice include *Daat Kohen* (201); *Yabia Omer* (*Yoreh De'ah* 7:36:2); *Yaskil Avdi* (*Yoreh De'ah* 6:20); *Iggerot Moshe* (*Yoreh De'ah* 3:146).
79. *Iggerot Moshe*, ibid.
80. *Baḥ* 151.

or non-Jewish children in a Jewish cemetery.[81] Others grappled with sensitive questions regarding the burial of those who had not yet completed the process of conversion,[82] or those who underwent non-halakhic conversions.[83] In Israel, this question arises regarding the many immigrants from the former Soviet Union whose religious identities are undetermined [*safek yehudim*]. Local Jewish communities and cemeteries have different practices, and these decisions should be made, with great sensitivity, by a local halakhic authority.[84]

In a different context, the burial of non-Jewish soldiers killed in combat, defending the State of Israel, has also become a source of controversy. Interestingly, R. Shlomo Goren (1917–1994), Chief Rabbi of the Israel Defense Forces, and later the third Ashkenazic Chief Rabbi of Israel (1973–1983), permitted, at least theoretically, burying a non-Jewish soldier in a Jewish military cemetery.[85] He suggests that it is not only R. Sirkis who permits, in certain circumstances, burying Jews with gentiles, but that this may be the opinion of Rambam as well. R. Goren observes that in one place Rambam cites the obligation to tend to the burial of gentiles,[86] omitting the phrase "with the dead of Israel." Elsewhere, he writes: "The sages commanded to visit their (the gentiles') sick, and to bury their dead with [*im*] the Jewish dead."[87] Furthermore, R. Goren contends that gentiles who fight for the nation and land of Israel are even greater than the righteous gentiles [*ḥasidei umot haolam*], who have a portion in the World to Come.[88]

---

81. *Minḥat Elazar* 3:8; *Iggerot Moshe, Yoreh De'ah* 3:147.
82. See *Minḥat Elazar*, ibid., regarding one who was circumcised but died before immersing in the *mikveh*; see also *Mikhtav Shlomo* 3:6.
83. R. Moshe Feinstein (*Iggerot Moshe, Yoreh De'ah* 1:160, 2:149), taking into account how sensitive and divisive this issue can be, adopts a somewhat tolerant approach, and requires a separation of only eight *amot*. R. Yechiel Yaakov Weinberg (*Seridei Esh* 3:100) allows them to be buried in a separate row in the cemetery, which would not ordinarily be permitted for gentiles.
84. The *Aḥaronim* discuss burying Jews and gentiles in close proximity. Although one may not bury gentiles next to Jews, some write that one may distance the plot of a gentile from that of a Jew by eight *amot* (see *Gilyon Maharsha, Yoreh De'ah* 362, s.v. *etzel tzaddik*). Some rule that even a distance of four *amot* (*Iggerot Moshe, Yoreh De'ah* 2:149) or separation by a fence ten *tefaḥim* high (*Iggerot Moshe, Yoreh De'ah* 2:131; see also *Minḥat Elazar* 2:41) may suffice.
85. *Terumat HaGoren* 1:27, 2:79.
86. Rambam, *Hilkhot Avel* 14:12.
87. Rambam, *Hilkhot Melakhim* 10:12.
88. Rambam, ibid., 8:11.

Some cite the following passage from the Talmud.[89]

> Those executed by the [Roman] government, no creature can stand in their section [in heaven]. Who are these? If we say [that the reference is to] R. Akiva and his colleagues, is it only because they were executed by the government? Even without that [they would have attained that elevated status]. Rather, the reference is to the martyrs of Lod.

Rashi explains that this passage refers to Papos and Luliyanus, who, according to the Talmud, were killed defending the Jewish people.[90] It appears that the principle: "A wicked man is not buried next to a righteous man," would not apply to these soldiers.

In practice, special sections have been set aside in Israeli civilian and military cemeteries for non-Jews.

### AUTOPSIES AND POSTMORTEM EXAMINATIONS[91]

The Talmud teaches that the sanctity of a body is similar to that of a *sefer Torah*.[92] There are numerous laws that relate to and protect the human body even after death. For example, in addition to the obligation of burial discussed above, there is a prohibition to derive benefit [*issur hanaa*] from,[93] or to mistreat or mutilate, a corpse [*nivul hamet*].[94]

The *Aḥaronim* discuss whether one is permitted to perform forensic, clinical, or academic autopsies. They address the issues of *kevura* and

89. Bava Batra 10b.
90. See Taanit 18b.
91. Upon the death of a relative, the family members may have to face the question of whether to donate the organs of their loved one to people in need of organ transplants. The halakhic literature on this complex topic is extensive and is beyond the scope of this book. Although the overwhelming majority of halakhic authorities maintain that it is not only permitted, but also a mitzva to donate one's organs after death, they disagree regarding the exact definition and moment of death, especially regarding whether brain stem death is considered to be death, which impacts upon which organs may be harvested for transplant. This issue should be discussed with a competent halakhic authority.
92. Berakhot 17b.
93. See Avoda Zara 2b; Sanhedrin 47b. Most *Rishonim* (see Rashi, Sanhedrin, ibid., s.v. *pinehu*; Tosafot, ibid., 48b, s.v. *meshamshin*) explain that this is a Torah prohibition.
94. See Bava Batra 154a–b; Ḥullin 11b.

*halanat hamet,* the prohibition of deriving benefit from a corpse, and the prohibition of defiling a corpse.

Regarding clinical autopsies, some are lenient when the examination may provide information that may help an individual who is before us with the same disease or condition [*ḥoleh lefaneinu*].[95] R. Yechiel Yaakov Weinberg expands and broadens this leniency, and permits performing an autopsy when the information may benefit another potential patient, even if his identity is not currently known. *Ḥazon Ish,*[96] R. Eliezer Waldenberg,[97] and R. Bentzion Uziel[98] also adopt a somewhat lenient approach, permitting autopsies when they may benefit other patients. R. Yaakov Ettlinger[99] (1798–1871) and R. Moshe Feinstein[100] take more stringent positions. In practice, autopsies may be permitted to help identify or cure new diseases or epidemics,[101] diagnose a genetic condition or disease,[102] or even to help apprehend a murderer and prevent a future crime.[103]

The *Aḥaronim* also discuss whether students may perform cadaver dissection on the corpse of a Jew.[104] While most authorities prohibit performing autopsies for study,[105] others adopt a more lenient approach in certain circumstances.[106] Many of the *Aḥaronim* cited above also discuss whether autopsies may be performed in order to settle a monetary or insurance claim.

These questions should be discussed with a competent halakhic authority. In Israel, there is specific legislation that relates to when an autopsy

95. See *Noda BiYehuda, Yoreh De'ah* 210; see also Ḥatam Sofer, *Yoreh De'ah* 336.
96. *Hilkhot Avelut* 208:7.
97. *Tzitz Eliezer* 4:14.
98. *Mishpetei Uziel, Yoreh De'ah* 28–29.
99. *Binyan Tziyon* 1:170–71.
100. *Iggerot Moshe, Yoreh De'ah* 2:151.
101. *Ḥazon Ish,* ibid.
102. See *Nishmat Avraham, Yoreh De'ah,* vol. 2, 349:1.
103. *Tzitz Eliezer,* ibid.
104. Some distinguish between the corpses of Jews and those of non-Jews. See *Encyclopedia Hilkhatit Refuit,* vol. 4, p. 578.
105. See *Noda BiYehuda,* ibid.; Ḥatam Sofer, ibid.; Maharam Schick, *Yoreh De'ah* 347–48; *Binyan Tziyon,* ibid.; *Gesher HaḤayim* 1:5; *Tzitz Eliezer,* ibid.; *Iggerot Moshe,* ibid.; R. Shlomo Goren, *Meorot* 2; *Yabia Omer, Yoreh De'ah* 3:23:26, et al.
106. See *Yaskil Avdi, Yoreh De'ah* 6:19; *Mishpetei Uziel,* ibid; see also *Ḥavalim BaNe'imim, Yoreh De'ah* 4:64.

may be performed. When autopsies are performed, all body parts should be returned to the family and buried with the body.

## CREMATION[107]

Since ancient times, Jews have rejected the practice of cremation. In fact, Tacitus, a Roman historian in the first century CE, records: "[Jews] are wont to bury rather than to burn their dead."[108]

In the modern era, a practical and efficient means of cremation was first introduced in the 1870s by Professor Lodovico Brunetti of Padua. Within a few years, cremation facilities were opened in Germany and across Europe. To this day, cremation is viewed by many as a convenient, inexpensive, and environmentally friendly alternative to burial. Halakhic authorities almost[109] unanimously oppose cremation and even prohibit the interment of ashes in Jewish cemeteries, as we will discuss below.

The halakhic authorities of the late nineteenth century and twentieth century[110] discuss the reasons why cremation is not an acceptable alternative to burial, and whether or not (and how) ashes may be buried in a Jewish cemetery. They even discuss whether the laws of mourning are observed

107. Several academic articles address the historical and even polemical aspects of the relevant halakhic literature. See David Malkiel, "*Tekhnologiya VeTarbut BeInyan Serefat HaMetim: Nituaḥ Histori UFenomonologi*," *Italia* 10 (1993), pp. 37–69; Adam Ferziger, "The Hamburg Cremation Controversy and the Diversity of German-Jewish Orthodoxy," *Leo Baeck Institute Year Book* 56, no. 1 (2011), pp. 175–205; Adam Ferziger, "Ashes to Outcasts: Cremation, Jewish Law, and Identity in Early Twentieth-Century Germany," *AJS Review* 36, no. 1 (April, 2012), pp. 71–102.

108. *Histories* 5:5.

109. R. Moses Israel Tedeschi of Trieste ("*Gutachten uber Leichenverbrennung*," *Monatsschrift fur die Literatur und Wissenschaft des Judenthums* 2 [1890], pp. 149–53) permits, and even recommends, cremation. R. Chaim (Vittorio) Castiglioni, Chief Rabbi of Rome, was cremated in 1911, per his request. See Ferziger, "Ashes to Outcasts," p. 71.

110. Rabbinic leaders were outspoken against cremation, and even against the interment of ashes. For example, in 1886, R. Eliyahu Benamozegh, Chief Rabbi of Livorno, wrote a treatise on the topic of cremation, titled *Yaaneh BaEsh* (Livorno). In 1901, R. Yisrael Chaim Braun published a pamphlet titled *Beit Yisrael*, which collected letters from Central European rabbis who prohibited cremation. In 1905, Dr. Meir Lerner of Altona, Germany, published *Ḥayei Olam*, which contains over 150 letters from rabbis across the world who prohibited cremation. In 1911, the Orthodox rabbis of Germany met at Frankfurt am Main and reaffirmed their opposition to cremation, and in 1935 the rabbis of Jerusalem issued a similar declaration (*Daat Kohen, Yoreh De'ah* 197).

for one who chooses to be cremated. We will briefly summarize the arguments against cremation and their practical ramifications.

Some proponents of cremation point to biblical verses that appear to indicate that cremation was an accepted Jewish practice. For example, they cite the Bible's description of the death of Asa, the third king of Judea.

> And Asa lay with his fathers, and died in the forty-first year of his reign. They buried him in his graves that he had excavated for himself in the city of David. And they laid him on a couch that he had filled with spices and diverse kinds [of spices], prepared with the perfumer's art, and they kindled an exceedingly great fire for him. (II Chr. 16:13–14)

Similarly, they cite the biblical depiction of the death of King Jehoram of the Kingdom of Israel.

> It was that from year to year, at the conclusion of two years' time, his innards emerged with his illness, and he died of dire diseases. They did not make a conflagration for him, like the conflagration of his fathers. (II Chr. 21:19)

These verses appear to indicate that kings were burned. Indeed, when describing the death of Zedekiah, Jeremiah predicts:

> You will not die by sword; you will die in peace; and like the conflagrations of your fathers, the former kings who were before you, so they will burn for you; and woe, lord, they will eulogize you, for I have spoken a statement, the utterance of the Lord. (Jer. 34:4–5)

However, as indicated in the first verse cited, it was customary to burn a conflagration of spices and diverse kinds. Furthermore, the Tosefta[111] teaches: "They mark the death of kings by burning a pyre … and what is it that they burn on the pyre on his account? His bed and the items he would use."

The story of Saul's death is more troubling. The Bible relates that after Saul and his sons were killed during a battle with the Philistines, the people of Jabesh Gilead

111. Tosefta, Shabbat 7:18.

> took the body of Saul and the bodies of his sons from the wall of Beit She'an. They came to Jabesh and they burned them there. They took their bones, and they buried them beneath the tamarisk in Jabesh, and they fasted seven days. (I Sam. 31:12–13)[112]

The commentaries offer different interpretations of this story. Some suggest that they burned their possessions, as described above.[113] Others suggest that they burned perfumes, and even their inner organs, in preparation for embalmment.[114] R. David Kimchi suggested that their bodies had already begun to decay, and the people of Jabesh Gilead deemed it disrespectful to bury their bodies in that condition.[115]

A closer look indicates that the Bible viewed burning bodies as a sign of great disrespect. For example, when Achan and his children are executed for taking the spoils of Jericho, the Bible relates: "All Israel cast stones upon him, and they burned them with fire" (Josh. 7:25). Similarly, when King Josiah executes the priests of idol worship [*kohanei bamot*] he burns their bones on the altar (II Kings 23:20). Finally, the prophet Amos says that God will not forgive Moab: "For his burning of the bones of the king of Edom into lime" (Amos 2:1).

The *Aḥaronim* raise numerous objections to the practice of cremation. R. David Zvi Hoffmann (1843–1921), for example, writes that cremation runs counter to the biblical obligation to bury the dead, and is a form of desecrating the deceased [*nivul hamet*].[116] R. Avraham Yitzchak HaKohen Kook (1865–1935) suggests that cremation may even be a form of: The ways of the gentiles [*ḥukot hagoyim*].[117] Some add that just as burial is an affirmation of the belief in the resurrection of the dead [*teḥiyat hametim*], destroying the body through cremation may constitute a rejection of this fundamental principle.[118] Some note that after millions of Jews were murdered and then

112. Interestingly, the parallel passage in the Book of Chronicles states only that: "They buried their bones" (I Chr. 10:12).
113. Radak, ibid.
114. Radak, ibid.; *Tosafot Yom Tov*, Pesaḥim 4:9.
115. Radak, ibid.
116. See *Melamed LeHo'il, Yoreh De'ah* 2:114; see also *Gesher HaḤayim* 1:16:9. See *Aḥiezer* (3:72), who adds that one thereby violates the prohibition of *bal talin*, delaying the burial.
117. *Daat Kohen, Yoreh De'ah* 197. R. Kook adds that even if burial were only a custom, it is a custom that is sufficiently authoritative to prohibit cremation for that reason.
118. *Beit Yitzḥak, Yoreh De'ah* 1:155; *Aḥiezer*, ibid.; *Daat Kohen*, ibid.

cremated by the Nazis during the Holocaust, cremation has become an even more objectionable practice.

Many authorities prohibit burying the ashes of a cremated person in a Jewish cemetery, to demonstrate the community's disapproval of cremation.[119] Some suggest that the ashes should be interred, but in a separate area of the cemetery.[120] With regard to one who is burned against his dying wish, accidentally, or *al kiddush Hashem*, e.g., those murdered in the Holocaust,[121] his ashes are certainly afforded a proper burial in a Jewish cemetery.

Some rule that if a person specifically requested to be cremated, his children should not honor this last wish and should bury the body.[122] Furthermore, some insist that one should not observe the laws of mourning for one who was cremated by choice.[123] Most authorities maintain that the Mourner's Kaddish is recited in any case. These complex, sensitive issues should be discussed with a halakhic authority.

## BURIAL IN ERETZ YISRAEL

There is an ancient tradition, tracing back to biblical times, that one makes every effort to be buried in the Land of Israel. Indeed, the Book of Genesis concludes with both Jacob[124] and Joseph[125] requesting that their bodies be taken from Egypt to Eretz Yisrael for burial.

---

119. *Beit Yitzḥak*, ibid.; *Aḥiezer*, ibid.; *Gesher HaḤayim* 1:6:9; *Sefer Kol Bo al Avelut* 1:3:21; *Daat Kohen*, ibid.; *Iggerot Moshe, Yoreh De'ah* 3:147:2; *Teshuvot Ivra* 65, et al. Others, such as R. Marcus Hirsch (cited in *Beit Yisrael*) and his son-in-law R. Chanoch Ehrentrau (*Ḥeker Halakha*, 1904) permitted burying the ashes (see *Seridei Esh* 2:95, 98). Similarly, R. Nathan Marcus Adler and his son R. Herman Adler permitted burying ashes in Jewish cemeteries in England. See R. Tzvi Rabinowicz, *A Guide to Life: Jewish Laws and Customs of Mourning* (Jason Aronson, 1989), pp. 18–19.
120. *Seridei Esh* 2:95:98.
121. *Har Tzvi, Yoreh De'ah* 275; *Tzitz Eliezer* 8:35; *Gesher HaḤayim* 1:16:8.
122. *Sefer Kol Bo al Avelut*, ibid.; *Gesher HaḤayim* 1:16:9, based on Y. Ketubot 11:1.
123. See *Minḥat Elazar* (2:34), in accordance with the ruling of the *Shulḥan Arukh* that one does not mourn for those who deviate from the ways of the community (*Yoreh De'ah* 345:5). Some rule that since nowadays the choice to be cremated is most often taken due to ignorance, mourning is observed, and begins immediately upon hearing about the death.
124. Gen. 47:29. Some suggest that Jacob's request related more to the specific aspects of the Exodus story than to his will to be buried in Eretz Yisrael. See *Mishnat Rabbi Eliezer*, chap. 19; and Rashi on Gen. 47:29 (based on Ketubot 111a).
125. Ibid., 50:25.

The Talmud[126] relates different reasons for burial in Eretz Yisrael. One source indicates that burial in Eretz Yisrael may atone for one's sins.

> R. Anan said, Anyone buried in Eretz Yisrael, it is considered as though he was buried beneath the altar; it is written here: "You shall make for me an altar of earth [*adama*]" (Ex. 20:21), and it is written there: "And His land [*admato*] will atone for His people" (Deut. 32:43).

This source indicates that Eretz Yisrael shares the atoning capability of the altar. R. Anan's statement may be viewed as a continuation of the previous passage in the Talmud: R. Elazar said: Anyone who resides in Eretz Yisrael dwells without iniquity. Although this statement seems to refer to the greater spiritual potential of living in Eretz Yisrael,[127] one might suggest that it relates to the greater proximity between man and God in Israel;[128] proximity to God purifies one's soul, in life and after death. A similar version of R. Anan's statement points to this understanding.

> Anyone buried in Eretz Yisrael is considered as though he were buried beneath the altar, because all of Eretz Yisrael is suitable for the altar, and anyone buried beneath the altar is considered as though he were buried beneath the Throne of Glory [*kiseh hakavod*].[129]

The significance of being buried under the altar lies in its proximity to the Throne of God.

Another passage[130] indicates that burial in Eretz Yisrael may be auspicious during the resurrection of the dead [*teḥiyat hametim*].

> R. Elazar said: The dead [buried] outside Eretz Yisrael will not be resurrected... According to R. Elazar, will the righteous outside Eretz Yisrael not be resurrected? R. Ela said: By means of rolling.

126. Ketubot 111a.
127. See, for example, Ramban, Lev. 18:25.
128. Deut. 11:12.
129. *Avot DeRabbi Natan* 26:2.
130. Ketubot 111a.

> R. Abba Sala Rabba objected: Rolling is an ordeal that entails suffering for the righteous. Abaye said: Tunnels are prepared for them in the ground.

Similarly, the Yerushalmi[131] teaches:

> "I shall walk before God in the land of the living" (Ps. 116:9). R. Shimon b. Lakish said in the name of bar Kappara: The land whose dead will live first in the days of the Messiah... But if this is the case, our rabbis in the Diaspora will be at a disadvantage. R. Simi said: God will smooth the ground before them, and they will roll like jugs, and when they arrive in Eretz Yisrael their souls will return to them.

Setting aside the differences between these passages, and between the righteous and the ordinary Jew, these passages clearly indicate that burial in Eretz Yisrael may be advantageous during *teḥiyat hametim.*

Many pious individuals instruct their children to bury them in Eretz Yisrael.[132] Some authorities even say that unless a parent indicated otherwise, one may assume that he would have preferred to be buried in Eretz Yisrael.[133] One should certainly not bury a parent in Eretz Yisrael against his stated will.

Although the halakha does not generally permit reinterment,[134] one may move the remains of one who was buried outside of Eretz Yisrael, to Eretz Yisrael.[135] The *Aḥaronim* even permit reinterment in Eretz Yisrael in a case where the deceased did not explicitly request to be reburied there.[136]

---

131. Y. Kilayim 9:3.
132. Some even discuss whether it is preferable to be buried in Jerusalem; see *Tzitz Eliezer* 14:79; *Shevet HaLevi* 2:207:2; see also Radbaz 732.
133. See *Pitḥei Teshuva* 363:2.
134. Y. Mo'ed Katan 2:4; *Shulḥan Arukh, Yoreh De'ah* 363:1.
135. *Shulḥan Arukh,* ibid., based on Ramban, *Torat HaAdam, Shaar HaKevura.* See Shakh (ibid., 3) who relates this to the verse: "And His land will atone for His people" (Deut. 32:43).
136. *Pitḥei Teshuva* (ibid., 2) cites R. Levi ibn Habib (1480–1545), known by the acronym *Maharlbaḥ* (*Maharlbaḥ* 63).

In more recent years, halakhic authorities have dealt with numerous interesting cases regarding the reinterment of remains in Eretz Yisrael. For example, in 1956 R. Yochanan Perlow, the Grand Rebbe of Karlin-Stolin in America, died and was buried in New York. Over the next year, a debate erupted among his followers in America and Israel whether to bring his remains to Israel for burial. R. Tzvi Pesach Frank,[137] based upon the ruling cited above, permitted his reinterment. His remains were moved the next year, and he was reburied in Tiberias. Similarly, in 1970, the Israeli government raised the possibility of moving the remains of Sir Moses Montefiore (1784–1885), and those of his wife, from Ramsgate, England, to Jerusalem. R. Ovadia Yosef[138] contended that it would be permitted to move their remains. R. Moshe Feinstein[139] ruled that it was prohibited to transfer the remains of Sir Moses Montefiore to Israel. He insisted that even if one's children may move their parent's remains, this right is not extended to others. Sir Moses Montefiore's remains were not relocated to Israel.

We should note that not everyone agrees with regard to the merit of being buried in Eretz Yisrael. The Yerushalmi[140] teaches:

> Rabbi b. Kirya and R. Lezer were strolling in Istrina. They saw coffins arriving in Eretz Yisrael from *Ḥutz LaAretz*. Rabbi b. Kirya said to R. Lezer: What have they accomplished? I apply to them the verse:[141] "My heritage you rendered an abomination," in your lifetime; "You came and defiled My land," in your deaths. He said to him: When they arrive in Eretz Yisrael they take a clod of earth and place it on the coffin, as it is written: "And His land will atone for His people" (Deut. 32:43).

The *Or Zarua*,[142] cited by Rema,[143] derives the widespread custom of burying the deceased with dirt from Eretz Yisrael from this passage.

Furthermore, some contemporary authorities criticize the growing phenomenon of burial in Eretz Yisrael. For example, R. Yosef Eliyahu

137. *Har Tzvi, Yoreh De'ah* 274; see also *Ḥoveret Beit Aharon VeYisrael*, vol. 42, pp. 138–51.
138. *Ḥazon Ovadia, Avelut*, vol. 1, p. 420; see also *Yabia Omer, Yoreh De'ah* 6:31.
139. *Iggerot Moshe, Yoreh De'ah* 3:153.
140. Y. Kilayim 9:3.
141. Jer. 2:7.
142. *Or Zarua* 2:19.
143. Rema 363:1; see *Gesher HaḤayim* 1:27:10.

Henkin (1881–1973) strongly criticizes the practice of ordinary people spending large sums of money on funeral arrangements, including burial in Israel, instead of giving money to charity and supporting Torah study.[144] He even describes the phenomenon as presumptuousness [*yuhara*]. Others object to burying the deceased in Eretz Yisrael when his relatives live elsewhere. They cite *Sefer Ḥasidim*,[145] who describes how it is beneficial for the deceased when relatives visit their graves and pray for their souls.

Although the prevailing sentiment in the Talmud supports the merits of burial in Eretz Yisrael as stated above, numerous sources emphasize that it is preferable to die in Eretz Yisrael, and not just to be buried there. For example, the Yerushalmi[146] also cites the following incident:

> Ulla would regularly descend [from Eretz Yisrael to Babylonia]; the time for his death arrived there (outside Eretz Yisrael), and he began to cry. They said to him: Why are you crying? We will take you up to Eretz Yisrael. He said to them: What will that accomplish for me? I am losing my gem (my soul) in an impure land. There is no comparison between one who loses it in his mother's bosom and one who loses it in the bosom of a strange woman.

Rambam[147] succinctly summarizes this issue:

> The sages said: Anyone who dwells in Eretz Yisrael, his sins are forgiven, as it is stated: "A dweller will not say: I am sick, the people in it are forgiven iniquity" (Is. 33:24). Even one who walked four cubits there merits the World to Come; and likewise, one who is buried there receives atonement as though the place where he is is an altar of atonement, as it is stated: "His land will atone for His people" (Deut. 32:43)…There is no comparison between one who is absorbed there alive and one absorbed there after his death; nevertheless, the prominent sages would bring their dead there. Go out and learn from our patriarch Jacob, and Joseph the righteous.

---

144. *Teshuvot Ivra* 86, 88:3; see also *Divrei Yoel, Vayeḥi*, pp. 515–16.
145. *Sefer Ḥasidim* 710.
146. Y. Kilayim 9:3.
147. Rambam, *Hilkhot Melakhim* 5:11.

* * *

As mentioned above, the human body is likened to the parchment of a *sefer Torah*. Indeed, the Talmud[148] teaches:

> R. Shimon b. Elazar states: One who stands over the deceased at the time of the departure of the soul is obligated to rend [his garments]. To what is this similar? To a *sefer Torah* that is burned, for which one is obligated to rend [one's garments].

Ramban, in his commentary to the passage cited above, explains:

> It seems to me that the soul in the body is like the names of God on the parchment. It is merely a parable to convey the message that it is a great loss and cause for alarm and that one must rend his garments as though a *sefer Torah* was burned before him.

Just as the names of God sanctify the parchment on which it is written, so too, the soul sanctifies the body. We are commanded to respect the human body when alive, and after the soul departs as well. Just as a *sefer Torah* is buried, so too, a human body is not cast away, burned, or destroyed, but interred in the most respectful manner possible, as it waits until it will once again serve as a receptacle for the human soul, which will one day return to it.

148. Mo'ed Katan 25a.

*Chapter 3*

# Burial Customs and the Laws of *Keria*

## HONORING THE DEAD AND PREPARATIONS FOR BURIAL

The Talmud likens the human body to a *sefer Torah*.[1] The body is the receptacle that contains the soul, similar to the *sefer Torah*, which carries the names of God.[2] The body of the deceased is treated with the utmost respect; one must behave appropriately in its presence, it is carefully guarded, and it is meticulously prepared for burial.

The Talmud teaches that one should not eat or drink in the presence of the deceased.[3] Furthermore, the Gemara even expresses concern that certain behaviors may be viewed as mocking the deceased.

> One may not walk in a cemetery with *tefillin* on his head and a Torah scroll in his arm and read from it. If one does so he commits a transgression due to the verse: "He who mocks the poor [*lo'eg larash*] blasphemes his Creator" (Prov. 17:5). As the deceased is incapable of fulfilling mitzvot, fulfilling a mitzva in his presence is seen as mocking him…when one walks in a cemetery, within four cubits

1. Mo'ed Katan 25a.
2. Ramban, *Torat HaAdam, Inyan HaKeria*, p. 52.
3. Berakhot 17b; see *Shulḥan Arukh, Yoreh De'ah* 341:1; Shakh 3. *Taz* (1) explains that it is only the *onen* who is prohibited from eating in the presence of the deceased.

> of a grave, that is prohibited. However, beyond four cubits from a grave, one is obligated in prayer and *tefillin.*

Due to this concern of "*lo'eg larash*" one may not recite words of Torah, the *Shema, Shemoneh Esreh,* or *berakhot,* nor may he don *tefillin* or exposed *tzitzit,* within four *amot* (two meters) of the deceased, or in a cemetery.

It is proper to appoint a "*shomer,*" a guard to watch the body until it is given to the *ḥevra kadisha.* There are numerous reasons given for this practice. The Talmud mentions protecting the deceased from "a weasel or from mice."[4] This appears to be the primary reason.[5] In addition, other sources indicate that watching the body is an act of respect, so that the deceased does not appear to be "an unwanted vessel" (Jer. 22:28).[6] It is proper for those watching the deceased to recite psalms and other prayers, and not to engage in idle conversation. Those who watch the deceased are exempt from *Shema* and *Shemoneh Esreh;*[7] if two people are watching the deceased they should alternate reciting the *Shema* and *Shemoneh Esreh.* One may receive payment for watching a body, even on Shabbat.[8]

There is an ancient Jewish custom to wash and prepare the body for burial.[9] The *ḥevra kadisha* is entrusted with performing this task, known as the "*tahara,*" during which its members wash and dress the body in burial shrouds (*takhrikhin*). Just as when a person enters this world, his body is washed and cleaned, that should be the case when a person leaves this world as well.

There are three stages of the *tahara*: the *reḥitza* (washing the body), the *tahara* (spiritual purification, during which nine *kavim* [20 L] of water are poured over the body), and the *halbasha,* when the body is dressed in *takhrikhin.* The *tahara* is performed with the utmost modesty and sensitivity; those engaged in preparing the body for burial recite biblical verses

---

4. Shabbat 151b; see also Berakhot 18a.
5. See *Iggerot Moshe, Yoreh De'ah* 1:225; *Shevet HaLevi,* 5:178. R. Moshe Feinstein adds that if there is no fear of mice the body does not require constant supervision.
6. See *Gesher HaḤayim* 5:4:4. He cites an additional reason, based on the Zohar, which asserts that watching the body protects the deceased from various spiritual impurities.
7. See *Shulḥan Arukh, Oraḥ Ḥayim* 71:3 and *Yoreh De'ah* 341:6; see also 403:9 regarding one who transfers remains from one grave to another.
8. *Nitei Gavriel, Hilkhot Avelut,* vol. 1, p. 90.
9. Shabbat 151a; see also *Shulḥan Arukh, Yoreh De'ah* 352:4.

relating to the *tahara*. The details of the *tahara* differ from community to community and are beyond the scope of this chapter.

There are situations when a *tahara* is not performed. For example, R. Yaakov b. Moshe Moelin (1387–1427), known as Maharil, writes that a person murdered by non-Jewish bandits is buried in his clothing, in order to "provoke anger and [divine] vengeance."[10] Furthermore, a *tahara* is not performed for one who was found dead where blood flowed from the body, e.g., in the case of a person who fell from a roof, as the blood that flowed from the body should not be washed away.[11] The *Aḥaronim* discuss whether a *tahara* is performed for those who die naturally in a manner involving significant bleeding, such as a woman in childbirth.[12]

Finally, the Talmud[13] relates that the deceased is dressed in simple burial shrouds.

> Likewise, at first taking the dead out for burial was more difficult for the relatives than the actual death [as it was customary to bury the dead in expensive shrouds, which the poor could not afford]. The problem grew to the point that relatives would sometimes abandon the corpse and flee. This lasted until Rabban Gamliel came and acted with frivolity, [meaning that he waived his dignity, instructing that he be] taken out for burial in linen garments. And the people adopted this practice after him, to go out for burial in linen garments. R. Pappa said: And today, everyone follows the practice of burying the dead even in plain hemp garments [*tzerada*] that cost only a dinar.

Similarly, it is customary to bury the deceased in a simple, wooden coffin [*aron*]. In Israel, the burial is performed without an *aron*. The Israeli Military Rabbinate buries soldiers in coffins.

## RENDING ONE'S GARMENTS [*KERIA*]

Rending one's garments is one of the earliest expressions of mourning. The Torah relates that Reuben rent his garments after returning to the pit and

10. Ecclesiastes Rabba 3:16:1.
11. Maharil 65.
12. See Rema, *Yoreh De'ah* 364:4; *Taz* 3; Shakh 11; see also *Gesher HaḤayim* 11:4.
13. Mo'ed Katan 27b.

discovering that Joseph was missing,[14] as did Jacob upon hearing of Joseph's disappearance.[15] Similarly, David and his servants rent their garments after Amnon's murder,[16] as did Job after the death of his children.[17]

The Talmud[18] derives the obligation to rend one's garments from a biblical passage that relates to the death of Aaron's sons, Nadav and Avihu.

> R. Taḥlifa b. Avimi said that Shmuel said: A mourner who did not let his hair grow wild and did not rend his garments is liable to receive the death penalty [at the hand of Heaven], as it is stated [following the deaths of Nadav and Avihu, concerning the surviving sons of Aaron]: "Let the hair of your heads not grow loose, neither rend your garments, that you not die" (Lev. 10:6). From here it may be inferred that any other mourner who did not let his hair grow wild or rend his garments is liable to receive the death penalty.

God instructs Aaron, due to his status and responsibilities as the High Priest, not to observe mourning practices such as rending his garments and letting his hair grow. Despite the apparent biblical source for *keria*,[19] most *Rishonim*[20] maintain that the obligation to rend one's garments is only rabbinic. Some *Rishonim*, however, cite Raavad, who insists that there is a biblical obligation to rend one's garments as an expression of mourning over one's close relatives.

The commentaries offer several insights into this practice. While rending one's garment may be viewed as an expression of outrage and intense grief, Rambam[21] explains that rending one's garment ultimately relieves one's anger and calms one's soul. Rending the garment that covers

---

14. Gen. 37:29.
15. Ibid., 34.
16. II Sam. 13:31.
17. Job 1:20.
18. Mo'ed Katan 24a.
19. See Raavad, cited by Rosh (Mo'ed Katan 3:3).
20. See, for example, Ramban, *Torat HaAdam, Inyan HaKeria*, p. 63.
21. Rambam, *Hilkhot Shabbat* 10:10; see Commentary on the Mishna, Shabbat 13:3 and Bava Kama 8:5. See also *Torah Temima* (Lev. 10:6), who explains that this positive outcome justifies the apparent violation of the prohibition of *bal tashḥit*, causing wanton destruction.

the heart, in response to the death of a parent, may symbolize one's broken heart, as the prophet Joel says, "And rend your heart, and not your garments" (Joel 2:13). Interestingly, the Yerushalmi[22] explains that when rending for a deceased parent, one rends the shirt until he reveals his heart, emphasizing the additional anguish he feels as he can no longer fulfill the commandment of *kibbud av va'em* (honoring one's parents).[23]

One performs *keria* upon the death of a parent, spouse, child,[24] or sibling, i.e., anyone for whom one is obligated to mourn.[25] Regarding a child under the age of bar or bat mitzva, the Talmud teaches that "[the relatives] rend the garment of a child to arouse grief."[26] The *Gesher HaḤayim*[27] writes that the garment of a small child is rent only slightly, while the shirt of a child who has reached the age of *ḥinukh* is rent in accordance with the laws of *keria*.

Why are the garments of a child rent? R. Yitzchak ibn Ghiyyat[28] (1038–1089) explains that the obligation of the child in *keria* is like his obligation in all other mitzvot, due to the requirement of *ḥinukh*. Rashi explains that the child's garment is rent "so that those who see will cry and they will enhance their respect for the deceased, [but] not because he is a mourner."[29]

It appears that the original custom was to perform *keria* shortly after the death, after reciting the *tziduk hadin* (justification of [divine] judgment) prayer and the *Dayan HaEmet* blessing.[30] In most communities, it is customary to perform *keria* at the funeral service. R. Yechiel Michel Tukachinsky, in his *Gesher HaḤayim*,[31] questions this practice and suggests several explanations. First, he suggests that since most people are not well versed in the

22. Y. Mo'ed Katan 3:8.
23. *Penei Moshe* adds that one rends his shirt until he reveals his heart, as the honor one gives to a parent "is dependent upon the heart."
24. One does not perform *keria* for a child who passes away within thirty days of birth; see chapter 5.
25. Although an adopted child, adoptive parent, and adoptive sibling are not obligated to mourn (see chapter 5), they may certainly perform *keria*. Similarly, they may recite the *Dayan HaEmet* blessing.
26. Mo'ed Katan 26b. See *Shulḥan Arukh, Yoreh De'ah* 340:27.
27. *Gesher HaḤayim* 1:4:20.
28. See *Tur, Yoreh De'ah* 340.
29. Rashi, Mo'ed Katan 14b, s.v. *mekar'in*.
30. *Shulḥan Arukh, Yoreh De'ah* 339:3.
31. *Gesher HaḤayim* 4:6.

laws of *keria*, the mourner waits until the funeral service, when the members of the *ḥevra kadisha* can offer halakhic guidance and instruction. Second, it is customary for others to begin the rending of the garment, and the *ḥevra kadisha* is available to assist at the funeral. Finally, since all of the mourners are assembled together at the funeral, that may be a more appropriate time for the *keria*. Others suggest that since the grief is often felt most acutely at the funeral, that moment, known as "*shaat haḥimum*," is the most appropriate time for *keria*. One who does not attend the funeral should perform the *keria* upon hearing the news or when beginning the seven-day mourning period.

Although there is no inherent connection between the blessing and the *keria*, it is customary to say "*Barukh ... dayan ha'emet*" when rending one's garment. If one did not rend his garment when hearing of the death, or at the burial, he may rend his garment during the entire week of mourning,[32] but he should not say the *Dayan HaEmet* blessing after the third day.[33] If, however, a person is ill and is unable to fully comprehend what happened, when he recovers and understands his loss he may recite the blessing and rend his garments.[34] As we will learn in chapter 6, if one heard about the death of a relative after the *shiva*, but within thirty days of the death, he may still perform *keria*.[35] If he hears about the death of a parent he rends his garments even after thirty days.[36]

Before the funeral, a mourner may change his shirt, donning one that he would prefer to rend.[37] He should keep in mind that this is the shirt that he will most likely wear for the entire week. During the week, one who is mourning the death of a parent may not change his shirt, and if he does, he is required to rend the second shirt. One who is mourning other relatives may change into a different shirt,[38] although it is customary to wear a rent shirt for the entire week of mourning.

---

32. See *Nitei Gavriel, Hilkhot Avelut*, vol. 1, p. 300.
33. *Gesher HaḤayim* 4:26.
34. Shakh 396:1.
35. *Shulḥan Arukh, Yoreh De'ah* 340:18.
36. *Shulḥan Arukh, Yoreh De'ah* 396:1. It seems that on the seventh day, after the mourner concludes the *shiva*, he may no longer perform the *keria*. See *Ḥiddushim UBiurim, Hilkhot Keria* 27.
37. *Gesher HaḤayim* 4:1. Some suggest (*Har Tzvi* 263) that for a parent, one should rend the shirt that he was already wearing.
38. *Shulḥan Arukh*, ibid., 14.

*Keria* is performed while standing.[39] One who tears while seated did not fulfill his obligation and is required to rend again.[40] When rending for relatives other than one's parents, one may perform the *keria* privately, but when rending over the death of one's parent, one should rend publicly.[41] Although some record a practice of others rending the mourner's shirt, it is proper for the mourner to fulfill this mitzva by himself. It is customary for another to begin cutting the garment, and the mourner then performs the *keria*; a man begins cutting the garment for a man, and a woman for a woman.

The Talmud teaches that the *keria* performed upon the death of a parent differs from the *keria* for other relatives. For other family members, one rends only the outer garment,[42] on the right side,[43] and one rends it at least one *tefaḥ* (8–10 cm),[44] with either a knife or with one's hand.[45] For one's parent, one rends all of the garments, except the innermost garments that absorb perspiration, the overcoat, and a sweater worn for warmth. One tears on the left side,[46] until the tear exposes his heart. He should do so with his hand, which reflects a more intense bitterness.[47]

One should begin rending at the edge of the garment,[48] at the neck, and rend along the length of the garment, vertically, not horizontally.[49] When rending a suit jacket, one should rend the entire lapel. A woman should perform the *keria* in a modest manner, rending only the outer layer,

39. Mo'ed Katan 21a.
40. *Shulḥan Arukh, Yoreh De'ah* 340:1. R. Ovadia Yosef (*Ḥazon Ovadia, Avelut,* vol. 1, p. 217) rules that a person who is unable to stand may tear while sitting.
41. Ibid., 13.
42. *Shulḥan Arukh,* ibid., 9–10. One does not rend an outer garment that is worn for dignity, or a jacket or overcoat.
43. Maharshal; see *Taz,* ibid., 6; Shakh, ibid., 19.
44. Mo'ed Katan 22b.
45. Ibid.
46. *Baḥ* (see *Taz,* ibid.) explains that when rending for one's parents, one rends until he reveals his heart, which is on the left side.
47. Me'iri, Mo'ed Katan 24a.
48. Mo'ed Katan 22b. The *Rishonim* dispute whether this applies only to *keria* for one's parents (Rambam), or to *keria* for other relatives as well (*Mordekhai*). While the *Shulḥan Arukh* rules in accordance with Rambam, Rema relates that it is customary to always rend from the edge of the garment.
49. See *Pitḥei Teshuva,* ibid., 2.

and should either close the tear with a safety pin or wear a shirt beneath the outer garment.

If one must perform *keria* for more than one relative, one tear is sufficient. If one rent for one relative, and another dies within the seven-day mourning period, he must rend an additional tear for the second relative. If he rends after the end of the seven days of mourning, he may extend the original tear. For one's parents, one must tear until he reveals his heart; extending the original tear is not sufficient.[50]

Of course, *keria* is not performed on Shabbat or Yom Tov. Furthermore, in preparation for Shabbat one removes the rent garment. Regarding one whose relative passes away on Ḥol HaMo'ed, in which case the formal period of mourning does not begin until after the final day of the festival, the *Rishonim* disagree as to whether one should perform *keria* on Ḥol HaMo'ed. Most *Rishonim*[51] rule that one may perform *keria* on Ḥol HaMo'ed for a relative, when one hears of the death of an "*adam kasher*" or a Torah scholar, or if he is present at the time of death of any person. Other *Rishonim*[52] prohibit performing *keria* on Ḥol HaMo'ed. R. Yisrael Isserlin (1390–1460), in his *Terumat HaDeshen*, relates that the custom in Ashkenaz was to rend for one's parent, but not for other relatives, on Ḥol HaMo'ed. While *Shulḥan Arukh*[53] adopts the lenient view and permits *keria* in all the cases listed above, Rema cites the view of *Terumat HaDeshen* but adds that in a place where there is no set custom one should rend for all relatives on Ḥol HaMo'ed. *Gesher HaḤayim*[54] relates that in Israel it is customary to rend on Ḥol HaMo'ed only for one's parent. Elsewhere, one may perform *keria* for all of one's close relatives on Ḥol HaMo'ed.[55] One should then remove the rent garment immediately, and replace it after the festival, when the seven-day mourning period begins.

In addition to rending one's garment as an expression of mourning over the death of a close relative, the Talmud cites numerous other instances where one is required to rend one's garments. For example, the Gemara teaches that one who is present at the moment of death of any

---

50. *Shulḥan Arukh, Yoreh De'ah* 340:3.
51. See Rambam, Commentary on the Mishna, Mo'ed Katan 3:7; Ramban, *Torat HaAdam, Inyan HaKeria*, p. 66; *Mordekhai*, Mo'ed Katan 884.
52. Raavya, *Hilkhot Avel* 3:841; *Semak* 97.
53. Ibid., 31.
54. *Gesher HaḤayim* 4:34.
55. See, for example, *Nitei Gavriel, Hilkhot Avelut*, vol. 1, p. 311.

person should perform *keria,* just as one does upon seeing a burning *sefer Torah.*[56] Furthermore, the Gemara teaches:

> One rends his garments for his teacher who taught him Torah, or for the *Nasi,* or for the president of the court, or upon hearing evil tidings, or hearing God's name being cursed, or when a Torah scroll has been burned, or upon seeing the cities of Judea that were destroyed, or the destroyed Temple or Jerusalem in ruins.[57]

It is not customary to rend one's garment in most of these instances.

## BEHAVIOR AND CUSTOMS IN THE CEMETERY

The Talmud[58] teaches that upon entering a cemetery one recites a special blessing:

> Blessed... who revives the dead. The sages taught: One who sees graves of Israel recites: Blessed... who formed you in judgment, and who nourished you in judgment, and who sustained you in judgment, and collected your soul in judgment, and in the future will raise you from the dead in judgment. And Mar, son of Ravina, concludes the formula of this blessing in the name of R. Naḥman: And who knows the number of you all, and who in the future will restore you to life and sustain you.

Some recite the second blessing of the *Shemoneh Esreh,* "You are eternally mighty, my Lord," until "You are faithful to resurrect the dead," after the blessing.[59]

This blessing is recited only once every thirty days.[60] The mourners do not recite this blessing, as they do not recite blessings before the burial.

56. Mo'ed Katan 25a. Nowadays it is customary for those present at the moment of death not to rend their garments. Some suggest that the concern is that people will be unwilling to be with a person in his final moments, to avoid performing *keria* (*Gesher HaḤayim* 4:9).

57. Mo'ed Katan 26a.

58. Berakhot 58b.

59. *Kitzur Shulḥan Arukh* 198:13.

60. *Mishna Berura* 224:17.

As mentioned above, one must display extreme sensitivity in the cemetery, which includes appropriate conduct,[61] and even showing consideration for the deceased. Therefore, one should not wear *tzitzit* outside of his shirt or don *tefillin* on his head.

### *LEVAYAT HAMET* AND THE FUNERAL SERVICE

Each morning, we recite the following passage, based upon a passage from the Talmud.[62]

> These are the matters whose fruits we eat in this world but whose full reward awaits us in the World to Come: Honoring parents, acts of kindness, arriving early at the house of study morning and evening, hospitality to strangers, visiting the sick, helping the needy bride, attending to the dead, devotion in prayer, and bringing peace between people, but the study of Torah is equal to them all.

Attending to the dead, and escorting them to their burial, is perceived as a selfless act, for which one is rewarded in this world and in the World to Come.

Rambam[63] teaches that participation in a funeral procession and in a burial service are a fulfillment of a positive commandment.

> There is a positive commandment of rabbinic origin to visit the sick, comfort mourners, to prepare for a funeral, prepare a bride, accompany guests, attend to all the needs of a burial, carry the deceased on one's shoulders, walk before the bier, eulogize, dig a grave, and bury the dead, and also to bring joy to a bride and groom and help

61. *Shulḥan Arukh, Yoreh De'ah* 368:1.

62. The Talmud (Shabbat 127a) states: "These are the matters that a person does them and enjoys their profits in this world, and nevertheless the principal exists for him for the World to Come, and they are: Honoring one's father and mother, and acts of loving-kindness, and bringing peace between a person and another, and Torah study is equal to all of them. These matters, yes; other matters, no? These too, hospitality toward guests and visiting the sick, are in the category of acts of loving-kindness." Maharshal (*Teshuvot Maharshal* 64) notes that the text that appears in the Siddur adds "attending to the dead."

63. Rambam, *Hilkhot Avel* 14:1.

> them in all their needs. These are deeds of kindness that one carries out with his person that have no limit. Although all these mitzvot are of rabbinic origin, they are included in the Torah commandment: "Love your neighbor as yourself" (Lev. 19:18). That mitzva instructs that whatever you would like others to perform on your behalf, you should perform for your colleague in Torah and mitzvot.

Furthermore, the Talmud[64] teaches that accompanying the deceased to burial justifies interrupting the study of Torah. Indeed, the Talmud[65] criticizes those who fail to do so.

> Raḥava said that R. Yehuda said: One who sees the deceased taken to burial and does not escort him has committed a transgression due to the verse: "He who mocks the poor blasphemes his Creator" (Prov. 17:5). And if he does escort him, what is his reward? R. Asi said: The verse says about him: "He who gives to the poor gives a loan to the Lord [and the Lord will repay him]" (ibid., 19:17), and: "[He who oppresses the poor blasphemes his Creator] but he who is gracious to the poor honors Him" (ibid., 14:31).

This mitzva refers not only to participating in the funeral service, but also to walking with and accompanying the deceased to his final resting place. One who encounters a funeral procession and cannot accompany the body to the burial should walk with the deceased for at least four *amot* (approximately two meters).

There is a great mitzva to properly eulogize the deceased,[66] just as Abraham eulogized his wife, Sarah.[67] The Gemara[68] questions whether the purpose of the *hesped* is to honor the dead or to honor the living.

> A dilemma was raised before the sages: Is the eulogy delivered for the honor of the living relatives of the deceased, or is it delivered for the honor of the dead? What is the practical difference? There

64. Ketubot 17a.
65. Berakhot 18a.
66. Rambam, *Hilkhot Avel* 14:1.
67. Gen. 23:2.
68. Sanhedrin 46b.

> is a difference in a case where one said before he died: Do not eulogize that man, i.e., me. Alternatively, the difference is with regard to whether it is possible to collect the eulogist's fee from the heirs.

The Gemara suggests that if the purpose of the *hesped* is to honor the deceased, then if a person explicitly requests that *hespedim* should not be recited, his wishes are honored. Furthermore, since the *hespedim* are to honor the deceased, the estate is responsible for defraying the costs. The halakha is in accordance with this opinion.[69] *Shulḥan Arukh*[70] describes the appropriate content and delivery of a *hesped*.

> There is a great mitzva to appropriately [*kara'ui*] eulogize the deceased. There is a mitzva to raise one's voice in saying words that break the heart, in order to increase crying and to mention his praise. It is prohibited to overly exaggerate his praise; rather, one mentions his good qualities, and embellishes a bit, without overstating it. And if [the deceased] had no good qualities at all, he should not mention anything... One who mentions [the good qualities] of one who had none at all, or who overly exaggerates those that he had, causes harm to himself and to the deceased.

The eulogy is intended to elicit appropriate sadness and to highlight the qualities and traits of the deceased that others can study and emulate.

Eulogies, in their full-fledged sense, are not delivered on festivals (i.e., Ḥol HaMo'ed),[71] Rosh Ḥodesh,[72] Ḥanukka,[73] Purim (fourteenth and fifteenth of Adar),[74] or Purim Katan (fourteenth and fifteenth of I Adar).[75] Likewise, they are not delivered during the entire month of Nissan,[76] or on Tu BiShevat, Lag BaOmer, or other days on which *Taḥanun* is not recited.

---

69. *Shulḥan Arukh, Yoreh De'ah* 344:9–10.
70. Ibid., 1.
71. *Shulḥan Arukh, Oraḥ Ḥayim* 547:1 and *Yoreh De'ah* 401:5.
72. *Shulḥan Arukh, Oraḥ Ḥayim* 420:1.
73. Ibid., 670:3.
74. Ibid., 696:3.
75. Ibid., 697:1.
76. Ibid., 429:2.

There are many different customs regarding the funeral procession. For example, it is customary in some places to break an earthenware vessel as the procession begins, and recite the verse: "The snare is broken, and we have escaped" (Ps. 124:7).[77] At some funeral services, the *ḥazan* recites:

> Akavya b. Mahalalel says: Reflect on three matters, and you will not come to transgression: Know from where you came, and to where you are going, and before whom you are destined to give an account and a reckoning. From where you came, from a putrid drop; and to where are you going, to a place of dust, worms, and maggots; and before whom are you destined to give an account and a reckoning? Before the King of kings, the Holy One, Blessed be He. (Avot 3:1)

Some also recite another mishna (Avot 4:29), as well as the verses of *tziduk hadin.*[78] It is customary to say the psalm: *Yoshev beseter elyon* (Ps. 91), while escorting a man, and *Eshet ḥayil* (Prov. 31:10–31), while escorting a woman. The procession pauses a few times and the mourners recite the standard Mourner's Kaddish.

After the body is lowered into the grave, it is customary and appropriate for the mourner and the guests to participate in filling the open grave with dirt. The shovel is not handed directly from one person to another, to avoid the appearance of handing a symbol of tragedy to another.[79] The final *tziduk hadin* is recited, and the mourners recite the special burial Kaddish, known as *Kaddish HaGadol.*[80] This Kaddish is unique in that it expresses the hope for redemption and *teḥiyat hametim.* The *El Maleh Raḥamim* prayer is recited, and a representative of the *ḥevra kadisha* then asks forgiveness from the deceased, lest they treated the body with less than proper respect.

After interment, the seven-day period of mourning, the *shiva,* begins. The first act of mourning is usually performed at the cemetery, when those attending the funeral form two rows. The mourner walks between the rows, and those standing in the rows console him. This is known as the *shura.* In some communities, men form rows to console the male mourners and women form rows to console the female mourners.

---

77. *Gesher HaḤayim* 12:4:1.

78. Jer. 32:19; Ps. 92:16; Job 1:21; Ps. 78:78.

79. *Maavar Yabok, Maamar Sefat Emet* 27.

80. *Shulḥan Arukh,* ibid., 4.

After a funeral, it is customary to wash one's hands as one leaves the cemetery,[81] or at least before returning home.[82] Some write that one should wash each hand three times, alternating between right and left, as one washes his hands in the morning.[83] It is also customary not to dry one's hands after a funeral, and not to pass the cup directly to another person.[84]

It is important to keep in mind that while it is a great honor to accompany the deceased to his final resting place, the mishna[85] teaches us that there are more important escorts that accompany him.

> R. Yosei, son of Kisma, said: Once, I was walking along the way and a man met me and greeted me and I returned his greetings. He said to me: "Rabbi, from where do you come?" I said to him: "From a great city of sages and scholars." He said to me: "Rabbi, if you are willing to live with us in our place, I will give you a million gold dinars, precious stones, and pearls." I said to him: "If you give me all the silver, gold, precious stones, and pearls in the world, I would not dwell anywhere except in a place of Torah. Likewise, it is written in the Book of Psalms by David, king of Israel: 'I prefer the Torah of Your mouth over thousands of gold and silver pieces' (Ps. 119:72). Furthermore, when a person passes from this world neither silver, nor gold, nor precious stones, nor pearls accompany him; rather, only Torah and good deeds, as it is stated: 'When you walk it will guide you; when you lie it will guard you; and when you awaken it will be your conversation' (Prov. 6:22). 'When you walk it will guide you' – in this world; 'when you lie it will guard you' – in the grave; 'and when you awaken it will be your conversation' – in the World to Come. And it is stated (Hag. 2:8): 'Mine is the silver and Mine is the gold, the utterance of the Lord of hosts.'"

Ultimately, Torah and good deeds accompany a person when he leaves this world.

---

81. See, for example, Maharil 23.
82. See Rema, *Yoreh De'ah* 376:4.
83. *Peri Megadim* 2:20; see also *Mishna Berura* 4:39.
84. R. Akiva Eiger, *Yoreh De'ah* 376:4; see also *Kitzur Shulḥan Arukh* 199:10.
85. Avot 6:9.

## AFTER THE BURIAL

After the burial, the *shiva* begins, and the mourner is once again obligated to perform mitzvot. When starting the period of *shiva,* there are often certain rituals that he was unable to perform as an *onen* that it is now incumbent upon him to perform. We discussed above whether the mourner should don *tefillin* after the burial.

Regarding *birkot hashaḥar,* the morning blessings, the *Aḥaronim* discuss whether, and until when, one may recite them. R. Shneur Zalman of Liadi (1745–1813), in his *Shulḥan Arukh HaRav,*[86] rules that since the *onen* was not obligated to perform mitzvot when he awoke, which is when one becomes obligated to recite the morning blessings, he is exempt for that entire day. R. Yaakov Lorberbaum of Lissa (1760–1832), in his *Siddur Derekh Ḥayim,*[87] disagrees and maintains that the mourner is obligated to recite the morning blessings after the burial.

According to those who posit that the mourner should recite the morning blessings after the burial, until when may the blessings be recited? *Magen Avraham*[88] explains that the *onen* may no longer recite the *birkot hashaḥar* if the burial concludes after the fourth halakhic hour of the day. Since the *onen* was exempt during the morning, which was when the obligation takes effect, there is no point in reciting the *berakhot* later in the day. Others maintain that that one may recite the blessings until midday.[89] R. Yosef Chaim b. Eliyahu al-Chacham of Baghdad (1835–1909), in his Responsa *Rav Pe'alim,*[90] claims that fundamentally the obligation to recite the blessings is in effect throughout the day, and therefore the mourner may recite the blessings after the burial, when his obligation to perform positive commandments resumes, until dark. Gra rules that one may recite the morning blessings even until he goes to sleep.[91] Although many accept the view of *Magen Avraham,*[92] one who recites all of the morning blessings until midday, evening, or the time that he goes to sleep, has authorities upon whom he may rely. The mourner should recite the *birkot haTorah,* and the three "who did not make me" blessings. He should also recite the blessing over his *tzitzit* after the funeral.

---

86. *Oraḥ Ḥayim* 71:1.
87. *Siddur Derekh Ḥayim, Hilkhot Aninut* 4.
88. *Magen Avraham, Oraḥ Ḥayim* 71:1.
89. See *Mishna Berura* 52:10.
90. *Rav Pe'alim* 2:8.
91. *Maase Rav, Hilkhot Birkot HaShaḥar* 9.
92. See also *Gesher HaḤayim* 18:2:4; *Mishna Berura* 71:4.

The *Rishonim* discuss whether or not one who was an *onen* on Motza'ei Shabbat must recite Havdala after the burial. Maharam of Rothenburg[93] writes that after the funeral the mourner may not eat until he recites Havdala, in accordance with the talmudic ruling[94] that one who does not recite Havdala on Motza'ei Shabbat may recite Havdala up until and including Tuesday. Rosh[95] disagrees and rules like his son, R. Yehuda, who explains that the ruling in the Talmud concerns a case where one was obligated yet unable to recite Havdala. Since the *onen* was not obligated to recite Havdala on Motza'ei Shabbat, he is not obligated to recite it later.

*Shulḥan Arukh*[96] rules that the mourner must recite Havdala after the burial. On Motza'ei Shabbat, that would include the blessings over the *besamim* (spices) and the fire, but from Sunday to Tuesday it does not. If an *onen* inadvertently recited Havdala on Motza'ei Shabbat, he does not repeat Havdala after the burial.[97]

Furthermore, *Shulḥan Arukh* adds that one who was an *onen* on Motza'ei Shabbat recites Shaḥarit the next morning, after the burial (before midday); however, he does not recite a *tefillat tashlumin* (a second, compensatory *Shemoneh Esreh*) for the previous evening's Maariv prayer that he missed. R. Yechezkel Landau, in his comments on the *Shulḥan Arukh, Dagul Merevava,* rules that one is exempt only if he was an *onen* for the entire period of that prayer. However, if he became an *onen* at night, after the obligation to recite the evening prayer had already taken effect, he must recite a second prayer, a *tefillat tashlumin,* after Shaḥarit the next morning, after the burial.[98] *Arukh HaShulḥan*[99] cites this ruling and disagrees, exempting the *onen* from reciting compensatory prayers, arguing that if one is exempt from a prayer at the end of its time period (*sof zeman*), he need not recite a *tefillat tashlumin.*

As the burial approaches, the mourner begins the transition from the period of *aninut,* during which the *onen* often bears responsibility for the burial of his relative, to a period of profound sadness and emptiness, which

---

93. *Hilkhot Semaḥot* 145.
94. Pesaḥim 107a.
95. Berakhot 3:2. The *Beit Yosef* (341) notes that in his responsa, Rosh rules in accordance with Maharam of Rothenburg.
96. *Shulḥan Arukh, Yoreh De'ah* 341:2.
97. *Pitḥei Teshuva* 341:19.
98. See *Dagul Merevava* 341:2; see also *Pitḥei Teshuva* 341:18.
99. *Arukh HaShulḥan, Yoreh De'ah* 341:24.

come with the sense of loss. At the burial, the *onen* confronts death in the most stark and intense manner, at which point it is customary to fulfill the obligation of *keria* (rending one's clothing), and he then begins the gradual, multistage process of mourning. The laws and customs of these stages, like those of *aninut,* reflect the mourner's experience and help him to muster the strength to be comforted and look toward the future.

### *SEUDAT HAVRAA*

The Talmud[100] teaches that the mourner should not eat his own food after the burial.

> R. Yehuda said in the name of Rav: A mourner on the first day of his mourning is prohibited from eating of his own bread. From where is this derived? From what the Merciful One says to Ezekiel when the latter is in mourning: "And do not eat the bread of people" (Ezek. 24:17) [from which it is inferred that other mourners must eat the bread of others]. It was related that when Rabba and R. Yosef were in mourning they would exchange meals with each other.

This meal is known as the *seudat havraa,* based on the verse that describes the meal King David ate after the death of Abner: "All the people came to feed David food [*lehavrot*] while it was still day" (II Sam. 3:35).

The commentaries suggest numerous reasons for this custom. Some *Rishonim* imply that the neighbors are obligated to provide the *seudat havraa* out of concern for the mourner. For example, Rabbeinu Yeruḥam[101] explains:

> The verse states: "Nor eat the bread of men" (Ezek. 24:22), from which it is inferred that other [mourners] are obligated to eat the bread of other people. The reason is that the mourner is worried and moaning over the death [of his relative]. He does not want to eat, because he desires death as well. Therefore, he was commanded to eat the food of others.

---

100. Mo'ed Katan 27b.

101. Rabbeinu Yeruḥam (*Toldot Adam VeḤava* 28:2:233) attributes this reason to Rosh.

This idea that eating the food of others is intended to ease one's suffering appears in other *Rishonim* as well.[102] Indeed, some[103] cite the Yerushalmi,[104] which states: "A curse should come upon his neighbors" who do not provide him with food, as it is their responsibility to tend to the mourner.

R. Yehuda Ayash (1700–1760), in his *Shevet Yehuda,*[105] expresses concern that if the mourner is left alone on the difficult first day of mourning, he may eat and drink and become intoxicated to ease his pain, and he will forget about the deceased. In other words, the *seudat havraa* facilitates preservation of the honor of the deceased [*kevod hamet*].

Other sources indicate that the *seudat havraa* may be an expression of *niḥum avelim* [comforting the mourners]. For example, Ramban[106] cites R. Yitzchak ibn Ghiyyat, who cites a *baraita*: "In a place where it is customary to comfort the mourner with eggs and lentils we feed them [eggs and lentils]; in a place where it is customary [to comfort mourners] with meat and wine we feed them [meat and wine]; we act in accordance with the custom." Similarly, R. Mordekhai Yoffe (1530–1612), in his commentary on the *Shulḥan Arukh*, the *Levush,*[107] explains that "all of this is included in the comforting [of the mourner], as they demonstrate to the mourner that they are concerned about him and that they will not cast him off."

Some suggest a practical difference between these reasons. In a case where the burial is during a festival (on Ḥol HaMo'ed), and the period of mourning begins after the festival, is there a mitzva to provide the mourner with a *seudat havraa* after the burial? Some *Rishonim* assume that one's friends and neighbors provide him with a *seudat havraa* on Ḥol HaMo'ed, although in a somewhat different manner. Other *Rishonim*[108] insist that they do not provide a *seudat havraa* on Ḥol HaMo'ed. Tosafot[109] cite two opinions: The first is that there is a *seudat havraa* on Ḥol HaMo'ed. The second is that since there is no mourning on the festival, and the period of

---

102. See *She'iltot, Parashat Ḥayei Sara* 15; *Or Zarua* 2:430.
103. See Rosh, Mo'ed Katan 3:89.
104. Y. Mo'ed Katan 3:5.
105. *Shevet Yehuda* 378.
106. *Torat HaAdam, Inyan HaAvelut.*
107. *Levush, Yoreh De'ah* 378:1.
108. Rambam, *Hilkhot Avel* 11:1; Ramban, *Torat HaAdam, Inyan HaKeria,* p. 66; Rosh, Mo'ed Katan 3:59.
109. Mo'ed Katan 20a, s.v. *shekevar.*

mourning begins days after the burial, there is no *seudat havraa*. If the *seudat havraa* eases the suffering of the mourner or even comforts him, then it should certainly be provided during Ḥol HaMo'ed. If the meal is considered the first meal of the mourning period, intended for the preservation of the honor of the deceased, it may not be relevant on the festival.

In practice, *Shulḥan Arukh*[110] rules that a *seudat havraa* is provided for the mourners on Ḥol HaMo'ed, with the mourners sitting on regular chairs. Some *Aḥaronim* note that the meal should not consist of food typically associated with mourning, such as eggs and lentils.[111]

As mentioned above, the Talmud teaches: "A mourner on the first day of his mourning is prohibited from eating of his own bread." The mourner's friends and neighbors send him food for the meal. If the mourner is alone, or if no one sends him food, he is not required to fast and he may eat his own food.[112] In many communities, it is customary to send the mourner food throughout the *shiva* period.[113] The *Aḥaronim* discuss whether the mourner should refrain from eating bread and even from drinking before the *seudat havraa*.[114] *Gesher HaḤayim* writes that since the *seudat havraa* is supposed to be a meal, consisting of bread or cake, it is permitted to drink coffee or tea before the *seudat havraa*.[115]

Rema[116] rules that if the burial took place late in the day, and the mourner did not eat a *seudat havraa*, he may eat from his own food, as there is no *seudat havraa* at night.

What food should be eaten at the *seudat havraa*? The Talmud[117] teaches:

---

110. *Shulḥan Arukh, Yoreh De'ah* 401:4. Some *Aḥaronim* relate that in Jerusalem it is customary to provide a *seudat havraa* only for one mourning a parent (*Penei Barukh* 28:11; *Ḥazon Ovadia, Avelut*, vol. 3, p. 134).
111. *Ḥokhmat Adam, Kuntres Matzevet Moshe* 2.
112. *Taz, Yoreh De'ah* 378:1. Some rule that in this case the mourner should refrain from eating until nightfall (*Kitzur Shulḥan Arukh* 205:2).
113. *Ḥokhmat Adam* 163:5.
114. See *Arukh HaShulḥan, Yoreh De'ah* 278:2; *Divrei Shalom, Yoreh De'ah* 152; *Kitzur Shulḥan Arukh* 196:10.
115. *Gesher HaḤayim* 20:2:4; see also *Yabia Omer* (*Yoreh De'ah* 2:25), who rules that one should also refrain from eating fruits and cooked dishes before the meal.
116. Ibid., 3.
117. Bava Batra 16b.

> A *baraita* taught: On that day, Abraham our forefather passed away, and Jacob our forefather prepared a lentil stew to comfort Isaac, his father. What is different about lentils that it is fed to mourners? They say in the West in the name of Rabba b. Mari: Just as this lentil has no mouth, so too, a mourner has no mouth [to speak]. Alternatively, just as the lentil is round, so too, mourning comes around to all the inhabitants of this world. What is the practical difference between the two explanations we adopt? There is a practical difference between them with regard to whether it is appropriate to comfort the mourner with eggs (which have no mouth but are not completely round).

*Shulḥan Arukh*[118] writes that one begins the meal with these foods, which symbolize mourning, and follows them with a regular meal. Before partaking of the *seudat havraa,* it is appropriate for the mourner to recite the prayers and blessings that he failed to recite in the morning.

118. Ibid., 9.

*Chapter 4*

# The Obligation of *Avelut*: Source, Nature, and Reasons

The ancient Jewish practice of mourning the death of a close relative appears numerous times in the Bible. Jacob "rent his garments, and placed sackcloth on his loins, and mourned his son many days" (Gen. 37:34), Joseph "observed mourning for his father seven days" (Gen. 50:10), and the Jewish people observed days of "weeping of the mourning" (Deut. 34:8), after the death of Moses. Similarly, David was "weeping and mourning over Absalom" (II Sam. 19:2), and the prophet Jeremiah describes some of the mourning practices of his time (Jer. 16:1–8).

The Talmud teaches that after burial, the mourner is obligated to observe a seven-day period of mourning, known as *shiva*, which includes mourning practices and prohibitions. This chapter will explore the source, nature, and reasons for this obligatory seven-day mourning period.

## THE SOURCE AND ORIGINS OF *AVELUT*

The commentaries discuss whether the obligation to mourn is of biblical or rabbinic origin. On the one hand, the Talmud, in several places, indicates that there is a Torah obligation to mourn. For example, the Gemara[1] derives the obligation to mourn for seven days from a verse in the Bible:

> From where is it derived that the rites of mourning are observed for seven days? As it is written: "And I will turn your festivals into mourning" (Amos 8:10). Just as a festival lasts seven days, so too, mourning lasts for seven days.

The Yerushalmi[2] also seeks a Torah source for the seven days of mourning:

> From where is it derived that mourning from the Torah is seven days? The verse states: "And he observed mourning for his father seven days" (Gen. 50:10).

The Yerushalmi rejects this suggestion: "Do we derive matters from before the giving of the Torah?" Nevertheless, some *Geonim* derive from this passage the notion that the entire seven-day mourning period is of Torah origin.[3]

Although the *Rishonim* reject this possibility, some maintain that mourning on the day of the death and burial is of biblical origin. Rambam,[4] for example, in the wake of Rif,[5] writes:

> There is a positive commandment to mourn one's relatives, as it is stated: "Had I eaten the sin offering today, would it have been satisfactory in the eyes of the Lord?" (Lev. 10:19). There is mourning by Torah law only on the first day, which is the day of death and the day of burial. The rest of the seven days of mourning are not by Torah law. Although it is stated in the Torah: "And he observed mourning for his father seven days" (Gen. 50:10), the Torah was given and the halakha was renewed. Moses our teacher instituted for the Jewish people seven days of mourning and seven days of wedding celebrations.

1. Mo'ed Katan 20a.
2. Y. Mo'ed Katan 3:5.
3. Rif, Berakhot 9b–10a; see also *Behag* 21.
4. Rambam, *Hilkhot Avel* 1:1; see also *Sefer HaMitzvot*, Positive Commandment 37.
5. Ibid.

Rambam rules that there is a Torah obligation to mourn only on the first day, the day of the death and burial. The obligation to mourn for an entire week was instituted by Moses.

*Rishonim* cite many sources from which it is derived that mourning is a mitzva by Torah law. Ramban,[6] for example, cites a passage that states that the communal mitzva to rejoice on festivals overrides the individual mitzva of mourning:

> A mourner does not practice his mourning on a festival, as it is stated: "And you shall rejoice in your festival" (Deut. 16:14). The Gemara explains: If it is a mourning period that had already begun at the outset of the festival, the positive communal mitzva of rejoicing on the festival comes and overrides the positive individual mitzva, i.e., the mourning.

In addition, *Rishonim* cite the opinion of R. Yehoshua, who prohibits donning *tefillin* on the first day of mourning: "What is the reason of R. Yehoshua? As it is written, 'And I will make it as the mourning for an only son, and its end as a bitter day' (Amos 8:10)," i.e., a single day.[7] These *Rishonim* agree that despite the Torah obligation to mourn on the day of the burial and funeral, observance of the seven-day period and of its mourning practices is a rabbinic obligation.

It appears that although Rambam and Ramban agree that the obligation to mourn on the day of death and burial is by Torah law, they disagree regarding the content and character of this obligation.

Rambam explains that the essence of *avelut*, or as R. Soloveitchik explains, the "fulfillment [*kiyum*] of *avelut*," is in the heart. Indeed, regarding those executed by the Jewish courts, for whom one is not permitted to mourn, Rambam[8] writes: "One does not mourn those executed by the court... Although they do not observe mourning rites, they mourn [*onenin*], as acute mourning [*aninut*] is only in the heart." Interestingly, Rambam[9]

---

6. Ramban, *Torat HaAdam, Inyan HaAvelut*, p. 207. Alternatively, Tosafot (Mo'ed Katan 14b, s.v. *aseh*) explain that this source may imply that nowadays the obligation to rejoice on the festival, *simḥat Yom Tov*, may also be a rabbinic obligation.
7. Mo'ed Katan 21a.
8. Rambam, *Hilkhot Sanhedrin* 13:6.
9. Rambam, *Hilkhot Avel* 5:1. He writes, "These are the matters that are prohibited for a mourner on the first day by Torah law and on the remaining days by rabbinic law. It is prohibited for him to cut his hair, launder his clothes, wash, anoint himself, engage

enumerates eleven activities prohibited for a mourner. Although he considers all eleven prohibitions as expressions of the mourner's inner sadness, they are not inherent to the mourning process, and even one who does not observe these eleven prohibitions is still considered to be a mourner.

Conversely, Ramban[10] writes: "Mourning by Torah law is primarily [refraining from] indulgences, among them washing, smearing oil, and sexual relations, and *tefillin*, which are characterized as *pe'er*, and laundering, and cutting one's hair, as these are joyful [*simḥa*] activities." He continues: "Mourning, by definition, means that one should not involve himself in matters of happiness, rather in matters of mourning. And this is the mourning of the heart, from which they derived that one may not engage in matters of happiness." Ramban appears to equate mourning of the heart with refraining from joyful activities. Therefore, it is not surprising that Ramban insists that these activities are prohibited even before the burial. These prohibitions are inherent to the fulfillment of the mitzva of mourning, which takes effect immediately after the death.

Other *Rishonim*, including Tosafot,[11] maintain that all mourning practices are of rabbinic origin. They rely on several talmudic passages, including one where the laws of mourning are explicitly described as rabbinic (*miderabbanan*),[12] and the halakhic principle *halakha kedivrei hamekil be'avel*, i.e., the ruling is in accordance with the lenient opinion with regard to mourning,[13] which appears to be a variation of the halakhic principle

---

in sexual relations, wear shoes, work, study Torah, stand his bed upright, uncover his head, and greet others – eleven matters in total." The *Aḥaronim* question how Rambam can describe these eleven prohibitions as being by Torah law when all but one (cutting one's hair) are derived from verses in Nevi'im. *Kiryat Sefer* (*Hilkhot Avel* 5:1) explains that the verses in Nevi'im reveal matters [*gilui milta*] of Torah origin. *Leḥem Yehuda* (ibid.) invokes the principle: "*mesaran hakatuv leḥakhamim*" (Ḥagiga 18a), i.e., at times the Torah teaches a general principle and the sages determine the specific details and applications, e.g., the prohibited labors on Ḥol HaMo'ed, and the afflictions of Yom Kippur (see Ran on Rif, Yoma 1a).

10. *Torat HaAdam, Inyan HaAvelut.*
11. See Ramban, ibid.; Rosh, Mo'ed Katan 3:3; *Mordekhai* 862. Rosh relates that Rabbeinu Tam maintained that the *Behag* was blind, and at times his students recorded opinions with which he himself did not agree.
12. Mo'ed Katan 11b; see also Nazir 15b.
13. Mo'ed Katan 17b; Eiruvin 46a.

*safek derabbanan lekula,* that the ruling is lenient in cases of uncertainty involving a rabbinic prohibition.

The *Rishonim*[14] suggest a practical difference between these two opinions. Once, the practice was to bury the deceased on the second day of the festival (Yom Tov Sheni), which is observed outside of Israel.[15] According to those who maintain that *avelut* is of biblical origin, the biblical obligation of mourning overrides the rabbinic obligation to observe Yom Tov Sheni, and one would begin observing mourning rituals on the final day of Yom Tov. Although this appears to be the subject of a dispute in the *Shulḥan Arukh,* in practice everyone agrees that no mourning rituals are observed on the last day of the festival.[16]

Although there may be no practical difference between these opinions, this dispute underscores different understandings of the relationship and transition between *aninut* and *avelut,* and the overall obligation of mourning.

It appears that Rambam, Rif, and Ramban hold that *avelut* is an extension or continuation of *aninut.* In other words, the death of a close relative commences the mourning process, which begins with *aninut* and transitions into *avelut.* Indeed, as we already learned, Ramban believes that during the period of *aninut,* one should observe mourning practices that do not interfere with the preparations for burial. Although in practice Rambam disagrees, he holds that fundamentally *avelut* derives from *aninut.*[17] In contrast, Tosafot do not see any direct conceptual relationship between *aninut* and *avelut.* The period of mourning begins at the time of the burial.[18]

14. Behag, *Hilkhot Avel,* p. 245.
15. Beitza 6a; See Tosafot, s.v. *veha'idana.*
16. *Shulḥan Arukh, Yoreh De'ah* 399:13.
17. *Rambam, Hilkhot Avel* 1:1.
18. This dispute may impact the understanding of a very halakhically relevant statement of Rava to the people of Mehoza: "Those of you who do not follow the coffin all the way to the place of interment should begin counting your days of mourning from when you turn your faces from the city gates to return home" (Mo'ed Katan 22a). While Rif and others would explain that the obligation to mourn begins at the moment of death, and therefore, when the mourner turns away from the coffin, there is no longer any reason to delay the full onset of the laws of *avelut,* Tosafot would understand that although generally the period of mourning begins with the burial, when the mourner does not participate in the burial, his separation and withdrawal from the burial process may also begin the period of mourning. We will discuss this topic in greater detail in chapter 5.

**THE NATURE OF *AVELUT***

Whether or not one views *avelut* as an extension of *aninut* may also shed light on the nature of the obligation to mourn.

On the one hand, those *Rishonim* who derive the biblical obligation to mourn from *aninut* (Rif, Rambam, and Ramban) understand that *aninut* and *avelut* share the same foundation: An inner experience of dejection and sadness.[19] The Torah relates to the ramifications of this intense grief and prohibits the *onen* from participating in the offering of sacrifices or partaking of *maaser sheni* (as we discussed in chapter 1). It is this psychological state, this grief and sadness, R. Soloveitchik explains, which cannot coexist with the obligation to rejoice on the festivals, and therefore the laws of mourning are negated by the festival.[20]

On the other hand, those who view *avelut* as completely separate from *aninut* maintain that while *aninut* connotes inner sorrow, mourning is an expression of one's respect for the deceased. Rashi,[21] for example, explains: "Although a mourner is obligated to observe mourning with regard to wearing shoes, washing, and anointing to demonstrate his respect for the deceased, he is not obligated to be sad [*lehitzta'er*]." Apparently, even the *Geonim*, who hold that the entire seven-day mourning period is of biblical origin, agree that mourning is an expression of respect for the deceased, and therefore, under extenuating circumstances, the seven-day mourning period may even be delayed.[22]

Interestingly, one may even trace these two understandings of the mourning period to the sources cited by the Talmud. The first source cited above, which draws a parallel between the seven-day festival and the seven-day obligation to mourn, based on the verse: "And I will turn your festivals into mourning" (Amos 8:10), from which it is derived: Just as a festival lasts for seven days, so too, mourning lasts for seven days, might view the mourning period

19. R. Soloveitchik, *Out of the Whirlwind*, p. 70. Similarly, Netziv (*Haamek She'ala* 15) explains that "the essence of the mourning on the first day… relates to private matters, in other words, to mourn in one's heart, and that which the mishna teaches, 'for grief is borne in the heart alone,' is known, and that includes partaking of sacrifices, which gladdens the soul, rejoicing, and studying Torah; but everyone agrees that public displays are prohibited by rabbinic law."

20. *Shiurim LeZekher Abba Mari*, vol. 2.

21. Rashi, Sukka 25a, s.v. *tirda dereshut*.

22. Ketubot 3b.

as a time of intense inner sorrow, in contrast to the festival, which is a time of inner rejoicing. According to the second source, which derives the period of mourning from the seven-day mourning period for Jacob (Gen. 50:10), which took place sometime after the conclusion of the "days of weeping" (Gen. 50:4), the mourning period is an expression of respect for the deceased.[23]

## REASONS FOR THE OBLIGATION OF *AVELUT*

Why does the halakha require a mourner to observe the laws and customs of *avelut*? What is the reason behind the obligation, whether biblical or rabbinic, to mourn?

As mentioned above, some sources indicate that mourning practices demonstrate respect and honor for the deceased, and provide others with an opportunity to learn from the person's actions and to engage in introspection. Other sources focus on the inner experience of the mourner, *avelut shebalev*. Apparently, the Torah not only acknowledges and accommodates this basic emotional response, but expects and obligates the mourner to engage in a staged process of *avelut shebalev*, regardless of whether or not the person feels this grief. Taken a step further, perhaps the halakha wants the mourner to grieve, to experience the tragedy of death, and to feel the loss of his close relative. The implications of this fascinating point are far beyond the purview of this book, but are nonetheless worth noting.

There are two more aspects, or reasons for *avelut*, that are worth mentioning.

*Avelut* instills an appreciation for human life, which is imbued with the image of God.[24] The Talmud,[25] in discussing the obligation of overturning the bed [*kefiyat hamita*], which is no longer practiced, explains:

> A mourner is obligated to overturn his bed, as bar Kappara taught [that God stated]: I have placed the likeness of My image [*deyokan*] within humans, and owing to their sins I have overturned it (as when

23. R. Akiva Eiger (*Yoreh De'ah* 344:1) questions whether the obligation to mourn should be understood as a form of "respect for the deceased" or "respect for the living." He cites several practical differences, including whether one may instruct his children not to mourn him after his death.
24. See also *Gesher HaḤayim* 19:2.
25. Mo'ed Katan 15a–b

> this person died the divine image in him was removed). Therefore, you too must overturn your beds on account of this.

The Gemara indicates that *kefiyat hamita* is an expression of our shock caused by the loss of the divine image [*tzelem Elokim*]. R. Soloveitchik explains that for this reason, it is customary to cover the mirrors, and the pictures of the deceased, in the house of the mourner.

Finally, some suggest that observing mourning practices leads a person to introspection and ultimately to repentance.[26] On the one hand, the encounter with death moves the mourner to reassess his or her own life trajectory and conduct. On the other hand, remembering one's relationship with the deceased may give rise to feelings of guilt and regret, and remind the mourner of human imperfection.[27]

These themes, respect and honor for the deceased [*kevod hamet*], sorrow and grief [*avelut shebalev*], appreciating human life, and repentance [*teshuva*], appear throughout the various laws and customs of *avelut*. Of course, each mourner experiences *avelut* in a different way, based upon the individual, the circumstances, and the relationship to the deceased.

---

26. See *Sefer HaḤinukh* 264.
27. See R. Soloveitchik, *Out of the Whirlwind*, pp. 5–8: "The aching heart is a contrite heart, and a contrite heart is, of course, an atoning heart. Enlightened *avelut* contains a feeling of guilt... First, death per se is a consequence of sin or human imperfection... Second, the aspect of guilt is interwoven into the human time-consciousness... Man is always a latecomer as far as the formulation of value judgments is concerned... During the mourning stage we ask the questions we should have asked before: Who was he? Whom did we lose? His image fascinates us from afar, and we ask with guilt and regret the questions that are now overdue, the questions to which only our lives can provide the answers."

*Chapter 5*

# For Whom Is One Obligated to Mourn

The Torah teaches that a Kohen, for whom it is prohibited to come in contact with a corpse, is required to become impure [*tamei*] in order to bury his close relative.

> The Lord said to Moses: Speak to the Priests, sons of Aaron, and say to them: He shall not become impure from a dead person among his people. Only for his kin, who is close to him: for his mother; and for his father; and for his son; and for his daughter; and for his brother; and for his virgin sister, who is close to him, who has not been with a man; for her, he may become impure. (Lev. 21:1–3)

Some explain that this passage is the Torah source for the laws of mourning.[1]

1. Sifra, Lev. 21:3. See also Rambam (*Sefer HaMitzvot*, Positive Commandment 37), who writes, "The thirty-seventh mitzva is that we are commanded that Kohanim will impurify themselves for those relatives mentioned in the Torah … This mitzva is actually the commandment to mourn, i.e., that every Jew is required to mourn his relatives, i.e., the five deceased for whom there is a mitzva to mourn. The commandment is stated with regard to a Kohen to underscore its gravity: Even a Kohen, for whom it

In addition, the Talmud[2] derives the list of relatives for whom one is obligated to mourn from the obligation of the Kohen to become impure.

> The sages taught: With regard to all of the relatives mentioned in the Torah in the passage referring to Kohanim, for whom a Kohen becomes impure, a mourner must mourn for them. And they are: His wife, his father, and his mother, his brother and his unmarried sister from the same father, his son, and his daughter.
>
> The sages added other relatives to this list: His maternal brother and his unmarried sister from the same mother, and his married sister,[3] whether from the same father or from the same mother. One mourns for these relatives, although a Kohen would not become impure for them.

This passage teaches that one must observe the laws of mourning for seven relatives: One's spouse,[4] son, daughter, father, mother, brother, and sister.

In this chapter, we will discuss cases where there is uncertainty whether or not one is required to observe the laws of mourning, due to the nature of the relationship with the deceased, his conduct, or his age. We will conclude with unique cases of mourning, e.g., *avelut* for one's teacher.

## RELATIONSHIP BETWEEN THE MOURNER AND THE DECEASED

In this section, we will address several cases where one may be exempt from the obligation to mourn due to the nature of his relationship to the deceased.

---

is typically forbidden to become impure, is commanded in this case to act like any other Jew and become impure. [It is stressed in this way] in order to prevent the laws of mourning from being compromised." See also Rambam, *Hilkhot Avel* 2:6.

2. Mo'ed Katan 20b.
3. The *Mordekhai* (Mo'ed Katan 887) records that when Rabbeinu Yoel's married paternal half-sister died, he deliberately bathed, as he understood that the sages added only a married sister with whom one shares both a mother and father. Most *Rishonim* disagree (see *Mordekhai*; *Hagahot Maimoniyot, Hilkhot Avel* 2:2; see also Y. Mo'ed Katan 3:5) and understand that the sages obligated mourning one's sister, paternal or maternal, whether or not she is married.
4. While everyone agrees that one is obligated to mourn a spouse, the *Rishonim* disagree as to whether there is a Torah obligation for a Kohen to become impure for his wife, and consequently whether there is a Torah obligation to mourn a spouse; see Rambam, *Hilkhot Avel* 2:1, 7; *Kesef Mishneh*, ibid., 2:1.

In these cases, as we shall see, one may choose to adopt and observe certain mourning practices. At times, these decisions may be challenging and complicated, as the decision to mourn may depend not only upon the nature of one's relationship to the deceased, but on the mourner's community as well.

## Adopted Children

As mentioned above, one is obligated to mourn only for a close biological relative, i.e., a parent, sibling, child, or spouse. However, the Talmud teaches: "Anyone who raises an orphan in his house, the verse ascribes him credit as if he fathered the child."[5] Is it permitted for an adopted child to observe the laws of mourning for an adoptive parent? Should he mourn his adoptive parents?

Jewish law distinguishes between biological parents and adoptive parents regarding many laws, including those of personal status, prohibited relationships [*yuḥasin*], inheritance, and even honoring one's parents [*kibbud av va'em*]. On the one hand, one's basic obligation to honor his parents[6] is an expression of gratitude for their having brought him into this world.[7] There may be an obligation to honor the spouse of one's parent, but that appears to be an extension of the obligation to honor his parent.[8] On the other hand, the obligation to honor one's parent may also be an expression of gratitude for the effort the parent invested in raising the child. *Sefer HaḤinukh*,[9] for example, writes:

> Among the roots of the mitzva is that it is appropriate for a person to acknowledge and return kindness to people who were good to him, and not to be an ungrateful, alienated scoundrel, as that is a bad and objectionable attribute before God and people. And internalize that one's father and mother are the reason for his existence in the world, and therefore, it is truly appropriate to give them honor and any benefit that he can because they brought him into the world, *and worked hard for him when he was little.*

5. Sanhedrin 19b.
6. Ex. 20:12; Deut. 5:16; see also Lev. 19:3.
7. See Kiddushin 30b.
8. See Rambam, *Hilkhot Mamrim* 6:15; *Shulḥan Arukh, Yoreh De'ah* 240:20.
9. *Sefer HaḤinukh* 33.

*Sefer HaḤinukh* adds that the obligation to honor a parent is rooted not only in the fact that they gave him life, but also in the fact that they raised and cared for him in his childhood.

Furthermore, the adoptive parent teaches the child Torah or at least facilitates his Torah study. The Talmud teaches that the honor due a teacher is greater than the honor due a parent, "as his father brought him into this world, and his teacher, who taught him the wisdom of Torah, brings him to the World to Come."[10] Therefore, halakha recognizes the parental relationship between a child and an adoptive parent, and this is manifest in several areas of halakha.[11]

Should a child observe the laws of mourning for an adoptive parent?[12] Several recent authorities,[13] including R. Yosef Dov Soloveitchik[14] and R. Ovadia Yosef,[15] rule that a child may, and indeed should, observe the laws of mourning in this case. R. Soloveitchik even insists that although there may be no halakhic obligation to mourn, there is certainly a fulfillment [*kiyum*] of the mitzva of *avelut*.[16] R. Moshe Sternbach[17] concurs that it is appropriate to mourn for an adoptive parent, and cites a passage from the Talmud that relates that Rabban Gamliel accepted condolences after the death of his slave, Tavi.[18] Indeed, Rema permits observance of the laws of mourning even when there is no obligation.[19]

In addition to observing the laws of mourning, one may also recite Kaddish for an adoptive parent.[20] Some suggest that in this case, the adopted

10. Bava Metzia 33a.
11. For a more extensive treatment of this topic, see R. Melech Schachter, "Various Aspects of Adoption," *Journal of Halacha and Contemporary Society* 4 (Fall, 1982).
12. See R. Dr. Joel B. Wolowelsky, "Honoring and Mourning Adoptive and Step Parents," *Le'ela* 51 (June, 2001).
13. See also *Nishmat Avraham*, vol. 5, p. 141.
14. See *Shiurei HaRav*, p. 38; see also *Mesorah* 5 (Adar, 5751/1991), p. 47.
15. *Ḥazon Ovadia, Avelut*, vol. 1, p. 551.
16. He derives this from Rambam (*Hilkhot Avel* 13:4), who writes, "A deceased person who has no mourners to be comforted, ten upright men from the community at large come and sit in his place throughout the seven days of mourning. Others gather around them. If there are not ten fixed men, each day, ten are selected from among the rest of the people and they sit in his place."
17. *Teshuvot VeHanhagot* 3:374.
18. Berakhot 16b.
19. Rema, *Yoreh De'ah* 374:6.
20. Rema, Responsa 118; see also *Biur Halakha* 132; *Sedei Ḥemed*, vol. 4, *Maarekhet Avelut* 156; *Ḥazon Ovadia*, ibid.; *Halikhot Shlomo, Tefilla*, p. 226.

child does not take precedence in reciting Kaddish over those obligated to recite Kaddish. This is not relevant today, as in most places, all mourners recite Kaddish in unison, although he does not serve as the *sheliaḥ tzibbur* in place of other mourners.[21]

Although an adopted child is encouraged to observe the mourning practices, the laws of *aninut* are not completely in effect. Therefore, unless the mourner is actively engaged in burial preparations, he is not exempt from performing mitzvot,[22] and he should don *tefillin* privately.[23] Furthermore, he should not refrain from Torah study due to the mourning.

An adopted child may perform *keria*[24] and recite the blessing *Dayan HaEmet.*[25]

Ostensibly, this applies to mourning the passing of adopted children, adoptive siblings, stepparents, and stepsiblings as well. Of course, the decision to accept upon oneself some or all of the laws of mourning may be a function of the nature, extent, and depth of the relationship between the mourner and the deceased.

Finally, adopted children remain obligated to mourn their biological parents, if their identities are known.

### The Convert and Mourning a Non-Jewish Parent

The Talmud teaches that one who converts to Judaism is "like a newborn child."[26] From a purely legal perspective, despite the biological relationship, the halakha does not recognize pre-conversion familial relationships. Likewise, the Torah does not recognize the relationship between a person born of a Jewish mother, and his non-Jewish father. Of course, a convert should treat his or her non-Jewish parents with appropriate respect,[27] to avoid creating the impression that the convert left a culture of greater sanctity for one of lesser sanctity, and as an expression of gratitude for their having brought him into this world.[28]

21. *Nishmat Adam,* ibid.; see Ḥatam Sofer, *Oraḥ Ḥayim* 164.
22. See R. Akiva Eiger, *Yoreh De'ah* 374.
23. R. Shlomo Zalman Auerbach, cited by *Nishmat Avraham,* ibid.
24. See *Shulḥan Arukh, Yoreh De'ah* 340:8, 37.
25. See *Shulḥan Arukh, Oraḥ Ḥayim* 222:2.
26. Yevamot 22a.
27. *Shulḥan Arukh, Yoreh De'ah* 241:9.
28. See *Iggerot Moshe, Yoreh De'ah* 2:130.

Rambam[29] rules that a convert is not obligated to mourn even for a relative who converted with him. Although the *Mordekhai* (1250–1298) writes that one who converts with his mother must observe the laws of mourning after his mother dies,[30] even in that case *Shulḥan Arukh*[31] rules that a convert is not obligated to mourn for a relative. Of course, just as an adopted child is encouraged to mourn, so too in this case, it would be proper for the child to observe the laws of mourning.

The *Aḥaronim* discuss whether a convert may voluntarily observe some of the mourning practices for his gentile parents, including the recitation of Kaddish.

R. Aharon Walkin (1864–1942), in his *Zekan Aharon,*[32] suggests that just as a convert should show respect for his non-Jewish parent, so too, he should recite Kaddish after his parent's death, as failure to do so could be perceived as slighting his parent. R. Ovadia Yosef[33] concurs, and concludes that "a righteous convert may pray for the recovery of his non-Jewish father from illness, and is also permitted to recite Kaddish for him, for the elevation of his soul, after he passes away." R. Yaakov Ariel[34] also notes that the biblical model for Kaddish: "I will be glorified and I will be sanctified and I will become known before the eyes of many nations, and they will know that I am the Lord" (Ezek. 38:29), is stated in the context of gentiles. He suggests, however, that one should recite only the Kaddish after *Aleinu,* to distinguish between him and other orphans, and because it corresponds with the universal themes expressed in the *Aleinu* prayer.

As for the laws of mourning, some *Aḥaronim* suggest that while the convert should certainly not observe those laws that compromise his religious observance, e.g., refraining from Torah study, he may choose to observe some mourning practices, e.g., he may rend his garments.[35] In some cases, it may be appropriate to even observe *shiva* for a non-Jewish parent. Of course, the convert must take care to avoid participating in halakhically problematic burial or memorial services performed for the deceased.

29. Rambam, *Hilkhot Avel* 2:3; see also Yevamot 97b.
30. *Mordekhai,* Mo'ed Katan 904.
31. *Shulḥan Arukh, Yoreh De'ah* 374:5; see also Rema.
32. *Zekan Aharon, Mahadura Tinyana, Yoreh De'ah* 87.
33. *Yeḥave Daat* 6:60.
34. *BeOhalah Shel Torah* 1:60.
35. Ibid.

## THE ACTIONS OF THE DECEASED

### "Sinners"

The *Rishonim* grapple with a fascinating question: Are some people, due to their conduct, unworthy of being mourned? In this section we will discuss whether one mourns sinners, among them those who leave the Jewish faith or engage in prohibited or immoral behavior.

As we learned previously, a Kohen is commanded to become ritually impure [*tamei*] for the burial of his close relatives. The Talmud[36] teaches that a Kohen should become impure for the burial of his parent only if he "performs the actions of his people."

> One might have thought that even if his [the Kohen's] parents had dissociated themselves from the practices of the congregation, he may become ritually impure; therefore, the verse states: "Speak to the Priests, sons of Aaron, and say to them: He shall not become impure from a dead person *among his people*. Only for his kin, who is close to him: for his mother, and for his father, etc." (Lev. 21:1–2). "*Among his people*" teaches: Only if [the parent] performs the actions of his people.

A Kohen does not become impure for parents who have "dissociated themselves from the practices of the congregation," and have not followed the practices of his people. Elsewhere, we are taught that the laws of mourning are not in effect for those who deviate from the practices of the community [*poresh midarkhei tzibbur*].[37]

The *Rishonim* seek to define who, aside from heretics, apostates, and informants,[38] are considered to be those dissociated from the practices of the congregation. Rambam,[39] based upon a *baraita*,[40] writes:

> One does not mourn all those who deviate from the path of the community, i.e., people who cast off the yoke of the mitzvot from their necks and are not included within the Jewish people in terms

36. Sanhedrin 47a; italics added.
37. Semaḥot 2:8.
38. See Evel Rabbati 3:5.
39. Rambam, *Hilkhot Avel* 1:10.
40. Evel Rabbati, ibid.

> of observance of the mitzvot, honoring the festivals, and attendance at synagogues and study halls. Rather, they are free and independent like the other nations.
>
> Likewise, one does not mourn heretics, apostates, and informers on Jews to gentiles. Instead, their brothers and their other relatives wear white clothes, enrobe themselves in white, eat, drink, and celebrate, as the enemies of the Holy One, Blessed be He, have perished. In their regard, it is stated: "Those who hate You, God, I will hate" (Ps. 139:21).

This source, which describes one who has cast off the yoke of mitzvot, sharpens the question: What type of behavior renders one unworthy of being mourned?

Some *Rishonim*[41] cite Maharam of Rothenburg, who distinguishes between one who sins insolently [*mumar lehakhis*] and one who sins to sate his appetite [*mumar lete'avon*]. Maharam insists that the latter is mourned. From Rosh and the *Mordekhai* it appears, however, that even if one sins to sate his appetite, if he does so consistently, he is not to be mourned.

*Shulḥan Arukh*[42] cites Rambam, and rules that those who have cast off the yoke of mitzvot are not to be mourned. Rema, elsewhere,[43] writes that one who performs certain sins on a regular basis is also not mourned, in accordance with the opinion of Rosh and the *Mordekhai* cited above.[44]

The *Aḥaronim* are troubled by the ruling on numerous levels. First, they note that Rabbeinu Gershom, known as the *Meor HaGola*, the Light of the Exile, reportedly mourned for his son who converted to Christianity. R. Yosef Karo, in his *Beit Yosef*, cites the *Mordekhai* and *Hagahot Maimoniyot*,

41. See Rosh 3:59; *Mordekhai* 889.

42. *Shulḥan Arukh, Yoreh De'ah* 345:5.

43. Rema, *Yoreh De'ah* 340:5.

44. Interestingly, Rema also relates to an earlier dispute concerning whether one who does not pay taxes is considered to have "dissociated from the community." Rashba (1:763) writes that although one who does not pay communal taxes is considered a "sinner," he is not considered to be one who has severed ties with the community. *Nimukei Yosef* disagrees, and insists that "since they do not feel the anguish of the community and do not bear their weight in taxes," they are not to be mourned. Rema rules that they are mourned, but the community need not interrupt their work in order to tend to their burial.

who explain that "one should not learn from [the actions of] Rabbeinu Gershom, as he acted in this way as an expression of his great sorrow over the fact that [his son] did not merit to repent."[45] *Hagahot Asheri*[46] understands that Rabbeinu Gershom's son was killed by non-Jews, in which case his death was an atonement, and he was therefore worthy of being mourned. Still other *Rishonim* suggest that Rabbeinu Gershom's son converted and then died while still a child and therefore he should have been mourned.[47] Interestingly, *Or Zarua* further relates that he heard from his teacher, R. Shimshon, that Rabbeinu Gershom did not mourn when his son died, but rather when he converted. This is apparently the source for those who mourn when a close relative converts out of Judaism.[48]

In more recent times, halakhic authorities have discussed whether one must mourn for non-religious family members. Some offer somewhat technical arguments in favor of mourning. For example, R. Shimon Gruenfeld (1860–1930), known as Maharshag,[49] suggests in his responsa that instructing a family not to mourn for a non-religious relative may lead to animosity [*eiva*]. Some express concern that refraining from mourning a relative may bring shame upon the family.[50] Others note that nowadays we should not discourage mourning, as the mourning period often brings families closer to communal identification and religious observance. Finally, some authorities relate to a broader question regarding the status of those who violate Shabbat and other commandments nowadays. They assert that in our day violating Shabbat and other prohibitions is not intended, nor perceived as "dissociating from the congregation,"[51] and therefore close relatives are obligated to mourn.

45. *Beit Yosef, Yoreh De'ah* 345.
46. *Hagahot Asheri,* Mo'ed Katan 3:59.
47. *Or Zarua, Hilkhot Avelut* 2:428.
48. See *Ḥokhmat Adam* 156:6.
49. Maharshag, *Yoreh De'ah* 1:25.
50. See Ḥatam Sofer (*Yoreh De'ah* 326), cited below, regarding mourning for one who commits suicide.
51. This question is beyond the scope of this chapter, although it is sufficient to note that as early as the twelfth century, Rambam (Commentary on the Mishna, Ḥullin 1:2; *Hilkhot Mamrim* 3:3; see also *Iggeret HaShemad*) provided the legal basis to view the Karaites as *tinokot shenishbu,* a talmudic category that refers to those taken captive at birth, who were not raised to observe the commandments. In more recent times, halakhic authorities such as R. Yaakov Ettlinger (*Binyan Tziyon, HaḤadashot* 23),

In our times it is customary to mourn for almost all Jews, regardless of their religious commitment or level of observance.[52] That said, there are cases in which the *Aḥaronim* advise against observing mourning practices, such as for a person who arranged to be cremated, one who converted to another religion, and one who married a non-Jew.[53] As the details and context differ from case to case, one should consult a halakhic authority.

## Mourning for Abusive or Estranged Relatives

While mourning might seem to be the most natural reaction to the death of a close relative, at times, a person may wish not to mourn, either because their relationship to the deceased was strictly biological, or due to estrangement or conflict. We noted above, however, that an adopted child is required to mourn for his or her biological parent, as *avelut*, especially for a parent, is not dependent upon one's sense of loss, but rather upon an objective biological relationship.

In that context, it is interesting to note two possible exceptions, which are emotionally sensitive, halakhically complicated, and subject to debate. Any decision not to observe the laws of mourning in these cases should be made after consulting with a rabbinic authority.

The first case relates to an abusive parent.[54] Is a child obligated to observe mourning practices for an abusive parent? This question must be addressed on numerous levels, including whether there is an obligation to honor an abusive or wicked parent.[55] The type and extent of abuse (e.g., verbal, physical, sexual, etc.) is addressed, as well as whether this falls under the cat-

---

*Ḥazon Ish* (*Hilkhot Sheḥita* 2 and on Rambam, *Hilkhot Deot* 6:3), and R. Avraham Yitzchak HaKohen Kook (*Iggerot HaRaya* 138), have suggested new ways to understand and categorize the behavior of non-religious Jews.

52. See, for example, R. Ovadia Yosef, *Yalkut Yosef, Avelut* 14:17; *Yad Yitzḥak* 3:149; *Emet LeYaakov, Yoreh De'ah* 345:218; *Nitei Gavriel* 126:12.

53. See, for example, *Shevet HaLevi* 2:213; *Yalkut Yosef* 14:12.

54. R. Dr. Joel B. Wolowelsky, "Mourning Abusive Parents," *Ḥakirah: The Flatbush Journal of Jewish Law and Thought* 9 (2010), pp. 191–98; see also R. Mark Dratch, "Honoring Abusive Parents," *Ḥakirah: The Flatbush Journal of Jewish Law and Thought* 12 (2011), pp. 105–19.

55. See *Shulḥan Arukh, Yoreh De'ah* 240. While R. Yosef Karo appears to obligate the child in the mitzva of *kibbud av*, based on the opinion of Rambam (*Hilkhot Mamrim* 6:11), Rema disagrees, and cites those who believe that a child is obligated to honor a "wicked" parent only if the parent repents.

egory, discussed above, of those who "dissociated themselves from the practices of the congregation." It must be determined whether it is proper, and whether it might even be dangerous, psychologically or physically, for a child to mourn an abusive parent. Modern scholars have offered different perspectives.[56]

The second case relates to whether the laws of mourning apply to someone in the process of divorcing a spouse, or a victim of spousal abuse. R. Shlomo Luria (1510–1574), known as Maharshal, writes in his *Yam Shel Shlomo*:[57]

> Regarding someone whose wife passed away during [marital] strife, and he had intended to divorce her, he is not required to mourn for her... and a case once came to me in which a man was in conflict with his wife, and during [that time] she died, and I ruled that he should

56. See R. Wolowelsky, "Mourning Abusive Parents." R. Mark Dratch (ibid.) concludes: "Is mourning for abusive parents obligatory, discretionary, or prohibited? There is no obligation to mourn for an abusive parent. If the mourning is for the sake of the memory and honor of the deceased, then an abusive parent who is classified as a *rasha* should not be mourned. And if mourning is for the sake of the living, then it is up to the children to decide, in consultation with their rabbis and mental health professionals, on their psychological readiness and the appropriateness of engaging in traditional mourning practices. If the children decide that they are psychologically strong enough to mourn, and that sitting *shiva* is not perceived by them as a continuation of the burden of abuse they suffered during their parents' lifetimes, they may choose to observe these practices. However, if mourning would place too heavy an emotional burden on them, they should not sit *shiva* or observe other mourning practices. If, at sometime in the future, as part of their ongoing healing process they choose to mourn their abusive parent, they may determine the appropriate and meaningful ways to do so. The recitation of Kaddish, recitation of *Yizkor*, and observance of *yahrzeit*, which are understood by many to be demonstrations of filial honor, may also be omitted. Although children are obligated to honor their parents even after those parents have died, this obligation, as we have argued above, does not apply to abusive parents. Even the suggestion that abused children recite Kaddish for the full twelve-month period, a practice that would indicate that the deceased was a *rasha* who is in need of such prayers and the reason children otherwise recite Kaddish for only eleven months (so as not to imply that their parent requires such prayers), does not make the recitation obligatory. The children of one who was a *rasha* because of violations of other religious laws may recite a twelve-month Kaddish as a means of redeeming their parent; the additional emotional toll caused by the parent's status on the children may be minimal. However, the emotional, psychological, and spiritual price that abused children may pay by the daily recitation of Kaddish or the annual observance of *yahrzeit* may be overly demanding and, as a result of what we have argued above, not required."
57. *Yam Shel Shlomo*, Gittin 2:4.

> not observe the seven days of mourning ... How can one imagine compelling him to mourn when his heart is not mourning, and there is no "bitter day" before him. While it is true that regarding a regular case the rabbis did not distinguish between one who loves and who hates, here there is good reason to distinguish ... Furthermore, in those cases there is a [biological] relationship, and therefore even if he hates him he is still his flesh and he is overcome with mercy, and mourning and bitterness are present; but here all would agree that we take into account that there is nothing in his heart, and there is no mourning or bitterness.

Maharshal notes that his peers questioned this ruling, and he even consulted with the scholars of Jerusalem, from whom he received the approval of one elder.

Aside from whether or not this responsum reflects the accepted halakhic practice, this fascinating passage reveals much about the nature of *avelut* and relates to a fundamental question, raised previously, regarding the relationship between formal and experiential mourning.

This responsum led to further, related rulings. For example, *Pitḥei Teshuva*[58] cites the *Yeshuot Yaakov*, who insists that if a man whose wife has refused to accept the writ of divorce receives permission from one hundred rabbis to marry another woman [*heter me'ah rabbanim*],[59] then he is not required to mourn his first wife if she passes away. In addition, some conclude on the basis of that ruling that a woman is not required to mourn the death of her abusive husband.[60]

As mentioned above, these questions are complex and should be discussed with a halakhic authority.

### Suicide

Tragically, there are times when the burdens of life seem so onerous that a person chooses to end his own life. While aware of the tragedy of suicide, the Rabbis emphatically insisted that suicide is not a religiously acceptable or halakhically valid option. Some sources view suicide as falling under the

---

58. *Pitḥei Teshuva, Even HaEzer* 90:8.
59. A *heter me'ah rabbanim* is issued on rare occasions, in circumstances where one's wife is unwilling or unable to receive a *get*. The husband receives the permission of one hundred rabbis to marry, and this overrides the decree of Rabbeinu Gershom, who prohibited marrying more than one wife. The husband then writes a *get* and deposits it with a *beit din*.
60. *Nitei Gavriel, Hilkhot Avelut* 126:3.

broader prohibition of murder.[61] Others point to the following verse: "And surely your blood of your lives will I demand an account; at the hand of every beast will I demand it, and at the hand of man; at the hand of every man's brother will I require the life of man" (Gen. 9:5). Rashi explains, "Although I have permitted you to kill an animal, I will require your blood, from one who spills his own blood."[62] Indeed, Rambam[63] writes:

> A person who hires a murderer to kill his fellow man, one who sends his servants and they kill him, one who binds his fellow man and leaves him before a lion or the like and the beast kills him, a person who commits suicide, are all considered to be shedders of blood; the sin of bloodshed is upon their hands, and they are liable to be put to death at the hand of God. They are not, however, liable for execution by the court.
>
> Which source indicates that this is the law? The verse states: "One who sheds the blood of man, by man shall his blood be shed" (Gen. 9:6). This refers to a person who kills his fellow man by himself, without employing an agent. The previous verse: "And surely your blood of your lives will I demand an account" (Gen. 9:5), refers to a person who commits suicide.

The *Rishonim* also offer different explanations for this prohibition. R. David b. Solomon ibn Zimra, in his commentary to the *Mishneh Torah*,[64] explains that it is not permitted for one to endanger himself, or to take his own life, as "a person's life is not his property." Others suggest that the act of taking one's own life is, in essence, a denial of reward and punishment and the World to Come.[65]

In this context, the Rabbis teach:

> No mourning rites are observed for a person who commits suicide; one does not mourn him, nor eulogize him, nor rend his garments, nor remove his shoes, but people stand in line to comfort the mourners and recite the mourners' blessing, and do everything

---

61. See *Pesikta Rabbati* 24.
62. See also Bava Kama 91b; Genesis Rabba 34:13.
63. Rambam, *Hilkhot Rotze'aḥ UShmirat HaNefesh* 2:2–3.
64. Radbaz, *Hilkhot Sanhedrin* 18:6.
65. *Ḥizkuni*, Gen. 9:5; Ibn Ezra, Deut. 32:39.

> out of respect for the living. This is the principle: Anything that is to honor the living may be done; but everything that is not for them, it is not imperative for the congregation to do.[66]

The *Rishonim* disagree regarding the scope of this statement. Ramban[67] explains that the Talmud does not mean to imply that there are no mourning practices for a person who took his life, but rather that the mourning practices are limited. Rambam[68] disagrees and writes:

> When a person commits suicide, we do not take action on his behalf at all. We do not mourn him or eulogize him. We do, however, stand in line to comfort the relatives, recite the mourners' blessing, and perform any action that shows respect for the living.

Rambam rules that while no mourning rites are observed, those practices related to the living apply. *Shulḥan Arukh*[69] concurs, and rules that relatives do not eulogize, rend their garments, or observe the laws of mourning for one who commits suicide.

Interestingly, R. Moshe Sofer (1762–1839), in a lengthy responsum,[70] passionately expresses his concern for the honor of the family of the deceased. He writes:

> Regarding the practical law, who will challenge the agreement of the *Beit Yosef* in the *Shulḥan Arukh*, who rules in accordance with Rambam? Despite the principle that dictates that the law is in accordance with the more lenient opinion in matters of mourning, I say that whenever there is an honorable family whose dignity will be compromised and they would be eternally ashamed, as one [member of the family] has blemished his actions, and if the family is permitted to mourn then people will say that the rabbis are certain that the person

66. Semaḥot 2:1.
67. Ramban, *Torah HaAdam, Inyan HaHesped*, p. 83.
68. Rambam, *Hilkhot Avel* 1:11.
69. *Shulḥan Arukh, Yoreh De'ah* 345:1.
70. Ḥatam Sofer, *Yoreh De'ah* 326; see *Pitḥei Teshuva* 345:1; see also *Ḥazon Ovadia, Avelut*, vol. 1, p. 526.

> did not commit suicide, then the rabbi may rule that the family can mourn even if it is clear to him that the person knowingly ended his life.

Although the *Aḥaronim* rule in accordance with the ruling of *Shulḥan Arukh*, as we will see, the *posekim* have sought to understand the actions of the deceased and treat the family with concern and sensitivity.

The Talmud, and later halakhic authorities, attempt to determine which cases are defined as "suicide." In that attempt, they grapple with two important questions.

First, Tractate Semaḥot[71] teaches that one must be certain that the person took his life intentionally.

> Who is considered to be one who takes his life knowingly (i.e., a suicide)? Not one who climbed to the top of the tree and he fell and died or to the top of a roof and he fell and died. Rather, it is one who says: "Behold, I am going to climb to the top of the tree or the top of the roof and throw myself down and die," and they see him climb to the top of the tree and fall and die; he has the presumptive status of one who took his life knowingly, and one does not tend to him in any way.
>
> If one found him hanging from a tree, or slain and cast upon a sword, he has the presumptive status of one who took his life unknowingly and we tend to him and withhold nothing.

Ramban[72] explains that if the person explicitly expressed his desire to end his life, even if no one saw him die, the act is considered to be a suicide. Rambam writes that "if we see him climb immediately *in anger or know that he was distressed and see him fall and die,* we presume this person is one who committed suicide," indicating that although we may infer his intentions from his behavior, the act can be considered a suicide only if one witnesses the death. In contrast, in the second case: "If however, we see him strangled and hanging from a tree or slain and lying upon his sword, his presumptive status is like that of all other corpses." *Shulḥan Arukh*[73] rules in accordance

71. Semaḥot 2:2–3.
72. Ramban, *Torah HaAdam, Inyan HaHesped*, p. 83.
73. *Shulḥan Arukh, Yoreh De'ah* 345:2.

with Ramban. R. Yoel Sirkis[74] cites R. Shlomo Luria (Maharshal), who insists that the person's status is not determined on the basis of his words; rather, there must be certainty that he indeed intended to end his life.

In addition, some *Aḥaronim* suggest that even if one's intent was to end his life, but he dies only after a while, the suspicion is that perhaps he changed his mind, or repented, and therefore his death is not deemed a suicide.[75]

Second, this law relates to a person who "takes his life knowingly [*ledaat*]." If there is reason to believe that the deceased did not have knowledge or intent [*daat*] then his death is not deemed a suicide. Therefore, for example, Tractate Semaḥot[76] relates the following:

> There was an incident involving the son of Gorganos, who fled from school and his father threatened to box his ears; he feared his father and he went and lost his life in a pit. They asked R. Tarfon, who said that one does not withhold anything from him. And there was again an incident involving a child from Benei Berak who broke a bowl, and his father threatened to box his ears, and he feared him and lost his life in a pit. They came and asked R. Akiva, who said that one does not withhold anything from him.

The *Rishonim* understand that in this tragic case, the child's action is not considered to be intentional and therefore it is not considered a suicide. Furthermore, Ramban[77] and Rosh[78] add that just as the act of a child who ends his life is considered to be unintentional, so too, if an adult, under duress, takes his own life, it is not considered an act of suicide. They cite the apparent suicide of King Saul as an example.[79]

---

74. *Baḥ, Yoreh De'ah* 345.
75. *Gilyon Maharsha* 345; *Gesher HaḤayim* 25:3:2. Ḥatam Sofer (3:69) questions this assumption.
76. Semaḥot 2:4–5.
77. Ibid., p. 84.
78. Rosh, Mo'ed Katan 3:94.
79. See Genesis Rabba 34:5. Whether or not one can infer from the story of Saul that in certain extreme situations it is permitted to take one's own life is subject to debate. See, for example, Avoda Zara 18a; Tosafot, ibid., s.v. *ve'al*; Gittin 57b; Tosafot, ibid., s.v. *vekaftzu*; *Yam Shel Shlomo*, Bava Kama 8:59; Ramban, ibid., and the shocking incident alluded to by the *Daat Zekeinim*, Gen. 9:5.

This leniency is extended to those suffering from mental illness. One of the earliest sources to forward this approach was the *Besamim Rosh.*[80] He suggests distinguishing between philosophical and emotional motives. Ending one's life due to emotional duress is not considered, in relation to the laws of mourning, a form of suicide. Despite the controversial nature of this work,[81] several *Aḥaronim* agree with his approach.[82]

R. Yechiel Michel Epstein, in his *Arukh HaShulḥan,*[83] presents the dominant approach of modern authorities:

> The principle with regard to one who takes his life knowingly, we attribute it to any reason at all, e.g., fear, or pain, or insanity, or the belief that suicide is preferable to stumbling and committing other transgressions, etc. Suicide is truly a remote prospect for a person in his right mind. Learn from Saul the Righteous, who fell on his own sword so that the Philistines would not abuse him. Cases of exigent circumstances fall into the same category, and all the more so, in the case of a minor who commits suicide, which is considered involuntary.

This also appears to be the approach of R. Yechiel Michel Tukachinsky, in his *Gesher HaḤayim,*[84] who asserts:

> Most cases that appear to be suicide, God forbid, are not to be adjudged as suicide, as whenever it is possible to attribute his death to someone else, even if it is a far-fetched scenario, or if it is possible to attribute it to the fact that he was not sane and was confused for any of a number

80. *Besamim Rosh* 145.
81. *Besamim Rosh* was published in 1793 by Saul Berlin, who attributed it to R. Asher (Rosh). The authenticity of this work was challenged by leading rabbinic figures, including R. Moshe Sofer, who disagreed with this responsum as well (Ḥatam Sofer 3:69). Although it is generally assumed to be a forgery, several responsa made their way into rabbinic literature, and were judged on their merits. This responsum is an example.
82. See, for example, *Sho'el UMeshiv, Mahadura Kama* 3:217; *Beit Efraim, Yoreh De'ah* 76; and Maharsham 6:123. Ḥatam Sofer (ibid.), R. Shlomo Kluger (*Tuv Taam VaDaat, Mahadura Shlishit* 2:202), and others disagree.
83. *Arukh HaShulḥan, Yoreh De'ah* 345:5.
84. *Gesher HaḤayim* 25:3:1.

> of reasons, or if as he was in the throes of death he regretted his actions and repented, one attributes the case in a lenient manner and we accord him the presumptive status of one who did not take his own life.

Nowadays, it is customary to mourn and recite Kaddish[85] for those who took their own lives, in accordance with the reasons mentioned above.

## THE AGE OF THE DECEASED

### Miscarriage, Stillbirth, and Infant Death[86]

The Talmud, in numerous places, discusses the halakhic ramifications of the tragic, although at that time relatively common, cases of miscarriage, stillbirth, and infant death.

The laws of *avelut* are not observed after a miscarriage or a stillbirth.[87] Furthermore, the Gemara[88] rules in accordance with the opinion of Rabban Gamliel, who taught that during the first month an infant's chances of survival are somewhat uncertain, and therefore, regarding certain laws, infant death is likened to a stillbirth.

> Any child that remains alive thirty days after birth is no longer considered a stillborn. Proof is cited from that which is stated [with regard to the laws of redemption and valuations]: "And their redemption, from a month old you shall redeem according to your valuation, five shekels of silver, according to the shekel of the Sanctuary; it is twenty *gera*" (Num. 18:16), indicating that no value is ascribed to an infant less than one month old, as its viability is uncertain.

The Talmud adds that even if the child dies on the thirtieth day, mourning practices are not observed.[89]

---

85. See Ḥatam Sofer 3:69; see also *Yabia Omer, Yoreh De'ah* 6:36.
86. For further reading, see R. Avraham Stav, *KaḤalom Ya'uf: Hitmodedut im Ovdan Herayon* (Mossad HaRav Kook, 2000); R. Yamin Levi, *Confronting the Loss of a Baby: A Personal and Jewish Perspective* (Ktav Publishing House, 1998); see also R. Jason Weiner, "Jewish Guidance on the Loss of a Baby or Fetus," *Ḥakirah* 23.
87. Semaḥot 3:1; Shabbat 136a; *Shulḥan Arukh, Yoreh De'ah* 374:8. This is most likely derived from the Sifra (*Emor* 1:6).
88. Shabbat 135b.
89. Bekhorot 49a.

The *Shulḥan Arukh*[90] rules that regardless of whether the child dies due to illness or accident, the laws of mourning are not observed. The *Aḥaronim* add that the laws of *aninut* are also not observed,[91] although some suggest that it is proper to refrain from eating meat and drinking wine until after the burial.[92] This would apply only if the hospital, or local *ḥevra kadisha,* is not responsible for the burial.

In recent years, due to advances in technology and neonatal care, infants born prematurely are often placed in incubators and cared for until they are healthy enough to survive on their own. Unfortunately, some of these "preemies" still pass away, despite their parents' and communities' prayers and the valiant efforts of doctors and nurses. The *Aḥaronim* discuss whether in this case one should begin counting the thirty days from birth, or from when the infant leaves the incubator. While some maintain that *avelut* should be observed,[93] most authorities rule that it is observed only if the infant lived more than thirty days after being removed from the incubator.[94] If an infant was born after a full-term pregnancy and survived more than thirty days on a ventilator, mourning rites are observed.

Some *Aḥaronim* rule that one may recite the *Dayan HaEmet* blessing upon hearing of a miscarriage or the death of an infant for whom one does not observe the mourning rites.[95] Others suggest that one should recite the blessing but omit the name of God (i.e., *barukh dayan ha'emet*).[96] There is no obligation to perform *keria.*[97]

---

90. *Shulḥan Arukh, Even HaEzer* 155:4.
91. See *Pitḥei Teshuva;* R. Akiva Eiger, *Yoreh De'ah* 341:1.
92. *Tiferet LeMoshe,* cited by *Pitḥei Teshuva,* ibid.
93. R. Yosef Shalom Elyashiv, cited in *Torat HaYoledet,* p. 391.
94. R. Shlomo Zalman Auerbach, *Minḥat Shlomo* 2:96:5; R. Shmuel Wosner, *Shevet HaLevi* 7:188:2; R. Ovadia Yosef, *Ḥazon Ovadia, Avelut,* vol. 1, pp. 545–47; see also *Nitei Gavriel* 126:5.
95. R. Moshe Feinstein, cited in *Yesodei Semachos* (p. 2), rules that one should recite the blessing after hearing of the death of an infant. R. Gavriel Zinner, in his *Nitei Gavriel* (163:6, 135:6), also rules that one may recite the blessing. See also *Shulḥan Arukh, Oraḥ Ḥayim* 222:2; and *Biur Halakha,* ibid., s.v. *dayan.*
96. *Gesher HaḤayim* 4:21. Some explain that the blessing should be recited only when there is a concurrent obligation to rend one's garments (see *Magen Avraham* 223:4), while other's explain that the blessing is recited only when an entity that existed in the world is lost (see *Biur Halakha* ibid.).
97. *Shulḥan Arukh, Yoreh De'ah* 340:30.

Regarding a newborn who died, there are different customs regarding burial. For example, the *Rishonim* cite a geonic practice to circumcise a child who died before his *Brit Mila,* and to name the child before the burial.[98] The *Tur* explains that the infant is named so that after the resurrection of the dead [*teḥiyat hametim*] it will be known who the child's father is.[99] In some communities a *tahara* is performed for the infant; in others, it is not.[100]

The Talmud[101] describes the unique characteristics of the burial of a newborn who died.

> Within the first thirty days [after birth], an infant that dies is taken out for burial in one's bosom... And for such an infant, people do not stand in a line to offer their condolences to the mourners, nor do others recite over him the mourners' blessing, nor is the usual formula for the consolation of mourners recited.

There is no bier, and the burial is done without the mourning elements of a funeral. Newborns who died are often buried together with miscarried fetuses in a special plot. In some communities, the infant is buried discreetly, without parental participation, and at times without even marking the grave. Other communities allow parental participation, and some communities do mark the grave. There is no halakhic basis for denying parents the right to be present at the burial.[102]

### ONE'S TEACHER: A UNIQUE CASE OF MOURNING

The Talmud teaches that one should mourn his Torah teacher. One passage even questions whether a Kohen is required to become impure to honor his deceased teacher.[103] Regarding the laws of mourning, the Talmud[104] discusses the extent to which a person should mourn his teacher:

---

98. Rosh, Mo'ed Katan 3:88; *Kol Bo* 73; *Shulḥan Arukh, Yoreh De'ah* 265:5.
99. *Tur, Yoreh De'ah* 353.
100. See *Nitei Gavriel* 135:11.
101. Mo'ed Katan 24a.
102. R. Avraham Stav (*KaḤalom Ya'uf,* p. 39) relates that R. Aharon Lichtenstein strongly opposed the practice of denying the parents the right to be present at the burial.
103. Y. Berakhot 3:5.
104. Mo'ed Katan 25b.

> It was further related that when R. Yoḥanan passed away, R. Ami sat in mourning for him for seven days and for thirty days as though he had lost a close relative. R. Abba, son of R. Ḥiyya b. Abba, said: What R. Ami did, he did on his own [but this practice does not reflect the halakha]. For R. Ḥiyya b. Abba said that R. Yoḥanan said as follows: Even for the death of his teacher who taught him wisdom, one sits in mourning over him for only one day and no more.

This passage appears to conclude that one should mourn for a "teacher who taught him wisdom" for one day. The *Shulḥan Arukh*[105] cites this passage but adds that one should mourn for only part of the day that his teacher died or of the day that he hears of his death.[106] Furthermore, while Rema writes that until the teacher is buried the student should refrain from eating meat and drinking wine,[107] R. Shlomo Luria asserts that one should refrain from eating meat and drinking wine the entire day.[108]

The Talmud also teaches that one should perform *keria* over the death of one's teacher, just as one rends his garment over the death of a parent.[109] The *Rishonim* disagree as to the type of *keria* instituted for the death of one's teacher. The Talmud[110] teaches that one is not permitted to repair a garment rent upon losing his teacher, similar to a garment rent upon losing one's parents. Rambam[111] appears to infer from there that one is also required to rend his garment until he reveals his heart, as he does for a parent. Ramban[112] disagrees and insists that one tears only a *tefaḥ* upon hearing of the death of his teacher. The *Shulḥan Arukh* cites both opinions.[113]

---

105. *Shulḥan Arukh, Yoreh De'ah* 374:10.
106. Ibid., 242:25.
107. Ibid., 340:1.
108. *Taz,* ibid., 340:5.
109. Mo'ed Katan 26a; see also Bava Metzia 33a.
110. Mo'ed Katan 26a.
111. Rambam, *Hilkhot Talmud Torah* 5:9 and *Hilkhot Avel* 9:2.
112. *Torat HaAdam, Inyan HaKeria,* p. 59; see also Rosh, Mo'ed Katan 3:43.
113. *Shulḥan Arukh, Yoreh De'ah* 242:25, 340:7. Rambam's view is cited first, and then Ramban's, as the dissenting opinion, indicating that he adopts the first opinion.

## DO CHILDREN OBSERVE THE LAWS OF MOURNING?

The *Aḥaronim* dispute whether or not a child observes the laws of mourning at all. While some *Aḥaronim* insist that a child should observe the laws of mourning,[114] *Shulḥan Arukh*[115] rules that a child is exempt from the laws of mourning.[116]

The *Rishonim* also dispute whether a child who becomes a bar or bat mitzva after the burial assumes the obligation of fulfilling the laws of *avelut*. Maharam of Rothenburg asserts that if one becomes an adult within thirty days of the death, he assumes the obligation to observe *shiva* and *sheloshim*, similar to one who hears of the death of a close relative within thirty days of his death [*shemua kerova*]. Rosh disagrees and rules that since the child was exempt from *avelut* at the time of the burial he is completely exempt from the laws of mourning.[117] The *Shulḥan Arukh* rules in accordance with the opinion of Rosh.[118] Some *Aḥaronim* suggest that if the child becomes an adult during the *shiva*, he should observe the rest of the *shiva*.[119] The *Aḥaronim* also discuss whether the one who did not observe *shiva* and *sheloshim* observes the twelve-month period of mourning for his parents, as it is an expression of *kibbud av va'em*.[120]

Although children may technically be exempt from observing the laws of mourning, the child's clothes are rent, and a young boy recites Kaddish. Furthermore, one should demonstrate understanding and sensitivity with regard to young mourners. At times it may be appropriate for them to sit and participate in the *shiva* with the other mourners, and at times it may be better for them to feel released from the intensity of the *shiva*.

---

114. *Derisha, Yoreh De'ah* 340:12; *Taz*, ibid., 15.
115. *Shulḥan Arukh, Yoreh De'ah* 396:3; see also *Baḥ, Yoreh De'ah* 384; *Nekudot HaKesef* 340:15.
116. *Dagul Merevava* (comments on *Taz*, ibid.) explains that a child does not mourn as doing so would interrupt his Torah education. *Minḥat Ḥinukh* (264:8) suggests that *ḥinukh* is meant to educate a child in the mitzvot he will fulfill as an adult, and in this case there is no certainty that the child will one day be a mourner.
117. Rosh, Mo'ed Katan 3:96.
118. *Shulḥan Arukh, Yoreh De'ah* 396:3. *Baḥ* (ibid.) rules in accordance with Maharam.
119. See *Gesher HaḤayim* 19:3:3.
120. *Ḥokhmat Adam* (168:6; see *Pitḥei Teshuva*, ibid., 4) and *Arukh HaShulḥan* (*Yoreh De'ah* 396:5) rule that one should observe the twelve-month mourning period. R. Ovadia Yosef (*Ḥazon Ovadia*, vol. 2, p. 119) disagrees. See also *Gesher HaḤayim*, ibid.

*Chapter 6*

# The Beginning of the Seven-Day Mourning Period

The Talmud teaches that after the burial, the mourner begins a seven-day period of *avelut*, known as *shiva*, which is a time that involves particular mourning rites and prohibitions. Although the seven days of mourning typically begin immediately following the interment, at times, when the mourners do not attend the funeral, they begin observing *shiva* even before the burial. Indeed, it is not uncommon for different relatives to begin and end their seven-day mourning periods at different times. Furthermore, unfortunately, it is not always possible to have a burial, and in such a case, *shiva* begins when the mourners despair of finding or recovering the body. Finally, sometimes relatives are informed of the death only after the burial, in which case the laws of mourning may differ depending on when and how they receive the news. In this chapter, we will discuss these different cases.

## BURIAL [*SETIMAT HAGOLEL*]

The Talmud[1] cites a dispute between R. Eliezer and R. Yehoshua regarding the beginning of the mourning period:

---

1. Mo'ed Katan 27a; see also Sanhedrin 47b.

> The sages taught the following: From when do the mourners overturn their beds?[2] From when the deceased is taken out of the opening of his house; this is the statement of R. Eliezer. R. Yehoshua says: From when the tomb is sealed with the grave cover [*setimat hagolel*].

R. Eliezer and R. Yehoshua disagree whether it is the completion of the burial preparations, or the burial itself, that marks the beginning of the mourning period.[3]

Although the *Rishonim* rule in accordance with the opinion of R. Yehoshua, they disagree as to whether the sealing of the tomb [*setimat hagolel*] refers to closing the covering of the coffin[4] or sealing the grave with a large stone.[5] Rambam writes, "From when is a person obligated to mourn? From when the grave is covered."[6] The *Shulḥan Arukh* rules that the period of mourning begins when "the grave is covered with dirt."[7]

---

2. The "overturning of the beds," or *kefiyat hamita*, signified the beginning of the seven-day mourning period. It will be addressed in depth in chapter 7.
3. One might view this dispute as relating to the relationship between *aninut* and the mourning period: Does the obligation to mourn begin at the moment of death, although it is temporarily suspended due to the burial preparations (R. Eliezer), or does the burial formally obligate one to begin the mourning period? Alternatively, one might explain that R. Eliezer and R. Yehoshua simply disagree with regard to which moment obligates one to mourn, or until when the obligation to mourn is suspended. These themes are discussed throughout this chapter.
4. Rashi, Ketubot 4b, s.v. *golel*. Ramban (*Torat HaAdam, Inyan HaHatḥala*) explains that Rashi refers to a case where the coffin is sealed in the house. Shakh (*Yoreh De'ah* 373:11) disagrees and explains that Rashi refers to covering the coffin when it is placed in the ground.
5. Rabbeinu Tam, cited in Tosafot, ibid., s.v. *ad*.
6. *Beit Yosef* (*Yoreh De'ah* 375) asserts that Rambam agrees with Rabbeinu Tam.
7. *Shulḥan Arukh, Yoreh De'ah* 375:1. Interestingly, the *Mordekhai* (Mo'ed Katan 900) relates that when Rabbeinu Kalonymus the Elder (d. 1127) died, his city (Speier) was under siege. His body was sealed in a casket and placed in the building where there was a *mikveh*, with the intention of burying him at a later date. His relatives began observing the seven- and thirty-day mourning periods immediately. Based upon this incident, *Shulḥan Arukh* (375:3–4) rules that "if [the body] is placed in a casket and stored in another house because the city is under siege, the *shiva* and *sheloshim* begin immediately, even though their intention is to bury him in a cemetery after the siege, as the closing of the casket is akin to the burial and the laws of mourning apply immediately." R. Yoel Sirkis (*Baḥ* 375) questions how the *Shulḥan Arukh,* who previously ruled that the period of mourning does not begin "until the grave

Although in most cases, it is the burial that marks the beginning of the mourning period, there are circumstances when *shiva* begins even before the burial.

### "TURNING OF THE FACE": THOSE WHO DO NOT ATTEND THE BURIAL

The Talmud teaches that at times, the mourning period begins irrespective of the burial. The Gemara[8] relates the following:

> Rava said to the people of Mehoza: Those of you who do not follow the coffin all the way to the place of interment should begin counting your days of mourning from *when you turn your faces* from the city gates to return home.

In the days of the Talmud, the dead were often transported long distances and buried far from home,[9] and most of the mourners did not accompany their deceased relatives to the site of the burial. Therefore, Rava instructed them to begin mourning when they take their leave of the deceased.

This passage is somewhat curious, as if it is the burial that marks the beginning of the formal process of mourning, why would those relatives who remain behind begin *shiva* immediately? One might suggest that taking leave of the deceased is akin to the burial. Indeed, Rashi[10] explains that "although *avelut* does not begin until *setimat hagolel*, for you, who will not see [the covering of the grave], your return [to the city] is akin to the covering of the grave." Alternatively, just as one who has despaired of burying his relative mourns even without a burial, here too, when a relative cannot

is covered with dirt," can rule that in this case mourning begins after the body is sealed in a casket. He concludes that the halakha is actually in accordance with the opinion of Rashi, as understood by Ramban, who maintains that the *shiva* begins when the coffin is sealed, although the custom developed to delay the beginning of mourning until the actual burial. Shakh (*Yoreh De'ah* 275:5) disagrees and explains that this case is similar to the case where one despairs of burying the deceased [*nityaashu milekovro*], discussed below, in which case *shiva* begins immediately.

8. Mo'ed Katan 22a; italics added.
9. Rashi (s.v. *delo*) explains that the Talmud refers to those who send the body from Babylonia to Eretz Yisrael for burial.
10. Rashi, s.v. *atḥilu;* italics added.

attend the burial, and the burial is no longer on his mind, he begins mourning immediately.

The *Rishonim* suggest different understandings of Rava's ruling to the people of Mehoza. Some claim that even Rava agrees that whenever possible, one should begin mourning only after the burial. However, if one is unaware of the time of burial, as in the case cited by the Talmud, the Rabbis instituted that mourning begins when he takes his leave of the deceased. Indeed, Rambam[11] writes that Rava is referring to a case where "they do not know when the burial will take place." Some *Aḥaronim*[12] insist that Rambam (and the *Shulḥan Arukh*)[13] maintains that one begins mourning immediately only in a case where he does not know the time of burial; however, if one can ascertain the time of burial, he begins mourning only after the burial.

Others, including Ramban,[14] explain that Rambam simply distinguishes between a burial in another city, and a burial in proximity to the city where they are, in which case even those who do not attend the burial begin mourning only after the burial, "as his thoughts are upon them, and it is as though he is entrusted with the burial."[15] In other words, when the burial takes place nearby, one's mind is still on the burial, and therefore mourning begins only after interment. However, when the burial is far away, even if the mourner knows when the burial will occur, this is similar to the case of one who despairs of burying the deceased [*nityaashu milekovro*], as mentioned above, and the *avelut* begins when he takes his leave of the body.

Finally, *Behag*[16] does not make the above distinctions, and maintains that whenever one does not attend the burial, one begins mourning immediately. He apparently views "turning one's face" from the body as akin to burial, as Rashi explained above.

Practically, when the mourner does not accompany the body for burial in a different city or country, the mourning period begins immediately after the mourner takes his leave of the deceased, often at the airport or funeral home.[17] When one of the relatives accompanies the body to the

---

11. Rambam, *Hilkhot Avel* 1:5.
12. See, for example, *Baḥ, Yoreh De'ah* 375:3; Radbaz 4:1135; Maharsham 2:260.
13. *Shulḥan Arukh, Yoreh De'ah* 375:1.
14. See *Tur, Yoreh De'ah* 375.
15. See also *Arukh HaShulḥan, Yoreh De'ah* 375:7–8; *Iggerot Moshe, Yoreh De'ah* 1:253.
16. *Behag, Hilkhot Avel* 245.
17. R. Shraga Feivel Cohen, in his *Badei HaShulḥan* (*Yoreh De'ah* 375:2, *Biurim*, s.v. *veyesh*),

burial, he begins *shiva* after the burial.[18] If he returns to join those already sitting *shiva*, he concludes *shiva* with them, even though he observed fewer than seven days of mourning.[19]

If the cemetery is near the city, those who remain behind do not begin mourning until they are informed of the burial,[20] or when they estimate that the burial has occurred.[21]

## ONE WHO HEARS OF THE DEATH OF A RELATIVE IN A DIFFERENT CITY AND DOES NOT ATTEND THE FUNERAL

When does one who hears about the death, in another city, of a close relative, and who does not attend the burial, begin to observe *shiva*? This question arose somewhat recently in halakhic literature, as before the age of telecommunication, it was rare to receive the news, before the burial, of a close relative's passing in a distant city. In our day, however, it is common. For example, when should a person in New York, who hears of the death of a relative in Israel but is unable to attend the burial, begin mourning?

---

suggests that "those who are still involved in burial preparations by telephone, etc., in this situation they still have the status of an *onen*." See below regarding one who hears of the death of a relative and doesn't attend the funeral.

18. The Yerushalmi (Mo'ed Katan 3:5) comments on this case that "everything follows the head of the family" [*hakol holekh aḥar gedol hamishpaḥa*]. The *Rishonim* disagree, based upon different textual variations, with regard to when this principle applies, i.e., when the *gedol hamishpaḥa* determines the beginning of the *shiva*. Rosh (Mo'ed Katan 3:39), for example, maintains that the beginning of the mourning period is always determined by the *gedol hamishpaḥa*. Therefore, if he accompanies the deceased to the burial, all the mourners begin *shiva* after the burial. If he remains behind, even those who accompany the body begin *shiva* from when he takes his leave of the body. Tosafot (Mo'ed Katan 22a, s.v. *mehadritu*) disagree and explain that although if the *gedol hamishpaḥa* does not accompany the body, those who remain behind begin mourning immediately and those who accompany the body begin after the burial, if the *gedol hamishpaḥa* accompanies the body, all mourners begin *shiva* after the burial. The *Shulḥan Arukh* (*Yoreh De'ah* 375:2) rules in accordance with the opinion of Tosafot; therefore, if the *gedol hamishpaḥa* travels to the funeral and does not return, even those who remained behind begin mourning only after the funeral. Shakh (ibid., 3) adds, based on Raavan, that this is only if the burial will take place within three days.
19. R. Akiva Eiger, ibid., s.v. *ve'im gedol* (based on Shakh 375:12).
20. Shakh, *Yoreh De'ah* 375:1.
21. See *Kitzur Shulḥan Arukh* 204:2.

R. Naftali Tzvi Yehuda Berlin, known as Netziv, rules that in this case, one begins to observe the rites of mourning only after the burial.[22] Indeed, he cites the *Shulḥan Arukh,*[23] who rules that one who heard that a relative was crucified in a different city begins mourning only after the burial. He notes, however, that *aninut* would last until the burial, in accordance with the opinion of Rosh, cited above.[24]

R. Berlin's son-in-law, R. Refael Shapiro, disagrees. In a responsum printed in R. Chaim Chizkiyah Medini's (1834–1905) encyclopedic collection of rabbinic rulings, the *Sedei Ḥemed,*[25] R. Shapiro insists that just as one who does not accompany the body to burial in a different city begins observing the laws of *avelut* when he "turns his face" and parts from the deceased, here too, the mourner does not need to wait until the burial, and begins mourning immediately. He explains that unlike the case of the relative who was crucified in another city, where the authorities had not yet allowed the body to be buried, and therefore one does not begin mourning until the burial, here, the body is scheduled to be buried but the mourner cannot attend.[26] In the middle of the responsum, he relates:

> And this is so obvious to me that I ruled accordingly, and when the telegram from Warsaw arrived informing that the burial of my father-in-law, the *gaon,* would be the next day, I instructed my wife to begin observing *avelut* immediately.

R. Shapiro instructed his wife to begin mourning her father immediately, against the explicit ruling of her father, Netziv.

22. *Meshiv Davar* 2:72.
23. *Shulḥan Arukh, Yoreh De'ah* 375:6, based on Rosh (Responsa 27:8).
24. See above, chapter 1.
25. *Sedei Ḥemed,* vol. 8, *Pe'at HaSadeh, Maarekhet Avelut* 14.
26. R. Shapiro also relates to the story, cited in chapter 1, in which Rabbeinu Tam's sister passed away in another city and he did not observe *aninut* since he did not plan on attending the burial, indicating that the actual obligation to mourn did not begin until the burial. He cites Rabbeinu Yona (Berakhot 11a, s.v. *kol zeman*), who explains that in that case, the body was brought to Rabbeinu Tam's city for burial, and as a result, he could not consider the body as having already been buried. Therefore, he did not observe the laws of *aninut,* and he began mourning only after the burial.

This interesting and very practical debate continues to this day. Some *Aharonim* rule in accordance with the opinion of Netziv and instruct those who hear about the death of a relative and their upcoming burial to wait until the burial and only then begin mourning.[27] Others accept the view of R. Refael Shapiro and rule that the mourner begins sitting *shiva* immediately.[28] In practice, it is customary in America to rule in accordance with the opinion of R. Refael Shapiro, i.e., to begin mourning upon receiving the news that a close relative has died in a different city in a case where one does not plan on attending the burial.[29]

This ruling is especially significant in a case when the mourner takes his leave of the deceased before Yom Tov. In this case, the mourner begins observing the period of mourning before Yom Tov, and then Yom Tov cancels the seven-day mourning period, even if the burial occurs after Yom Tov.[30]

## ONE WHO DESPAIRS OF BURYING THE DECEASED

Tractate Semaḥot[31] teaches that one begins mourning for those who cannot be buried from the moment he despairs of recovering or finding the body.

---

27. See *Arukh HaShulḥan, Yoreh De'ah* 341:12; *Imrei Yosher* 21; *Gesher HaḤayim* 1:19:10. *Shevet Sofer* (*Yoreh De'ah* 106), R. Shlomo Zalman Auerbach (see *Penei Barukh*, chap. 8, n. 23), and R. Ovadia Yosef (*Yabia Omer, Yoreh De'ah* 4:28), concur, and add that one does not observe the laws of *aninut* before the burial.

28. Maharsham 2:60; *Ḥelkat Yaakov* 1:188; *Iggerot Moshe, Yoreh De'ah* 1:253. See also *Ḥazon LaMo'ed Hilkhot Semaḥot* (2:33; and in *Noam*, vol. 4), who cites R. Tzvi Pesach Frank and R. Yosef Eliyahu Henkin as concurring with this view as well.

29. If the mourner continues to be involved in the burial preparations from afar, and certainly if he delivers a *hesped* (eulogy) over the telephone or via a live video call or similar, then even R. Refael Shapiro might agree that he should begin mourning after the burial. See R. Asher Bush, "*Hathalat Avelut LeMi SheEino Nimtza BeKevurat Aviv Umishtatef al yedei Telefon,*" *Beit Yitzḥak* 46 (5775/2015). I heard this from R. Mordechai Willig as well.

30. *Shulḥan Arukh, Yoreh De'ah* 399:1. In a recent example, R. Shmuel Wosner (1913–2015), author of the *Shevet HaLevi*, passed away on Erev Pesaḥ, Friday, April 3, 2015. He was buried on Saturday night, April 4, during Ḥol HaMo'ed Pesaḥ; therefore, his relatives did not begin mourning until after the festival. His son, R. Yosef Wosner, who was in New York and did not attend the funeral, began mourning on Friday, and the festival canceled the seven-day mourning period.

31. Semaḥot 2:9.

> From those who are executed by the government, nothing is withheld. From when does one begin to count for them? From the time that they have despaired of requesting (*nityaashu milishol*) [the body], but not of stealing [it].

Similarly, the mishna continues:

> Those who drowned in the sea or a river, or were consumed by a wild beast, nothing is withheld. From when does one begin to count for them? From the time they despaired of seeking [the body].

The *Shulḥan Arukh* rules that in these cases, and others, one begins mourning upon despairing of retrieving the body for burial,[32] even if this occurs more than thirty days after the death.[33]

The *Aḥaronim*[34] cite the *Ittur,* who rules that if a person drowns in a large body of water [*mayim she'ein lahem sof*], his relatives do not begin observing the laws of *avelut* until a Jewish court [*beit din*] establishes that he has died and that his wife may remarry. This higher standard is necessary to avoid a situation where his wife remarries, after observing the mourning period, even though it has not been unequivocally proven that her husband died and that it is permitted for her to remarry. The *Aḥaronim*[35] discuss whether this precaution, which actually overrides the laws of mourning, applies even when this concern is not relevant, e.g., if the one who drowned was a single man or a single woman. They also discuss whether Kaddish should be recited.[36] In recent years, we have seen these principles applied in numerous tragic incidents, such as in the aftermath of the 9/11 attack on the World Trade Center, and in Israel with regard to soldiers who are missing in action.

32. *Shulḥan Arukh, Yoreh De'ah* 341:4, 375:5–7.
33. Shakh, *Yoreh De'ah* 375:6, based on Rosh (Mo'ed Katan 3:56) and *Mordekhai* (Mo'ed Katan 899).
34. See Shakh, ibid., 6; *Taz,* ibid., 3.
35. See Ḥatam Sofer, *Yoreh De'ah* 2:344; *Shevut Yaakov* 1:102; see also *Ḥazon Ovadia, Avelut,* vol. 1, p. 532.
36. See *Pitḥei Teshuva* 375:3.

### ONE WHO HEARS ABOUT A RELATIVE'S DEATH: *SHEMUA KEROVA* AND *SHEMUA REḤOKA*

Until somewhat recently, cases where people heard days, weeks, or even months after the death and funeral that a relative had passed away were relatively common. The Talmud[37] discusses two scenarios: Where one receives the news within thirty days, and where one receives the news after thirty days.

> The sages taught the following: In the case of recent tidings (*shemua kerova*) of a relative's death, mourning applies for the seven- and thirty-day periods. In the case of distant tidings (*shemua reḥoka*), it applies for only one day. What are considered recent tidings and what are considered distant tidings? Recent tidings are news that arrives within thirty days of the person's death. Distant tidings are news that arrives after thirty days; this is the statement of R. Akiva.

R. Akiva maintains that one who hears about the death of a close relative within thirty days observes a full seven-day mourning period, as well as the thirty-day period [*sheloshim*], while one who hears after thirty days observes only one day of mourning. The *Aḥaronim* disagree as to whether the reference in the Talmud is to thirty days after the death[38] or after the burial,[39] if the funeral took place on a different day. *Gesher HaḤayim*[40] rules that "one who wishes to be lenient has [authorities] upon whom he can rely," and this is the custom.[41]

Regarding one who hears that a close relative has passed away within thirty days of the death, the *baraita*[42] teaches: "The day of hearing [of the recent death of a relative] is like the day of burial with regard to rending and mourning, for the mitzva of *shiva* and the mitzva of *sheloshim*." The mourner rends his garments,[43] does not don *tefillin*,[44] and does not eat his own food at the first meal after hearing of the recent death of a relative [*seudat havraa*]. The mourner recites the blessing of *Dayan HaEmet* upon hearing the news,

---

37. Mo'ed Katan 20a.
38. Maharshal cited by *Baḥ* 399; *Derisha* 399; *Taz* 402:6; Shakh 402:5.
39. *Dagul Merevava* 402; *Even HaEzer* 402.
40. *Gesher HaḤayim* 1:24:1.
41. *Penei Barukh* 26:3.
42. Semaḥot 12:1; see also Rambam, *Hilkhot Avel* 7:1; *Shulḥan Arukh, Yoreh De'ah* 402:1.
43. Ibid. See also Mo'ed Katan 20b.
44. *Taz* 402:1.

even if he hears it on Shabbat or Yom Tov.[45] The *Aḥaronim* discuss the basis for this law. Some understand the law of *shemua kerova* as a form of *tashlumin,* redress for the missed mourning period, during the period proximate to the death and burial.[46]

One who receives the news, at least thirty days after the death, that his close relative has died, mourns for "one day." Due to the principle: "The legal status of part of the day is like that of the entire day" [*miktzat hayom kekhulo*], which is typically applied on the seventh and thirtieth days, the mourning lasts for only a "brief period" [*shaa aḥat*],[47] consisting of a representative act of mourning, e.g., removing one's shoes or sitting on a low chair. A person who receives a *shemua reḥoka* about the death of a parent does not rend his garments (see chapter 3), but he recites the *Dayan HaEmet* blessing.[48] He does not eat a *seudat havraa.* The laws of mourning for twelve months, including the prohibition of cutting one's hair until "his colleagues have rebuked him," and not attending *semaḥot,* are observed. One counts the twelve-month mourning period from the day of the death.[49]

If one receives a *shemua kerova* on Shabbat, Shabbat is the first day of mourning and the *shiva* concludes on Friday morning. The mourner observes the inconspicuous laws of mourning [*devarim shebetzina*] on Shabbat, refraining from marital relations, bathing, and Torah study. After Shabbat, the mourner rends his garments and begins observing the mourning rites of *shiva.*[50] If one receives a *shemua reḥoka* on Shabbat, he is not obligated to observe any rites of mourning that day, and after Shabbat, he observes a single act of mourning.[51]

What if one receives news on Shabbat that a close relative has passed away, and after Shabbat, when he would begin mourning, thirty days will have already elapsed since the death? The Talmud[52] teaches:

---

45. *Shemirat Shabbat KeHilkhata* 2:65:49.
46. *Taz* (*Yoreh De'ah* 396:3) writes, "Observing the *shiva* and *sheloshim* for a *shemua kerova* is not a mitzva in and of itself; rather, it is redress for the mourning that should have been observed immediately after the burial, had he known. Since he did not know, the sages instituted compensatory mourning for thirty days."
47. *Shulḥan Arukh,* ibid.
48. *Gesher HaḤayim* (24:2:3) writes that if one did not recite the blessing within twenty-four hours of receiving the news, he should not recite it.
49. *Shulḥan Arukh,* ibid.
50. *Shulḥan Arukh,* ibid., 402:7.
51. *Shulḥan Arukh,* ibid., 402:6.
52. Mo'ed Katan 20b.

> R. Yosei b. Avin said: If one received recent tidings of a relative's death during a festival, when it is prohibited to mourn, and after the festival they became distant tidings, as after the festival thirty days had already elapsed since the relative's passing, the festival counts for him toward the number of days that make it a belated report. And, consequently, after the festival he observes only one day of mourning.

In this case, since one did not actually begin mourning during the thirty days, it is considered a *shemua reḥoka.*[53]

### MOURNING DURING THE WEEK AFTER A WEDDING

Tragedies are unpredictable and can occur at the most unfortuitous moments. The Talmud[54] discusses a case in which the preparations for a wedding were already completed, and before the wedding, the father of the groom, or the mother of the bride, passed away. As this case entails a financial loss, because those two relatives are deemed crucial for making the wedding feast happen, the Gemara rules that the couple should wed, and observe the seven festive days after the wedding [*sheva berakhot*], and then begin the seven days of mourning.

The *Aḥaronim*[55] rule that today there is no distinction with regard to which relatives pass away. In any case, the wedding is postponed until after the seven days of mourning.[56] In this case, the wedding may be performed immediately after the *shiva,*[57] even on the seventh day, and the couple then observes the seven-day festive period [*sheva berakhot*].

---

53. Similarly, *Taz* (402:7), based on a scenario similar to the one cited in the *Shulḥan Arukh* (365:11, 402:11), rules that if one hears of the death of a relative on the thirtieth day, after reciting Maariv but before dark, it is considered a *shemua kerova* and he is still required to observe the *shiva.*
54. Ketubot 3b.
55. See Shakh, *Nekudot HaKesef* 342; *Ḥokhmat Adam* 154:3.
56. R. Moshe Feinstein (*Iggerot Moshe, Yoreh De'ah* 1:227) insists that when there is a great financial loss, and the couple will not be able to rent the hall on another date, one may rely upon the ruling of the Talmud and perform the wedding before the burial. In his previous responsum (ibid., 226), he discusses whether the bride may choose to waive the seven-day marriage celebration and begin mourning immediately; see *Taz, Yoreh De'ah* 342:1.
57. Although the *Tur* (342) suggests that unless the groom has small children, or does not yet have any children (and has not yet fulfilled the commandment of procreation),

If the death occurred after the wedding, during the seven days of feasting [*shivat yemei mishteh*], neither the bride nor the groom observes the laws of *aninut*,[58] and they do not observe the laws of mourning until after the seven days of feasting. This means that they may launder their garments and cut their hair during the seven days of feasting.[59] In the case of the second marriage for both the groom and bride, only three festive days are observed after the wedding, and the seven-day period of mourning begins on the fourth day. Although the *Dayan HaEmet* blessing is recited, the *Aḥaronim* dispute whether the mourner should rend his garments. *Gesher HaḤayim* writes that the proper practice is to postpone *keria* until after the days of feasting.[60] In this case, the thirty-day *sheloshim* period begins on the first day of mourning, and not on the day of death or burial.[61]

If during the seven days after the wedding a close relative dies and then a festival occurs, some authorities rule that the festival abrogates the *shiva*, even though in practice the mourner did not begin to observe *shiva*.[62] Others insist that since the mourner did not yet begin observing the seven-day mourning period, the festival does not abrogate the *shiva*.[63]

The *Aḥaronim* discuss whether the law mentioned above, that one who attended the burial and then joins his relatives who began mourning

---

the wedding should be delayed until after the *sheloshim*, the *Shulḥan Arukh* (342) rules that in any case the wedding may be performed immediately after the *shiva*.

58. See *Gesher HaḤayim* 19:7:10. He also rules (19:7:8) that the groom is not exempt from *tefillin*. R. Moshe Feinstein, cited in *Yesodei Semachos* (p. 13), rules that the bride or groom observes the laws of *aninut*.

59. *Shulḥan Arukh, Yoreh De'ah* 342. The *Aḥaronim* discuss whether the *avelut* period is postponed even if the couple had not yet engaged in marital relations. Many authorities (*Taz* 342:1; Shakh, *Nekudot HaKesef* 342; *Dagul Merevava* 342; *Ḥokhmat Adam* 154:3) rule that the *ḥuppa* alone is not sufficient to delay *avelut*. Most Sephardic authorities rule that the *shiva* is postponed, and the couple may engage in relations. Some agree that the mourning is postponed but that the couple may not engage in marital relations during the seven festive days; see *Gesher HaḤayim* 19:7:10.

60. *Gesher HaḤayim* 19:7:5.

61. *Shulḥan Arukh*, ibid.

62. R. Akiva Eiger, in his comments to the *Shulḥan Arukh* (*Yoreh De'ah* 342), cites this view and appears to disagree, but notes that he did not see the original responsum and therefore the matter requires further investigation. *Sefer Kol Bo al Avelut* (p. 66), as well as R. Ovadia Yosef (*Yalkut Yosef, Avelut* 44:5), rule that the festival abrogates the *shiva*.

63. *Gesher HaḤayim* 19:7:2.

before the burial, and begins mourning with them, concludes his mourning period with them, applies in this case. In other words, if the bride or groom finishes the seven days of feasting and then joins the other relatives who are already sitting *shiva*, does he or she conclude the mourning period with them? While some rule that he must observe a complete mourning period,[64] others insist that the mourner joins the others and that if the primary member of the household is there, the mourner concludes *shiva* with them.[65]

## REINTERMENT [*LIKUT ATZAMOT*]

The Yerushalmi[66] describes the two-phase burial procedure that was employed in talmudic times. The bodies were first placed in deep pits, where the flesh would decompose. Afterward, the bones were removed and placed in an ossuary and then in a burial cave. The Talmud relates that on the day that the bones were gathered [*likut atzamot*], the laws of mourning were observed. Today, bodies are, as a rule, buried with the intention not to move them, and indeed, it is prohibited to transfer remains from one grave to another.[67] However, in certain circumstances, it may be permitted, necessary, or even a mitzva to do so.[68]

Regarding the day on which the bones are gathered, or when a body is reinterred, the Talmud teaches that "one who gathers the bones of his father or his mother mourns for them the entire day, but he does not mourn for them in the evening."[69] One observes all of the restrictions of a mourner, and rends his garment, on the day of *likut atzamot*.

The *Rishonim* disagree whether the laws of *aninut* apply in this case, and discuss when the laws of mourning begin. Maharam of Rothenburg[70]

---

64. *Har Tzvi, Yoreh De'ah* 265.
65. *Gesher HaḤayim* 19:7:4.
66. Y. Mo'ed Katan 1:5.
67. Y. Mo'ed Katan 2:4.
68. The *Shulḥan Arukh* (363:1) permits reinterring a body in order to bury it in a family plot or in Eretz Yisrael, or due to a fear lest the grave will be violated by non-Jews or damaged by water. Elsewhere, the *Shulḥan Arukh* (364:5) permits moving a grave that causes damage to the public, and moving a body to a gravesite that the deceased had requested (363:2). Other scenarios are discussed by the *Aḥaronim*. Reinterment should be performed only after consulting a halakhic authority.
69. Mo'ed Katan 8a.
70. *Hilkhot Semaḥot* 68.

held that one is considered to be an *onen* between the disinterment and reburial. Rosh[71] maintains that there is no *aninut* in this situation.

The laws of mourning are observed only on the day of the reinterment, until nightfall. After dark, even if the reburial is not yet complete, one is no longer a mourner. Therefore, it is preferable not to begin the reinterment toward the end of the day.[72] Although some *Aḥaronim* insist that one should observe mourning practices from the disinterment until the reburial,[73] most authorities maintain that mourning is observed only on the day of the disinterment.[74] Even one who hears about the reinterment of a relative must observe the laws of mourning. However, he observes these laws only on the day that he receives the news.[75]

The *Aḥaronim* also dispute whether the mourning rites are observed when the disinterred corpse remains in the original coffin. Some maintain that provided that the remains were not removed from the coffin, *avelut* is not observed.[76] Others insist that *avelut* is observed whether the remains are moved in the coffin or outside the coffin.[77]

Some write that one should not inform other family members of the time of the disinterment.[78]

### INFORMING RELATIVES ABOUT A DEATH

Finally, it is important to note that there is no obligation to inform a person that his or her relative has passed away.[79] Although it is customary, in ordinary circumstances, to inform people of the passing of their relatives so that they can attend the funeral, mourn, and recite Kaddish, there are times when it may be appropriate to delay informing someone of the loss of his relative, or even to completely withhold the information from him.

---

71. Rosh, Mo'ed Katan 3:56; see Rema, *Yoreh De'ah* 402:1.
72. *Shulḥan Arukh, Yoreh De'ah* 402:1.
73. *Iggerot Moshe, Yoreh De'ah* 1:260; see also *Ḥazon Ish, Yoreh De'ah* 2213:4.
74. See *Gesher HaḤayim* 26:4:8; *Yeḥave Daat* 4:59.
75. *Shulḥan Arukh, Yoreh De'ah* 402:5.
76. *Har Tzvi, Yoreh De'ah* 296; *Gesher HaḤayim* 26:4:12; see also *BeMareh HaBazak* 2:91; *MeOlam VeAd Olam* 46:36.
77. *Ḥazon Ish*, ibid.; *Iggerot Moshe*, ibid.; see also *Ḥazon LaMo'ed* 30:6.
78. Ḥatam Sofer (*Yoreh De'ah* 296), cited by *Pitḥei Teshuva* 402:1.
79. See *Mordekhai*, Mo'ed Katan 993.

The *Shulḥan Arukh*[80] rules that one should not inform a person who is ill of the death of a relative in a case where it may be detrimental to the ill person's health. Similarly, there may be no reason to inform a person of the death of his relative if he will not mourn him in any meaningful or significant manner. *Pitḥei Teshuva* (402:2) cites R. Meir Eisenstadt (1670–1744), who rules in his *Panim Me'irot* that one should not inform a person of the death of a relative on Yom Tov, or on Purim, in order not to detract from the joyful observance of the holiday. One may also withhold news of the death of a relative from a person before his or her wedding, or before his or her participation in someone else's wedding, when this is deemed appropriate. Of course, this decision should be made carefully, in consultation with a halakhic authority, and one should avoid lying if asked directly.[81]

80. *Shulḥan Arukh, Yoreh De'ah* 337.
81. See *Shulḥan Arukh, Yoreh De'ah* 402:12.

*Chapter 7*

# The Prohibitions of the Week of Mourning [*Shiva*]

The laws of *avelut*, as discussed previously,[1] reflect a variety of themes, including respect and honor for the deceased [*kevod hamet*], inner sorrow and grief [*avelut shebalev*], appreciation for human life, and repentance [*teshuva*].

Rambam[2] enumerates eleven prohibitions observed by the mourner during the *shiva*.

> These are the matters that are prohibited for a mourner on the first day by Torah law and on the remaining days by rabbinic law. It is prohibited for him to cut his hair, launder his clothes, wash, anoint himself, engage in sexual relations, wear shoes, work, study Torah, stand his bed upright, uncover his head, and greet others – eleven matters in total.

These eleven mourning rites reflect, express, and create the mourning experience for the seven-day period of *avelut*. In this chapter, we will review

1. See chapter 4, which also discusses whether the obligation to mourn is biblical or rabbinic.
2. Rambam, *Hilkhot Avel* 5:1.

the prohibitions and practices observed during the first week of mourning – *shiva*.

### HAIRCUTS, SHAVING, AND NAIL CUTTING

Allowing one's hair to grow long reflects two aspects of mourning. First, cutting one's hair, trimming one's beard, and for some, shaving, are basic forms of hygiene. For one who is usually well groomed, neglecting his hair causes physical discomfort, reflecting and expressing the mourner's inner psychological experience. Second, the mourner who allows his hair to grow shuns societal convention, and as his hair grows longer and longer, he further flouts the communal norms and societal standards associated with proper grooming.[3]

The Talmud[4] teaches that during the week of *shiva* the mourner does not cut his hair.

> It is prohibited for a mourner to receive a haircut, [as it is] derived from the fact that the Merciful One states to the sons of Aaron: "Let the hair of your heads not grow loose" (Lev. 10:6). [It was prohibited for them to grow their hair long during the period of mourning over the death of their brothers, Nadav and Avihu.] By inference, it

3. R. Maurice Lamm, in *The Jewish Way in Death and Mourning* (pp. 122–23), explains: "Allowing the hair to grow is another indication of the withdrawal of the mourner from society. It is part of the general pattern of forsaking personal appearance and grooming, at a time of great personal loss. Indeed, one of the prime characteristics of the hermit or the ancient Nazirite, who was a spiritually-inspired rebel against the sinfulness of society, was the unrestrained growing of hair. It expressed, evidently, a rejection of civility. Similarly, in our day, many youngsters, not in the least spiritually-inspired, demonstrate their rebellion by wearing their hair excessively long. It is, in a sense, an abandonment of, and withdrawal from, society which impels the mourner not to cut his hair. While the mourner is never asked to become a recluse – religious or social – he is nevertheless in a state of social withdrawal. He does not go to business or parties; he does not even go out-of-doors. He does not wish to be bothered with the social amenities of 'hellos' and 'goodbyes.' He allows his hair and beard and nails to grow in a spirit of abandonment. He is disheartened by life's tragic twists and turns. Only upon his emergence from deep despair, when relatives or friends begin to comment upon his unkempt appearance, does the mourner begin to groom himself again."
4. Mo'ed Katan 14b.

> is teaching that for everyone else it is prohibited [to cut their hair during the period of mourning].

Furthermore, the mourner may not get a haircut during the thirty-day mourning period, or even afterward when mourning a parent, as we shall discuss. One may comb his hair even during *shiva*.[5]

Regarding one's mustache and beard, the Talmud relates that R. Yehuda HaNasi permitted a mourner to cut facial hair that interfered with his eating.[6] The *Shulḥan Arukh*[7] rules that after *shiva*, a mourner may trim hair that interferes with his eating.

The Talmud[8] cites a dispute whether the prohibition of cutting one's hair includes cutting one's nails.[9]

> And just as the sages said that it is prohibited for a mourner to cut his hair during the period of his mourning, so too, it is prohibited for him to cut his nails during the period of his mourning; this is the statement of R. Yehuda, whereas R. Yosei permits [a mourner to cut his nails].

The Gemara rules in accordance with the opinion of R. Yosei, yet explains that he prohibited cutting one's nails "with scissors [*genustera*] that are specifically for cutting nails." A mourner may, however, cut his nails in an alternative manner.

The *Shulḥan Arukh*[10] rules that although one may not cut his nails with a nail clipper for thirty days, he may cut them with his hands or teeth (i.e., in an alternative manner) even during *shiva*.[11]

---

5. *Shulḥan Arukh, Yoreh De'ah* 390:6. Some *Rishonim* (*Semak* 97; *Mordekhai*, Mo'ed Katan 917; *Or Zarua, Hilkhot Avelut* 446) prohibit even combing one's hair.
6. The *Rishonim* debate whether the mourner may trim his mustache during the *shiva* (Ramban, *Torat HaAdam, Inyan HaAvelut, BeTisporet Keitzad*), only after the *shiva* (*Ritz Ge'ut, Hilkhot Avel* 49), or not at all (Rambam, *Hilkhot Avel* 6:3).
7. *Shulḥan Arukh, Yoreh De'ah* 390:1.
8. Mo'ed Katan 17b.
9. The Gemara (ibid., 18a) says that this includes fingernails and toenails.
10. *Shulḥan Arukh, Yoreh De'ah* 390:7.
11. The *Aḥaronim* discuss whether a woman who is preparing for the *mikveh* during *sheloshim* should ask a non-Jewish woman (*Shulḥan Arukh*, ibid.), or even a Jewish

**BATHING AND ANOINTING**

The Talmud teaches that during the entire seven-day mourning period, a mourner refrains from bathing [*reḥitza*] and anointing [*sikha*].[12]

> A mourner is prohibited from bathing, as it is written: "Do not anoint with oil, [and you shall be as a woman mourning for a dead person for these many days]" (II Sam. 14:2). And bathing is included in the category of anointing.

The Talmud[13] further qualifies and defines the prohibition of bathing.

> It is prohibited for a mourner to bathe his entire body both in hot water and in cold water all seven days of mourning. However, with regard to his face, his hands, and his feet, although it is prohibited to bathe them in hot water, in cold water it is permitted. However, with regard to smearing with oil, even a minimal amount of smearing is prohibited. But if one does so to remove the dirt, it is permitted.

In other words, all bathing in hot water is prohibited, while bathing one's face, hands, and feet in cold water is permitted. Some allow the mourner to bathe his limbs in lukewarm water [*mayim poshrim*] as well.[14]

Only bathing or anointing for pleasure [*taanug*] is prohibited.[15] Therefore, it is permitted to bathe or anoint to remove dirt, filth, or perspiration. Furthermore, one may bathe for medicinal reasons, including washing one's hair or scalp to remove lice or to alleviate the discomfort of blisters, and bathing in warm water to heal a skin rash, infestation (scabies), or hemorrhoids. Similarly, a mourner who recently underwent surgery, or a woman who recently gave birth, may certainly bathe.[16]

---

woman (Rema, ibid.), to cut her nails with scissors, or whether she may cut them herself (see *Taz*, ibid., 3; *Ḥokhmat Adam* 165:30).

12. Mo'ed Katan 15b.
13. Taanit 13b.
14. *Pitḥei Teshuva* (381:1) cites the *Tiferet LeMoshe*, who prohibits washing in lukewarm water as well. However, other authorities permit washing in lukewarm water; see, for example, *Nitei Gavriel, Hilkhot Avelut*, vol. 1, p. 544; *MeOlam VeAd Olam*, p. 153.
15. Y. Berakhot 2:4; see also Tosafot, Berakhot 16b, s.v. *istenis*.
16. Tosafot, ibid.; Rosh, Mo'ed Katan 3:37; *Shulḥan Arukh, Yoreh De'ah* 381:3.

One who is especially delicate [*istenis*], and experiences great discomfort, may bathe. The Talmud[17] relates:

> [Rabban Gamliel] bathed on the first night after his wife died. His students said to him: Haven't you taught us, our teacher, that a mourner is prohibited from bathing? He answered them: I am not like other people; I am delicate [*istenis*].

*Shulḥan Arukh*[18] cites this leniency, but appears to limit its application. He writes that not every person who claims to be an *istenis* may wash; rather, only those who are known to be particularly fastidious may do so. Today, especially in warmer climates, a mourner who experiences extreme discomfort from not bathing may shower, briefly, in lukewarm water.[19]

A woman may wash to perform a *hefsek tahara*, but she does not immerse in the *mikveh* during the week of mourning. A woman whose husband is in mourning may immerse in the *mikveh*, despite the prohibition of marital relations. A person who experiences two consecutive mourning periods [*tekhafuhu avelut*] may bathe his entire body in cold water after the first week.[20]

In addition to the prohibition of bathing, a woman may not wear makeup during the week of mourning.[21] A married woman may wear makeup after *shiva*.[22] Similarly, a married woman may dye her hair after *shiva*. A new bride during the first thirty days of marriage,[23] as well as a woman of marriageable age,[24] may wear makeup even during the seven days of mourning.

17. Berakhot 16b.
18. *Shulḥan Arukh, Yoreh De'ah* 381:3. Ramban (*Torat HaAdam, Inyan HaAvelut, BeReḥitza Keitzad*) cites this formulation in the name of R. Hai Gaon.
19. R. Maurice Lamm (*The Jewish Way in Death and Mourning*, p. 121) writes, "One who is very sensitive, *istenis*, and is accustomed to showering every single day, and experiences discomfort at having to forgo that necessity (not for him a luxury), may shower even during *shiva*. He should be careful to do so inconspicuously. In general, in our society, people who customarily shower several times a week, and experience discomfort when they are prevented from doing so, may shower during *shiva*."
20. Taanit 13b.
21. See Mo'ed Katan 20b; Taanit 13b.
22. Rosh (Ketubot 1:6) and *Shulḥan Arukh* (*Yoreh De'ah* 381:6), "so that she should not become unattractive to her husband."
23. Ketubot 4a.
24. Taanit 13b.

As mentioned above, the prohibitions of bathing and anointing last for the seven days of mourning. Rema relates that there is an "ancient custom, established by *vatikin* [pious individuals]" to refrain from bathing for the entire thirty-day period [*sheloshim*] as well.[25] Today, this stringency is not observed, and it is customary to resume normal bathing after the week of mourning.[26] It is proper, however, to refrain from swimming for pleasure.[27]

Although anointing is prohibited, one may use medicinal lotions, moisturizers for dry skin, and deodorants. Children, who are not obligated to observe the laws of mourning, may bathe during the week of mourning.[28]

## LAUNDERING

The Talmud[29] teaches that it is prohibited for a mourner to launder clothing.

> It is prohibited for a mourner to launder his garments, as it is written: "Joab sent to Tekoa, and he took from there a wise woman, and he said to her: Please mourn, and please don garments of mourning, and do not anoint with oil, and you shall be as a woman mourning for a dead person for these many days" (II Sam. 14:2).

The Gemara derives the prohibition of laundering from the phrase, "and please don garments of mourning [*bigdei evel*]." The *Rishonim* differ as to the scope and nature of this law.

---

25. Rema, *Yoreh De'ah* 381:1. The *Aḥaronim* debate the scope of this stringency. Shakh (1) writes that it includes all bathing, while the *Dagul Merevava* limits this practice to bathing one's entire body. This stringency originally appeared in the *Or Zarua* (*Hilkhot Avelut* 435). There are different explanations for this practice. Some suggest that bathing during *sheloshim* may lead to a violation of the prohibition of cutting one's hair. For example, the *Or Zarua* (ibid.) writes: "We fear that we may come to comb his hair, which is prohibited for the entire thirty days" (his assertion that combing one's hair is also prohibited is most likely based upon the laws of the Nazirite [Nazir 42a], although in practice combing one's hair is permitted throughout the month [*Shulḥan Arukh, Yoreh De'ah* 390:6]). Maharshal, cited by *Taz* (2), writes that since one who enters the bathhouse generally gets a haircut as well, bathing is also prohibited. R. Aharon Lichtenstein (*Minḥat Aviv*, pp. 311–19) suggests that this custom is in line with the nature of the thirty-day mourning period in that it involves refraining from pleasure.
26. *Arukh HaShulḥan* (*Yoreh De'ah* 381:4) writes that one may wash without soap after *shiva*. It is customary to permit bathing even with soap after *shiva*.
27. See *Sefer Kol Bo al Avelut*, p. 356.
28. *Arukh HaShulḥan* 381:9.
29. Mo'ed Katan 15a.

Rashi[30] maintains that the Talmud prohibits only laundering garments, but that one may wear laundered garments. This prohibition may be related to the general prohibition of labor [*issur melakha*] in effect during *shiva*,[31] or to preventing the mourner from being distracted from his mourning. However, the verse that refers to *bigdei evel* indicates that the focus of this prohibition is on the garments, and not on the act of laundering. Therefore, another explanation may be suggested: When Joab tells the woman to "don garments of mourning," he is, in essence, telling her to diverge from her daily routine and refrain from caring for herself, which includes laundering her garments. This allows her to focus on mourning the deceased.

Other *Rishonim*[32] disagree, and explain that not only is the mourner obligated to refrain from washing his clothes, but the central obligation is to wear *bigdei evel*, meaning that it is prohibited to wear laundered clothing. *Shulḥan Arukh*[33] rules in accordance with this view. Interestingly, the *Laḥmei Toda*[34] rules that just as it is only bathing and anointing for pleasure that are prohibited, so too, it is only wearing laundered clothing for pleasure that is prohibited. If, however, one's garment becomes stained or dirty, one may change into laundered clothing.[35]

Which garments are included in the prohibition of laundering? Laundered clothing that is intended to absorb perspiration [*bigdei ze'a*], such as underwear and socks, may be worn. *Shulḥan Arukh*[36] rules that the prohibition includes laundering linens, towels, and even hand towels. One may wash the clothes of a child who is in mourning.[37]

30. Rashi is cited in Tosafot (Mo'ed Katan 24b, s.v. *birkat avelim*) and Ramban (*Torat HaAdam, Inyan HaAvelut, BeTikhboset Keitzad*).
31. See Ramban, ibid.
32. See Tosafot, ibid.; Ramban, ibid.
33. *Shulḥan Arukh, Yoreh De'ah* 399:1.
34. Cited in *Pitḥei Teshuva* 399:2. The *Laḥmei Toda* suggests that earlier authorities did not write this explicitly as it is "obvious." See also *Pitḥei Teshuva* 381:3.
35. *Penei Barukh* (18:4) writes that one may even wash the shirt, without soap, in order to remove the dirt. He cites *Sedei Ḥemed*, who writes that one who changes into laundered clothing should have another person wear the clothing first, as mentioned below regarding *sheloshim*. When mourning for a parent, one must rend the new shirt as well.
36. *Shulḥan Arukh, Yoreh De'ah* 389:1; see also Rosh, Mo'ed Katan 3:53; *Mordekhai*, Mo'ed Katan 905.
37. See *Mordekhai*, Mo'ed Katan 905; *Shulḥan Arukh*, ibid., 2.

Some *Rishonim* rule that one should not wear laundered clothing even on Shabbat;[38] however, it is customary to wear Shabbat clothing in order to avoid a public display of mourning.

### WEARING LEATHER SHOES [*NE'ILAT HASANDAL*]

The Talmud[39] teaches that during the seven days of mourning, the mourner is not permitted to wear leather shoes.

> A mourner is prohibited from wearing shoes. Since the Merciful One says to [Ezekiel with regard to how his mourning rites should differ from the accepted custom]: "And put your shoes upon your feet" (Ezek. 24:17), which shows by inference that everyone else, i.e., all other mourners, is prohibited [from wearing shoes].

Ramban[40] explains that although some of the laws of mourning,[41] including those regarding bathing, anointing, marital relations, and *tefillin*, as well as laundering and cutting one's hair, are intended to minimize physical indulgence [*idunim*] or joy [*simḥa*], refraining from wearing leather shoes is supposed to cause discomfort. Alternatively, refraining from wearing shoes may be a sign of withdrawing from standard, day-to-day life, similar to other expressions of mourning.

This prohibition includes only leather shoes,[42] or shoes that are made of another material but covered with leather. A woman within thirty days of

---

38. See *Kol Bo* 114; Rivash 67. Rema (*Yoreh De'ah* 389:3) records that some prohibit wearing Shabbat clothing for the entire thirty-day period of mourning. R. David b. Solomon ibn Zimra (Radbaz 2:693) rejects this custom, as it violates the honor and sanctity of Shabbat.
39. Mo'ed Katan 15b.
40. *Torat HaAdam, Inyan HaAvelut*. Rambam (*Hilkhot Avel* 1:1) appears to disagree with this distinction.
41. According to Ramban, these laws are of Torah origin, in contrast to *ne'ilat hasandal*; see chapter 4.
42. The *Rishonim* disagree, regarding Yom Kippur, whether the prohibition of *ne'ilat hasandal* includes all protective shoes (Baal HaMaor, Yoma 2a), only leather shoes (Rif, Yoma 2a), or shoes that protect one from feeling the hardness of the ground (Rambam, *Hilkhot Shevitat HeAsor* 3:7). Some write that it is preferable to refrain from wearing comfortable shoes made from other materials (see *Mishna Berura* 614:5). Regarding *avelut*, the *Shulḥan Arukh* (*Yoreh De'ah* 382:1) appears to prohibit only leather shoes; see also *Gesher HaḤayim* (21:4). *Penei Barukh* (20:1) suggests that it is proper to be stringent.

giving birth,[43] a person who is ill[44] or with a foot injury, as well was one who is traveling,[45] may wear leather shoes. It is customary to wear non-leather shoes to the funeral or to remove one's shoes immediately after the burial.[46]

## SEXUAL RELATIONS [*TASHMISH HAMITA*]

The Talmud[47] teaches that during *shiva,* the mourner must refrain from marital relations.

> A mourner is prohibited from engaging in sexual relations, as it is written: "David consoled Bathsheba his wife, and came to her, and lay with her" (II Sam. 12:24), [after their son had died]. This proves by inference that initially, [during the period of mourning, sexual relations] were forbidden.

Furthermore, the Gemara[48] relates:

> A sage taught in Evel Rabbati: A mourner is prohibited from engaging in sexual relations during his days of mourning. There was an incident involving one who engaged in sexual relations during his days of mourning and [he was punished, for after his death] pigs dragged away his corpse.

The Gemara apparently seeks to convey that just as one did not properly respect his deceased relative, he too will not be properly respected after his death.

What is included in the prohibition of marital relations? The Talmud[49] clearly states that other forms of intimacy that are prohibited when

43. See *Shulḥan Arukh, Yoreh De'ah* 382:2.
44. Shakh, ibid., 1. Some suggest that today, since non-leather shoes are often as comfortable as leather shoes, a woman who recently gave birth, and a person who is ill, should not wear leather shoes (*Nitei Gavriel, Hilkhot Yom HaKippurim* 47:11; *Penei Barukh* 20:2, n. 8). R. Ovadia Yosef (*Ḥazon Ovadia, Avelut,* vol. 2, p. 175) disagrees.
45. *Shulḥan Arukh,* ibid., 4.
46. Rosh (Mo'ed Katan 3:39) writes that the mourner removes his shoes when he returns home. Others rule that one should remove his shoes, when this is possible, immediately after the burial; see *Shulḥan Arukh, Yoreh De'ah* 375:1.
47. Mo'ed Katan 15b.
48. Mo'ed Katan 24a; see Semaḥot, *Beraitot MeEvel Rabbati* 1:3.
49. In Ketubot 4b it states: "In truth, they said that she may pour his drink into the cup; arrange his bed; and wash his face, hands, and feet."

one's wife is a *nidda* due to precautionary prohibitions [*harḥakot*], are not prohibited during *shiva*. This is also the ruling of *Shulḥan Arukh*.[50]

Most *Rishonim* rule that just as the other forms of intimacy are permitted, as there is no fear that the mourner will engage in marital relations during the week of mourning, so too, the couple may sleep in the same bed, clothed.[51] Raavad[52] suggests that one should be stringent in this regard.

> However, in the same way we say to a Nazirite: "Go around, go around; do not approach the vineyard," so too, a man should maintain distance and not sleep with his wife together in a bed at all [during this period of mourning].

*Shulḥan Arukh*[53] rules in accordance with the lenient opinion but does cite Raavad's concern.

Raavad[54] rules that there is no prohibition of physical contact, e.g., hugging and kissing [*ḥibuk venishuk*]. This ruling is cited by other *Rishonim* as well.[55] Rabbeinu Yeruḥam,[56] however, writes:

> It is appropriate to be strict and not permit any form of intimacy except for pouring his cup; spreading his bed linen; and washing his face, hands, and feet, since the Gemara did not explicitly permit anything else [besides these three].

Rabbeinu Yeruḥam appears to prohibit other forms of intimacy. R. Shlomo Luria (Maharshal)[57] supports this opinion, and explains that hugging and kissing, which typically lead to sexual relations, are prohibited.

---

50. *Shulḥan Arukh, Yoreh De'ah* 383:3.
51. See, for example, Rosh, Ketubot 1:9; Ramban, *Torat HaAdam, Inyan HaAvelut, Tashmish HaMita Keitzad*.
52. *Baalei HaNefesh, Shaar HaPerisha* 2.
53. Ibid.
54. *Baalei HaNefesh, Shaar HaPerisha* 3.
55. See Rosh, Mo'ed Katan 3:36; Ramban, ibid.
56. *Toldot Adam VeḤava*, 28:232.
57. Cited in *Baḥ* 383, s.v. *vekhatav haRaavad*.

Although this stringency does not appear in the *Shulḥan Arukh*, Rema[58] writes, "Regarding hugging and kissing it is appropriate to be stringent." Interestingly, R. Akiva Eiger (1761–1837), in his commentary on this Rema, cites the Aramaic translation (Targum) of Ecclesiastes (3:5), which explains:

> "A time to embrace and a time to refrain from embracing" – there is a time to embrace one's wife, and a time to refrain from embracing, during the seven days of mourning.

The *Aḥaronim*[59] explain that this is a stringency and not the actual law.

In summary, while marital relations are prohibited during the week of mourning, all other forms of intimacy are permitted. Although some suggest that the mourner should avoid physical contact of an intimate nature, this should be left to the discretion of the mourner and weighed against the value of the emotional support and comfort provided by that contact.

### WORK [*ISSUR MELAKHA*] DURING *SHIVA*

The Talmud[60] teaches that a mourner should not work during the seven-day period of mourning. The Gemara teaches that just as one should refrain from labor during the intermediate days of a festival (Ḥol HaMo'ed), so too, a mourner should refrain from labor.

> A mourner is prohibited from performing labor, as it is written: "And I will turn your festivals into mourning" (Amos 8:10). The Gemara infers: Just as a festival is a time when it is prohibited to perform labor, so too, a mourner is prohibited from performing labor.

Rambam[61] notes that unlike the other prohibitions, here the verse is merely an allusion [*remez*], and not a full-fledged source for the prohibition. This prohibition enables the mourner to focus on his loss, and not be distracted by his day-to-day routine. These laws are somewhat complex, and when in doubt, one should consult with his local halakhic authority.

---

58. Rema, ibid.
59. See, for example, *Shulḥan Arukh HaRav, Yoreh De'ah* 184, *Kuntres Aḥaron*, n. 1.
60. Mo'ed Katan 15b.
61. Rambam, *Hilkhot Avel* 5:7.

The Gemara[62] teaches that a poor person,[63] who is supported by charity, may work, although in a limited manner. It states:

> The sages taught: During the first three days[64] after his bereavement, a mourner is prohibited from labor, even if he is a poor person who is supported by charity. From this point forward, he may perform labor privately in his own home if he needs to do so. And similarly, a woman may spin thread on a spindle in her own home when she is mourning.

The Yerushalmi[65] warns that a "curse will fall upon a community that allows its poor to work" during the days of mourning. That said, authorities as recent as the *Arukh HaShulḥan* write that it is obvious that "as a result of our sins, when there is much poverty, [a poor person] can perform labor himself, even on the first day."

The *Aḥaronim* discuss whether a mourner's employees may continue to work during *shiva*, as not working would cause financial loss [*davar haaved*] for the mourner and/or the employee.[66]

One is not permitted to engage in business during the *shiva*.[67] A mourner should close his store or small business for the entire seven-day mourning period. The mourner's partner may not work in the store during *shiva*.[68] It is proper to arrange a halakhic "sale" of the business, or for the mourner to

---

62. Mo'ed Katan 21b.
63. The *Rishonim* disagree as to whether the leniency that appears in the Talmud applies to all mourners, or only to the poor; see *Beit Yosef, Yoreh De'ah* 380.
64. R. Yosef Karo (*Beit Yosef*, ibid.) cites a disagreement regarding the uniqueness of the first three days. While the Yerushalmi (Y. Mo'ed Katan 3:5) describes how the soul hovers over the body during the first three days after burial, Rabbeinu Yeruḥam explains that the first three days are described as "days of crying" [*shelosha yamim lebekhi*], and one who works during these days is perceived as being lax in properly grieving for his loss. Furthermore, the *Aḥaronim* dispute whether the principle of: The legal status of part of the day is like that of an entire day [*miktzat hayom kekhulo*] applies to this third day; see Rema, *Yoreh De'ah* 393:1.
65. Y. Mo'ed Katan 3:5.
66. See *Arukh HaShulḥan, Yoreh De'ah* 380:6; *Gesher HaḤayim* 21:2:3.
67. See *Shulḥan Arukh, Yoreh De'ah* 380:3.
68. *Shulḥan Arukh, Yoreh De'ah* 380:21. *Ḥokhmat Adam* writes that it is customary to be lenient after the first three days of mourning.

"remove" himself from the business and its profits[69] before the death, or if necessary, during the period of *aninut*. This is accomplished through a *kinyan sudar*. As this matter is complex the mourner should consult with his halakhic authority.

One is permitted to perform household chores, including cooking and cleaning, during the *shiva*.[70]

### TORAH STUDY [*TALMUD TORAH*]

The Talmud[71] teaches that a mourner should not engage in Torah study during the week of mourning.

> A mourner is prohibited from studying matters of Torah. This prohibition is derived from the fact that the Merciful One says to Ezekiel: "Sigh in silence" (Ezek. 24:17).

God commanded Ezekiel, after the death of his wife, to "sigh in silence." The Gemara understands that this silence includes refraining from Torah study. Elsewhere, the Gemara[72] elaborates on the prohibition.

> And he is prohibited from reading in the Torah, and in the Prophets, and in the Writings, and from studying in the Mishna, in the Midrash, and in the halakhot, and in the Talmud, and in the *aggadot*.

Seemingly the Talmud prohibits studying all of the major areas of Torah.

Studying Torah is also prohibited on Tisha B'Av, the day upon which we mourn the destruction of the First and Second Temples. The Talmud teaches that "All mitzvot practiced by a mourner are likewise practiced on the ninth of Av." Therefore, in addition to the prohibitions of eating, drinking, applying oil to one's body, wearing shoes, and sexual relations, the Gemara adds:

> It is prohibited to read from the Torah, from the Prophets, and from the Writings, or to study from the Mishna, from the Gemara, and from Midrash, and from collections of halakhot, and from collections

69. See *Gilyon Maharsha, Yoreh De'ah* 380.
70. *Shulḥan Arukh, Yoreh De'ah* 380:22.
71. Mo'ed Katan 15a.
72. Ibid., 21a.

> of *aggadot*... One may read from the Book of Lamentations; from the Book of Job; and from the sad portions of Jeremiah, i.e., his prophecies of doom. And schoolchildren interrupt their studies for the day, because it is stated: "The precepts of the Lord are just, rejoicing the heart" (Ps. 19:9).

On Tisha B'Av, it is permitted to study sections of the Torah that are consistent with the character of the day.

What is the nature of the prohibition of Torah study during the seven-day mourning period, and does the leniency mentioned above apply to *shiva* as well?

On the one hand, one might suggest that the obligation to refrain from Torah study is similar to the obligations to refrain from bathing, anointing, and wearing laundered clothing, i.e., activities that facilitate physical or spiritual comfort, in which case it would be permitted to study topics that are not "rejoicing the heart." On the other hand, while the Talmud explains that one may not study Torah on Tisha B'Av because "the precepts of the Lord are just, rejoicing the heart," the mourner's obligation to refrain from Torah study stems from a different source: "Sigh in silence." Indeed, Me'iri[73] writes:

> The mourner is prohibited from Torah [study], as God said to Ezekiel, "Sigh in silence," as we explained, and this prohibition lasts all seven days... The [prohibition] of the mourner is an expression of "silence," and on Tisha B'Av it depends upon anguish [*tzaar*].

Me'iri, therefore, explains that since refraining from Torah study expresses a much broader theme of mourning – silence – all Torah study would be included in the prohibition, while on Tisha B'Av one may study topics that do not arouse happiness.[74]

---

73. *Beit HaBeḥira*, Mo'ed Katan 15a.
74. Interestingly, some *Aḥaronim* suggest that whether or not one may contemplate Torah matters [*hirhur*] may also depend upon this question. Maharil (201) prohibits *hirhur* on Tisha B'Av and for a mourner, as contemplating Torah brings happiness. The *Shulḥan Arukh* (*Oraḥ Ḥayim* 554:4) cites this opinion regarding Tisha B'Av. Some *Aḥaronim* question whether to extend this to the laws of mourning as well, where the prohibition may be rooted in "silence," and not *simḥa*. See, for example, *Alei Tamar*, Mo'ed Katan, chap. 3.

Tosafot[75] grapple with this question as well. They relate that Rabbeinu Tam, in his youth, prohibited studying these topics during *shiva,* as the Talmud does not mention this leniency in the context of *avelut.* In his later years, however, he changed his mind and permitted studying those topics that may be studied on Tisha B'Av.

*Shulḥan Arukh*[76] permits studying the Books of Job and Lamentations, the sad portions of Jeremiah, and the laws of mourning. One may also study works of *mussar.*[77] In addition, one may issue halakhic rulings, if necessary.[78]

Interestingly, the Yerushalmi[79] rules that "one who is overcome by his desire to learn Torah [*lahut aḥar haTorah*]" may study Torah. Although this leniency is not cited in the Talmud Bavli, or by the classic halakhic authorities, the *Aḥaronim* offer different explanations of this passage.

R. Yechiel Michel Epstein, for example, in his *Arukh HaShulḥan,*[80] explains:

> One desires Torah like a starving person desires food and if they do not feed him he will be overcome with hunger pangs and will be in physical danger; similarly, a person who desires Torah is considered to be in a mild state of danger [*ketzat sakana*].

Alternatively, *Gesher HaḤayim*[81] likens this prohibition to the prohibitions of bathing and anointing:

> The prohibition to study Torah is similar to the prohibition to bathe and to anoint, which are prohibited only when they provide enjoyment [*taanug*]. This person, however, who is suffering, is similar to an *istenis,* who is permitted to bathe and anoint as he intends only to alleviate his discomfort; here too, the same is true regarding studying Torah.

---

75. Tosafot, Mo'ed Katan 21a, s.v. *ve'asur.*
76. *Shulḥan Arukh, Yoreh De'ah* 384:4.
77. *Gesher HaḤayim* 21:5:1.
78. Mo'ed Katan 21a; *Shulḥan Arukh, Yoreh De'ah* 384:4; see also *Arukh HaShulḥan, Yoreh De'ah* 384:6.
79. Y. Mo'ed Katan 3:5; *Penei Moshe* explains that he "desires and is attached to Torah and to learning it constantly."
80. *Arukh HaShulḥan, Yoreh De'ah* 384:3.
81. *Gesher HaḤayim* 21:2.

Interestingly, R. Yissachar Tamar (1896–1982), in his commentary to the Yerushalmi,[82] relates that R. Yosef Rosen (1858–1936), known as the Rogatchover Gaon, studied Torah [*haya mefalpel bedivrei Torah*] on Tisha B'Av, and when he was a mourner, based upon this passage.

The *Aḥaronim* discuss whether a mourner may recite the biblical verses and rabbinic passages that constitute the daily *korbanot* segment of the morning prayer. While the mourner may certainly recite the *Parashat HaTamid, Eizehu Mekoman,* and the *Baraita* of R. Yishmael,[83] some omit the other passages, e.g., *Pitum HaKetoret.*[84] R. Ovadia Yosef rules that the mourner may recite all of these passages.[85]

## GREETING [*SHE'ELAT SHALOM*]

The Talmud[86] teaches that a mourner must refrain from extending or returning greetings and inquiring into another's welfare during the seven-day period of mourning.

> A mourner is prohibited from greeting [others or being greeted]. This is derived from the fact that the Merciful One says to Ezekiel: "Sigh in silence" (Ezek. 24:17).

As will be explained below, others should refrain from greeting the mourner as well.

What is the reason for this prohibition? On the one hand, this prohibition, derived from the phrase "Sigh in silence," reflects and dictates the mood of the mourner and comforters. As R. Maurice Lamm articulates:[87]

> With the shocking disruption of normal life caused by a death in the family, the standard forms of social intercourse, its niceties and graces and minutiae of etiquette, are without significance. The mourning

82. *Alei Tamar,* Mo'ed Katan, chap. 3.
83. See *Shulḥan Arukh, Oraḥ Ḥayim* 554:4 (regarding Tisha B'Av). The *Mishna Berura* (7) relates that in some communities *Eizehu Mekoman* is not recited in the mourner's house, but he disagrees with this practice.
84. *Gesher HaḤayim* 21:5:3.
85. *Yalkut Yosef, Avelut* 29:7.
86. Mo'ed Katan 15a.
87. R. Maurice Lamm, *The Jewish Way in Death and Mourning,* pp. 117–18.

> heart has no patience for these formalities. Tradition, thus, scorns all types of greeting during *shiva.*
>
> The sages, who consistently demand that one greet all men graciously and courteously, regard greetings as out of place when spoken by, or to, the mourner. It is absurd to say to a man deep in anguish over someone he loved, "Hello. How are you feeling today?" This is not only a question that cannot be answered; it indicates a lack of compassion and understanding. The *shalom aleichems* and the hellos are hollow and purposeless, even offensive, to the despairing heart. Certainly, as Maimonides, the twelfth-century sage, taught, we must strongly discourage the misplaced small talk and lightheartedness of some mindless visitors. The rejection of greetings at this time, far from betraying a lack of cordiality, issues from a profound insight into man's nature and a deep compassion for his predicament. This law, as so many other laws of bereavement, originated with Ezekiel. God tells Ezekiel (24:17): "Sigh in silence." Indeed, how can one mourn more eloquently than by "sighing in silence"?

On the other hand, some focus on the greeting itself. The standard greeting in rabbinic literature is *shalom. Shalom* connotes completeness, which is certainly not appropriate for the mourner, who is experiencing loss. Furthermore, as R. Lamm continues,

> "*Shalom*" is one of the names of God, and greeting in the name of God at a time when God has taken a close relative could conceivably be, in the spirit of the mourner, an intimation of scoffing and an invitation to question God's justice, at a time when he is required to proclaim God's justice, as in the *tziduk hadin* prayer.

According to this second approach, we might be more inclined to permit standard, polite greetings such as "Good morning."[88] Furthermore, some insist that even other people in the house of the mourner should refrain from using the word *shalom.*[89]

88. See *Be'er Heitev, Yoreh De'ah* 385:2; see also *Gesher HaḤayim* 21:7:5.
89. See *Arukh HaShulḥan, Yoreh De'ah* 385:4.

The Talmud[90] enumerates the times during which the mourner and the comforters should refrain from exchanging greetings.

> The sages taught: A mourner, during the first three days [after his bereavement], is prohibited from extending greetings to others. From the third day to the seventh day, he may respond when other people address him, but he may not extend greetings to them. From this point forward, he may extend greetings and respond in his usual manner.

In summary, the mourner should not extend a greeting to others until after *shiva,* but may respond, if greeted, after the first three days. Others should refrain from greeting the mourner for the entire period of mourning, i.e., twelve months for one mourning a parent and thirty days for one mourning other relatives. The Gemara adds that the mourner may offer his greetings to a large group, as "deference to the public is different."[91]

When parting from a mourner during the *shiva,* it is customary to say "May God comfort you among the other mourners of Zion and Jerusalem."[92] In Sephardic communities, and in many communities in Israel, the comforters say "May you be comforted from the heavens." In some places, it is customary to shake the mourner's hand and wish him a "long life."[93]

How should one speak to the mourner after *shiva*? The Talmud[94] teaches:

> One who finds another in mourning during the first thirty days of that person's bereavement may still speak words of consolation to him, but he should not extend greetings toward him. If he finds him after thirty days, he may extend greetings toward him, but he should not speak words of consolation to him [so as not to remind him of his pain].

When one meets another who is mourning a parent, he may console him

90. Mo'ed Katan 21b.
91. See Rema, *Yoreh De'ah* 385:1.
92. See *Perisha* 393:3.
93. R. Tzvi Pesach Frank (*Har Tzvi, Yoreh De'ah* 290) and R. Yechiel Yaakov Weinberg (*Seridei Esh* 2:135), apparently responding to the same question, explain that this is not considered to be a form of *she'elat shalom*.
94. Mo'ed Katan 21b.

for the entire twelve months. After the thirty-day mourning period, or twelve months for one mourning a parent, one should avoid comforting the mourner in a manner that may cause him grief.

In practice, Rema[95] records that it is not customary to refrain from greeting the mourner after the thirty-day mourning period, regarding those mourning their parents. He observes that "there is no apparent reason for this practice unless our greetings are not considered to be the greetings from their (i.e., the Talmud's) time."[96]

The Yerushalmi[97] teaches that whether or not one extends greetings to a mourner on Shabbat depends upon the local custom [*minhag hamakom*]. *Shulḥan Arukh* cites this passage as well as Rambam, who insists that refraining from greeting a mourner on Shabbat would be considered a public display of mourning, which is prohibited. Maharil[98] records that the custom is not to extend greetings to mourners even on Shabbat.

Rema[99] writes that one should also refrain from sending the mourner gifts during the entire period of mourning, as sending gifts is similar to *she'elat shalom*. He also rules that one should not send *mishlo'aḥ manot* on Purim during the period of mourning.[100] One may, however, send *mishlo'aḥ manot* to the mourner's spouse, or to his entire family. One may also send *mishlo'aḥ manot* to a mourner as an expression of respect, such as to a rabbi or to one's parent.[101]

## TURNING OVER THE BEDS [*KEFIYAT HAMITA*] AND COVERING ONE'S HEAD [*ATIFAT HAROSH*]

In addition to the prohibitions discussed above, there are two active expressions of mourning – *kefiyat hamita* and *atifat harosh*. As we will see, neither of these practices, at least in their original form, is observed nowadays.

The Talmud[102] teaches that one must overturn one's chair or bed

95. Rema, *Yoreh De'ah* 385:1.
96. Shakh (2) disagrees, and contends that according to this rationale, which is not articulated by any earlier authorities, one should be lenient even earlier.
97. Y. Berakhot 2:7.
98. Maharil 31:1.
99. Ibid., 385:3; see Maharil 31:1.
100. Rema, *Oraḥ Ḥayim* 696:7.
101. See *Piskei Teshuvot* 696:10.
102. See Mo'ed Katan 21a; Semaḥot 11:15.

during the seven days of mourning. This practice is known as *kefiyat hamita*. The Gemara[103] explains:

> A mourner is obligated to overturn his bed, as bar Kappara taught [that God stated]: I have placed the likeness of My image (*deyokan*) within humans, and owing to their sins I have overturned it [as when this person died the divine image in him was removed]. Therefore, you too must overturn your beds on account of this.

Unlike other mourning practices, which interrupt the mourner's daily routine, and limit his physical and even spiritual pleasure, *kefiyat hamita* apparently symbolizes the loss of human life, of God's image.

In addition to overturning one's bed, there is a second aspect of *kefiyat hamita*: The mourner is supposed to sit and sleep on the overturned bed.[104] Indeed, the Yerushalmi[105] teaches:

> And from where do we derive the practice of *kefiyat hamita*? R. Kerispi said in the name of R. Yoḥanan: The verse states, "They sat with him to the ground [*laaretz*]" (Job 2:13). The verse does not say "on the ground [*al haaretz*]," but rather "to the ground," [indicating that they sat upon] something close to the ground. We derive from here that they slept on overturned beds.

The verse describes how Job's three friends come to comfort him, and sit with him close to the ground.

Perhaps there is a distinction: While overturning beds reflects the loss of human life, as described above, sitting on the overturned bed may reflect a different theme. Sitting on an overturned bed reflects a break from one's routine, and may even cause slight physical discomfort, appropriate for one in mourning.[106]

---

103. Mo'ed Katan 15a–b.

104. R. Yitzchak Ze'ev Soloveitchik, in his *Ḥiddushei HaRiz al HaRambam* (*Hilkhot Avel* 4:9), develops the theory that there are two distinct aspects of *kefiyat hamita* – the beds should remain overturned all week, and the mourner should sit on overturned beds.

105. Y. Mo'ed Katan 3:5.

106. The *Rishonim* disagree as to whether one is obligated to sit or sleep on the overturned

In practice, the *Rishonim*[107] record that it is no longer customary to observe this practice. Some suggest, based on a passage in the Yerushalmi, that *kefiyat hamita* was viewed by gentile neighbors as a form of witchcraft or magic. Others suggest that in the Middle Ages, beds were easily overturned and it was no longer clear whether one was sleeping on the underside of a bed, and therefore it was no longer a significant expression of mourning.

Although *kefiyat hamita* is no longer formally practiced, the *Aḥaronim* note that the custom not to sit on regular chairs remains. They even assert that it is proper to sleep on the ground.[108] *Gesher HaḤayim* writes that while it is proper to sit on a low stool or chair, it is no longer customary to sleep on the ground.[109] Furthermore, those who come to visit and comfort the mourner do not sit on low chairs.[110] Those who cannot sit on a low chair due to age or physical discomfort may sit on a regular chair.

Some explain that the widespread custom of covering the mirrors in the home of the mourner is a fulfillment of this practice, as we will explain in the next chapter.

The second mourning practice mentioned in the Talmud is *atifat harosh*. The Talmud teaches:

> A mourner is obligated to wrap his head [as a sign of mourning, covering his head and face]. This is derived from the fact that the Merciful One says to Ezekiel [while he is in mourning]: "And do not cover your upper lip" (Ezek. 24:17). [God commands Ezekiel not to display outward signs of mourning, which proves] by inference that everyone else is obligated [to wrap their heads in this manner.]

Elsewhere,[111] the Gemara describes this wrapping:

bed (Rambam), or under the bed (see *Tur* 387).

107. See, for example, Tosafot, Mo'ed Katan 21a, s.v. *elu*; Rosh, Mo'ed Katan 3:78.

108. See Shakh and *Taz* 387:1.

109. *Gesher HaḤayim* 20:5:10.

110. See *Yalkut Shimoni*, Job 893; Rif, Mo'ed Katan 18a; and *Shulḥan Arukh* (*Yoreh De'ah* 387:1), who rules that those who come to comfort the mourner should also sit on a low chair. Shakh (ibid., 1) relates that it is no longer customary for visitors to sit on low chairs.

111. Mo'ed Katan 24a.

> And any wrapping of the head that is not performed in the manner of the wrapping of the Ishmaelites [who wrap their heads on all sides], is not considered proper wrapping. R. Naḥman demonstrated [the procedure by covering his face to the] sides of the beard [leaving only the center of his face exposed].

The *Shulḥan Arukh*[112] rules that the mourner covers his head at all times, except in the presence of guests.

Here too, the *Rishonim* explain that *atifat harosh* is no longer performed. Tosafot[113] explain that in addition to the fear that gentiles may view *atifat harosh* as a form of sorcery, the manner in which one is supposed to wrap one's head may elicit laughter [*seḥok*]. Although one should not be embarrassed by those who scoff at him for worshipping God,[114] in this context levity would undermine the entire purpose of the mourning practice.

Interestingly, *Arukh HaShulḥan*[115] notes that although it is no longer customary to observe *atifat harosh* in the traditional sense, "the contemporary form of *atifa* is to pull one's hat down toward his eyes, and it is proper for a mourner not to remove his hat from his head the entire seven days and to sit that way if it is possible." The custom is not in accordance with this suggestion.[116]

## REJOICING [*SIMḤA*]

In addition to the eleven expressions of mourning enumerated by Rambam, and discussed above, there is a broad prohibition of "*simḥa*" during the entire period of mourning.[117] Aside from a few halakhic expressions of this prohibition during the week of *shiva*, e.g., refraining from playing with a baby,[118] refraining from reciting the blessing over the new moon [*Kiddush Levana*], which is supposed to be said in a festive mood,[119] and omitting the *pesukei simḥa*

112. *Shulḥan Arukh, Yoreh De'ah* 386:1.
113. Tosafot, Mo'ed Katan 21a, s.v. *elu*.
114. See Rema, *Oraḥ Ḥayim* 1:1.
115. *Arukh HaShulḥan, Yoreh De'ah* 386.
116. R. Moshe Sternbach (*Teshuvot VeHanhagot* 1:683) writes that a hat would not be considered a proper form of *atifa*.
117. See *Levush, Yoreh De'ah* 391.
118. Mo'ed Katan 26b. Of course, a parent must tend to his or her children during the mourning period; the Talmud refers to public displays of playful laughter [*seḥok*].
119. See *Pitḥei Teshuva* 391:1. He concludes that the mourner should not recite *Birkat*

recited before the Havdala blessings,[120] the prohibitions relating to attending social and festive gatherings are usually more relevant during the thirty-day period of mourning, or during the twelve months of mourning for one's parent.

However, there are occasions on which a mourner, during *shiva*, may participate in certain festivities. For example, a mourner may wear festive garments [*bigdei Shabbat*] and leather shoes to his son's *Brit Mila* during the seven-day mourning period[121] and may participate in the *seudat mitzva*, which ideally should be held in the mourner's house.[122] Some even permit the grandparents, if they are mourners, to attend the *seudat mitzva*.[123] A mourner may serve as the *mohel* or the *sandak*, wearing *bigdei Shabbat*, but should not participate in the *seudat mitzva*.[124] Similar to the case of a *Brit Mila*, the parents of a baby boy, together with a Kohen, may hold a *Pidyon HaBen* during the seven days of mourning, wearing *bigdei Shabbat*,[125] and may participate in the *seudat mitzva*.

The parents of a child whose bar mitzva occurs during the week of mourning may join the child as he is called to the Torah, but the *seudat mitzva* should be held after the *shiva*.[126] Finally, as we discuss in chapter 11, some *Aḥaronim* permit a parent who is in mourning to attend the wedding of his child, although the parent should not eat with the other guests.[127]

## THE SEVENTH DAY: THE CONCLUSION OF THE *SHIVA*

The Talmud[128] teaches that although one is required to observe seven full days of mourning, in practice, we apply the halakhic principle "The legal status of part of the day is like that of the entire day [*miktzat hayom kekhulo*]," and the mourner ends his observance of the laws of *shiva* in the morning,[129]

---

*HaLevana* during the first three days of mourning, and should refrain from reciting the blessing during *shiva* unless it will be too late to recite it after *shiva*.

120. *Pitḥei Teshuva*, ibid.

121. *Gesher HaḤayim* 21:8:8; see *Yalkut Yosef* (*Avelut* 20:7), who prohibits leather shoes.

122. Rema, *Yoreh De'ah* 391:2.

123. See *MeOlam VeAd Olam* 25:8.

124. See *Gesher HaḤayim* 21:8:11.

125. See *Shevut Yaakov* 2:102.

126. *MeOlam VeAd Olam* 25:11.

127. See *Iggerot Moshe, Yoreh De'ah* 2:169.

128. Mo'ed Katan 19b.

129. The *Rishonim* discuss whether this principle, *miktzat hayom kekhulo*, applies at night as well. Ramban (*Torah HaAdam, Inyan HaAvelut*) suggests that one may even bathe

after the comforters depart.[130] Similarly, the laws of mourning for thirty days end immediately after sunrise on the thirtieth day, as "The legal status of part of the day is like that of the entire day."

The *Rishonim* disagree regarding the scope and rationale of this principle. *Terumat HaDeshen*[131] rules that this principle does not apply on the last day of the twelve-month mourning period observed for the death of a parent.

> [The last day of the twelve months] is not like the seventh and thirtieth day, as regarding the seven and thirty days, the count is according to the days, while regarding the twelve-month mourning period, [the halakha] mentions only twelve months, and does not mention 354 days since the months are counted, and if we could apply the principle that "the legal status of part is like that of the entire unit," it would be permitted at the beginning of the twelfth month, and that is certainly not true.

Since the twelve months are counted by months, and not days, the principle of *miktzat hayom kekhulo* does not apply.

Some are accustomed to leave the house accompanied by the comforters and walk for a short distance, symbolizing the mourner's reentry into society after a week of mourning.[132] There is a custom to visit the cemetery on the seventh day of mourning, recite prayers[133] and, if there is a *minyan*, Kaddish, and say *El Maleh Raḥamim* (which does not require the presence of a *minyan*).

---

and wear leather shoes at night, as we apply the principle of *miktzat hayom kekhulo* at night. Other *Rishonim* (Rivam; Rosh, Mo'ed Katan 3:30) rule that *miktzat hayom kekhulo* applies only in the morning. Maharam of Rothenburg (*Hilkhot Semaḥot* 30) rules that although we only apply the principle of *miktzat hayom kekhulo* in the morning, if one hears of the passing of a close relative more than thirty days after the death [*shemua reḥoka*], at night, he concludes the short, symbolic period of mourning without waiting until morning. *Shulḥan Arukh* (*Yoreh De'ah* 395:1) rules accordingly.

130. *Shulḥan Arukh*, ibid. If there are no comforters, the mourning ends after the time of the local morning service, or if there is no local service, after the mourner prays.

131. *Terumat HaDeshen* 292.

132. *The Jewish Way in Death and Mourning*, p. 140.

133. It is customary to recite certain psalms (33, 16, 17, 72, 91, 104, and 130). In addition, verses (from Psalms 119) whose initial letters spell the first name of the deceased, and verses whose initial letters spell the word *neshama* (soul) are recited.

*Chapter 8*

# The House of the Mourner [*Beit Haavel*]

R. Yosef Dov Soloveitchik[1] explains that in addition to the mourning practices observed during *shiva*, described in detail in the previous chapter, there are also laws and customs that relate to the home of the mourner [*beit haavel*].

R. Soloveitchik cites numerous proofs to support this theory. For example, the Talmud[2] teaches:

> The sages taught: With regard to one who is in mourning and must overturn his bed, he overturns not only his own bed, but rather he overturns all the beds he has in his house.

When this practice of *kefiyat hamita* was observed, all of the beds in the house were to be overturned, apparently as an expression of mourning, and possibly to transform the house into a *beit haavel*. Similarly, regarding

1. See R. Zvi Schachter, "*Mekom Hadlakat Nerot Ḥanukka*," in *Sefer Kavod HaRav* (1984), pp. 277–79.
2. Mo'ed Katan 27a.

the prohibition of *Talmud Torah,* the Gemara[3] teaches that not only does the mourner refrain from Torah study, but those in the house too may not speak matters of Torah.[4]

Just as the mournful silence precludes speaking matters of Torah, so too, *Arukh HaShulḥan* explains, people should not greet each other in the house of the mourner, as "one should not mention *shalom* in this house."[5]

In this chapter, we will discuss some of the central and unique mourning customs observed in the mourner's home.

### THE CANDLE AND MIRRORS

It is customary to light a candle in the house of the mourner that will remain lit for the seven days of mourning. This candle is known as the *ner neshama.* R. Zedkia b. R. Avraham HaRofeh (1210–1275) mentions this practice in his *Shibbolei HaLeket.*[6] As R. Maurice Lamm explains:[7]

> During *shiva,* candlelight is the symbol of the human being. The wick and the flame symbolize body and soul, and the bond between them. The flame is the soul that strives ever upward, and brings light into darkness. Jewish mysticism has suggested profound and insightful analogies of the flame and the soul of the deceased in its comments on the *shiva* candle, *yahrzeit* lamp and *Yizkor* candle.

Even if the death is on Yom Tov or Ḥol HaMo'ed, a candle is lit after the funeral that remains lit until the conclusion of the seven days of mourning.[8]

---

3. Ibid., 23a.
4. Based on this source, R. Soloveitchik criticized the common practice of studying Mishna in the house of the mourner between Minḥa and Maariv; see also *Arukh HaShulḥan* 378:8.
5. *Arukh HaShulḥan, Yoreh De'ah* 385:4.
6. *Shibbolei HaLeket, Hilkhot Semaḥot* 21; see also Tanya Rabbati 67. Some trace this practice to a passage in the Talmud that describes the death of R. Yehuda HaNasi. The Talmud (Ketubot 103a) relates that R. Yehuda HaNasi gathered his sons before he died and said, "Be careful with the honor of your mother; my lamp should be lit in its usual place; my table should be set in its usual place; and the bed should be arranged in its usual place."
7. R. Maurice Lamm, *The Jewish Way in Death and Mourning,* p. 98; see also *Gesher HaḤayim* 20:1:1.
8. *Gesher HaḤayim* 20:1:2.

It is also customary to cover the mirrors during the seven days of mourning.[9] The earliest reference to this practice appears in the *Derashot* of R. Moshe Sofer, known as Ḥatam Sofer. He writes:

> It is customary to overturn the mirrors during the seven days of mourning. It seems to me that this originates from the Yerushalmi. Our Talmud (Mo'ed Katan 15b) explains that practice of *kefiyat hamita,* as such: "I have placed the likeness of My image [*deyokan*] within humans, and owing to their sins I have overturned it (as when this person died, the divine image in him was removed). Therefore, you too must overturn your beds on account of this." The Yerushalmi adds "Turn over your facilitator," and *Korban HaEda* explains that the bed is the facilitator for relations between a husband and wife to create new life. We are not accustomed to turn over our beds, for the reason mentioned by the *posekim,* but at least we turn over our mirrors, which also serve as facilitator of relations between a husband and wife.

R. Soloveitchik also viewed the custom of covering the mirrors as an outgrowth and substitute of *kefiyat hamita.* He explained that the mirror, which reflects the image of God [*tzelem Elokim*], should be covered, just as *kefiyat hamita* mourns the loss of the image of God.[10] Others suggest that mirrors represent, and encourage, a focus on beauty and vanity, themes far from the mind of the mourner.

Although the earliest sources describe *turning around* the mirrors, later sources relate that it is customary to *cover* the mirrors. Some[11] suggest that since the daily prayers are held in the house of the mourner the mirrors should be covered, as it is customary not to pray toward mirrors.[12] There is no need to cover mirrors on Shabbat.

9. Some are accustomed to cover pictures as well.
10. *Sefer Kevod HaRav,* ibid.
11. See R. Ovadia Yosef (*Yabia Omer, Yoreh De'ah* 4:35:3). He adds that according to this reason, if there is no *minyan* in the house, then there is no reason to cover the mirrors.
12. Radbaz (4:106) writes that one should not pray facing a mirror, as it appears as if he is bowing to himself. Some cite mystical or metaphysical reasons for covering the mirrors; see *Ginzei Yosef* (p. 320), cited by numerous *Aḥaronim.*

## PROPER DECORUM IN THE *BEIT HAAVEL*

In addition to lighting a *ner neshama* and covering the mirrors, it is proper to maintain an appropriate environment in the house of the mourner. Indeed, *Shibbolei HaLeket*[13] writes, "It is prohibited for the mourner to engage in conversation, as one who engages in conversation appears as if he has forgotten his sorrow and does not appear like a mourner." This is manifest in the prohibition of *she'elat shalom*, as mentioned above, and in the broader prohibition of Torah study in the mourner's house.

A mourner should not engage in activities that will distract him from properly mourning. For example, the Talmud teaches that "a mourner should not place a young child in his lap because the child will bring him to laughter, and he will be disgraced in the eyes of other people."[14] Some suggest that a mourner should not read newspapers or other periodicals, which may distract him from mourning.[15]

## *LIMMUD MISHNAYOT*

As mentioned above, although the Gemara[16] appears to explicitly discourage Torah study in the house of a mourner, it is customary to study *mishnayot* in memory of the deceased, as the letters that form the word mishna also form the word *neshama*, soul.[17] Some have the custom to study *mishnayot* that begin with the letters of the name of the deceased, and then four *mishnayot* whose first letters spell the word *neshama* (Mikvaot 7:4–7), and conclude with the *Kaddish DeRabbanan*.[18] The mourner should not actively participate in the study of Mishna, as it is prohibited for him to study Torah.

## *NIḤUM AVELIM*

The Talmud[19] teaches that comforting and consoling the mourners [*niḥum avelim*] is a form of *imitatio Dei*, imitating God.

13. *Shibbolei HaLeket, Hilkhot Semaḥot* 20.
14. Mo'ed Katan 26b.
15. *Arukh HaShulḥan, Yoreh De'ah* 384:9.
16. Mo'ed Katan 27a.
17. *Kitzur Shulḥan Arukh* 207:5.
18. *Gesher HaḤayim* 20:4:1.
19. Sota 14a.

> R. Ḥama, son of R. Ḥanina, says: What is the meaning of that which is written: "You shall follow the Lord our God, [and Him you shall fear, and His commandments you shall observe, and His voice you shall heed, and Him you shall serve, and to Him you shall cleave]" (Deut. 13:5)? But is it actually possible for a person to follow the Divine Presence? But hasn't it already been stated: "For the Lord your God is a consuming fire [a zealous God]" (Deut. 4:24), [and one cannot approach fire. He explains:] Rather, the meaning is that one should follow the attributes of the Holy One, Blessed be He. [He provides several examples.] Just as He clothes the naked, as it is written: "And the Lord God made for Adam and for his wife hide tunics, and clothed them" (Gen. 3:21), so too, you shall clothe the naked. Just as the Holy One, Blessed be He, visits the ill, as it is written with regard to God's appearing to Abraham following his circumcision: "The Lord appeared to him in the plains of Mamre" (Gen. 18:1), so too, you shall visit the ill. Just as the Holy One, Blessed be He, consoles mourners, as it is written: "It was after the death of Abraham, God blessed Isaac his son" (Gen. 25:11), so too, you shall console mourners. Just as the Holy One, Blessed be He, buries the dead, as it is written: "He buried him in the canyon [in the land of Moab]" (Deut. 34:6), so too, you shall bury the dead.

Rambam,[20] in a well-known passage, writes:

> There is a positive commandment of rabbinic origin to visit the sick, comfort mourners, to prepare for a funeral, prepare a bride, accompany guests, attend to all the needs of a burial, carry the deceased on one's shoulders, walk before the bier, eulogize, dig a grave, and bury the dead, and also to bring joy to a bride and groom and help them in all their needs. These are deeds of kindness that one carries out with his person that have no limit.
>
> Although all these mitzvot are of rabbinic origin, they are included in the Torah commandment: "Love your neighbor as yourself" (Lev. 19:18). That mitzva instructs that whatever you would like others to perform on your behalf, you should perform for your colleague in Torah and mitzvot.

20. Rambam, *Hilkhot Avel* 14:1.

Rambam explains that although *niḥum avelim* may be a rabbinic commandment, it is part of a broader biblical imperative of "Love your neighbor as yourself."

Regarding *niḥum avelim,* in addition to being an act of kindness toward one's fellow man, and in a broader sense, a form of emulating God's behavior, Rambam[21] writes:

> It appears to me that comforting mourners takes precedence over visiting the sick. For comforting mourners is an expression of kindness to the living and the dead.

*Niḥum avelim,* according to Rambam, is "an expression of kindness to the living and the dead." In what way is *niḥum avelim* a form of kindness to the dead? Seemingly, just as the Talmud suggests that the *hesped* may "honor" the dead,[22] so too, when people comfort the mourners, they are also honoring the deceased.

The Talmud[23] describes the manner in which one should seek to comfort the mourner.

> R. Yoḥanan said: The consolers are not permitted to speak words of consolation until the mourner opens [and speaks first]. As it is stated: "They sat with him to the ground seven days and seven nights, and there was no one speaking a word to him, as they saw that the pain was very great. Thereafter, Job opened his mouth" (Job 2:13–3:1). Afterward: "Eliphaz the Temanite answered and said" (ibid., 4:1).

The verse describes how Job, and his three friends who came to comfort him, were silent for seven days. The Gemara derives from this story that one coming to console should not speak until the mourner begins speaking.

R. Mordekhai Yoffe, in his commentary to the *Shulḥan Arukh, Levush,*[24] explains that one should wait until the mourner "expresses his sadness, and then one begins to comfort him; however, before [the mourner

21. Rambam, ibid., 14:7.
22. Sanhedrin 46b; see also Rambam, *Hilkhot Avel* 12:1; see also Shabbat 152a.
23. Mo'ed Katan 28b.
24. *Levush, Yoreh De'ah* 376:1.

expresses his sadness] it is not proper to comfort him, as it is possible that he is not feeling sad." Alternatively, as R. Maurice Lamm[25] describes:

> The fundamental purpose of the condolence call during *shiva* is to relieve the mourner of the intolerable burden of intense loneliness. At no other time is a human being more in need of such comradeship. *Avelut* means withdrawal, the personal and physical retreat from social commerce and the concern for others. It is the loss that he alone has suffered. All the traditions of mourning express this troubled loneliness in diverse ways, covering the spectrum of social life – from the excessive growing of hair in indifference to social custom, to the avoidance of greetings, the minimum social courtesy. Recognizing this state of mind, the visitor comes to the house of mourning, silently, to join the bereaved in his loneliness, sorrowfully to sit alongside him, to think his thoughts and to linger on his loss.

He explains further:

> The purpose of the condolence call is not to convince the mourner of anything at all. This is the time for accompanying him on his very own path, not for argumentation or debate. It is the time for the contemplation of disaster. While the mourner himself may wish to discuss it, it is not the prime purpose of this visit to relieve his fears for the future or his guilt for the past. It is not proper, say the sages (indeed it borders on sacrilege), to impress upon the mourner the inevitability of death, as though to doubt the true purpose and justice of a decree that God issued, but would change if only He were free to do so. It is not seemly, perhaps it is even entirely useless, to assure the mourner that others have suffered similar tragedies, or worse fates, as though by right he should be less despairing. "It could have been worse," is cold consolation. This is a time for subjectivity, for an intensely personal evaluation of life, and the mourners should not be deprived of even this indulgence. Some of the importuning of visitors that "life must go on," and that the mourner should be "thankful that worse did not occur," are well-meaning, but hollow and sometimes annoying expressions.

---

25. R. Maurice Lamm, *The Jewish Way in Death and Mourning*, pp. 132–33.

Silence, R. Lamm explains, does not express a lack of pain and sadness, but rather the deepest form of loneliness and contemplation.

Of course, if the visitors feel that it is more appropriate to approach the mourner and to begin comforting him before he begins speaking, doing so is certainly proper. Indeed, R. Eliezer Waldenberg, in his *Tzitz Eliezer*,[26] acknowledges that it is customary to express one's condolences and speak of the deceased, and relates that that was the practice of the *Ḥazon Ish*, when he felt it was appropriate.

It is customary, when parting from the mourners, to say: May God comfort you among the other mourners of Zion and Jerusalem.[27] Others say: May you be comforted from the heavens.[28]

### LEAVING THE *BEIT HAAVEL*

In addition to the laws and customs that reflect and create the proper environment for mourning, the Talmud[29] teaches that the mourner should remain in the *beit haavel* for the entire week.

> The sages taught: During the first week after his bereavement, the mourner may not leave his house. During the second week, he may leave, but he may not sit in his usual place in the synagogue. During the third week, he may sit in his usual place but he may not speak. During the fourth week, he is like any other person.

R. Yisrael Isserlin[30] explains that "[the mourner] may not leave his house so that he would not forget his mourning when he goes to other people; and when he is alone in his house, and there are no other people besides the members of his household, it is clear and apparent that he is in mourning."

There are several exceptions to this practice. For example, a mourner may leave his house to travel to join other mourners.[31] Also, a mourner may

26. *Tzitz Eliezer* 17:45:4.
27. *Perisha, Yoreh De'ah* 393:3
28. Evel Rabbati 4:13, Rambam (*Hilkhot Avel* 13:2), Ramah (Sanhedrin 19a), and others.
29. Mo'ed Katan 23a.
30. *Terumat HaDeshen* 290.
31. *Shaarei De'ah* 393; see *Nitei Gavriel* 112:4.

leave the *beit haavel* at night[32] and may sleep in a different house.[33] Although it is customary for a mourner not to leave his house, even after the first three days,[34] to attend another funeral, he may attend the funeral of a close relative.[35] A mourner may also leave his house in a case of potential financial loss, or another great need.[36]

It is proper for the mourner to pray with a *minyan* in the *beit haavel.* If the community cannot gather a *minyan* in the home of the mourner, and as a result, he would be unable to recite Kaddish, *Kedusha,* and *Barekhu,* he may leave his home to attend the *minyan* in a local synagogue.[37]

On Shabbat during the week of mourning, the mourner may leave his house to attend communal prayers.[38] We will discuss the laws of Shabbat during *shiva* in chapter 12.

### PRAYERS IN THE *BEIT HAAVEL*

It is customary, wherever possible, to hold daily prayer services in the *beit haavel* in the morning, afternoon, and evening. As mentioned before, ideally the mourner should remain in the house where he is sitting *shiva,* and therefore it is preferable to gather a *minyan* so that he can pray there as well, and recite Kaddish with a *minyan.* Participating in a *minyan* in a *beit haavel* is also a form of *niḥum avelim.* Some write that praying in the house where the deceased passed away brings contentment [*naḥat ruaḥ*] to the soul of the departed.[39]

There are several changes in the prayers, when recited in the house of the mourner, which reflect the uniqueness of the atmosphere there. For

32. *Terumat HaDeshen,* ibid.; Rema, *Yoreh De'ah* 393:2.
33. *Ḥokhmat Adam* 165:11; see also *Iggerot Moshe, Yoreh De'ah* 2:172.
34. Mo'ed Katan, ibid.
35. *Pitḥei Teshuva,* ibid., 1.
36. Rema 393:2, based on Tosafot, Mo'ed Katan 27a, s.v. *im.* For example, a female mourner may leave the *beit haavel* in order to nurse her child, and a husband may accompany his wife to the hospital if she is giving birth (see *Iggerot Moshe, Yoreh De'ah* 5:60). A doctor who is in mourning may visit a patient, if necessary (*Pitḥei Teshuva* 380:1).
37. *Ḥokhmat Adam* 167:3; *Kuntres Matzevet Moshe* 8. *Magen Avraham* (*Oraḥ Ḥayim* 699:8) disagrees. See *Pitḥei Teshuva* 393:8.
38. *Shulḥan Arukh, Yoreh De'ah* 393:3.
39. Rema, *Yoreh De'ah* 384:3. *Gesher HaḤayim* (20:3:3) writes that although some write that this is unnecessary if the deceased was less than a year old, it is customary to hold services in the house of the mourner even in that case, as the mourner may not leave the house.

example, *Shibbolei HaLeket*[40] writes that *Taḥanun* is not recited in the house of a mourner, as the days of mourning are described as having the potential to be festive days (Amos 8:10), when *Taḥanun* and *Viduy* are not recited. Some explain that the days of mourning, and the house of the mourner, are particularly inauspicious, as they are "under the influence of *midat hadin*," and therefore *Taḥanun* should be omitted.[41] For similar reasons, many omit the *El Erekh Apayim* passage recited before *Keriat HaTorah, Lamenatze'aḥ* (Psalms 20), and the verse "And for me, this is my covenant" in the *Uva LeTziyon* prayer, as well as abridging the *Seliḥot*.[42] *Avinu Malkeinu*, recited during the *Aseret Yemei Teshuva* and on public fast days, is said in the house of a mourner.[43]

**HALLEL**

Hallel is primarily recited on festival days, i.e., Sukkot, Pesaḥ, and Shavuot, when there is no mourning. It is also recited on the eight days of Ḥanukka, and it is customary to recite an abridged version on Rosh Ḥodesh. In addition, in many communities, Hallel is recited on Yom HaAtzma'ut and Yom Yerushalayim, days that commemorate the establishment of the State of Israel and the reunification of Jerusalem after the Six-Day War. Is Hallel recited on these days in the *beit haavel*? If not, should the members of the *minyan* recite Hallel elsewhere or individually upon returning home?

Hallel is not recited in the house of the mourner on Rosh Ḥodesh. Some suggest that it is inappropriate to recite there the verses: "This is the day that the Lord has made; we will rejoice and be glad in it" (Ps. 118:24),[44] and: "The dead do not praise the Lord" (Ps. 115:17).[45] Others note that just as Hallel is not recited on Rosh HaShana, as: "Is it possible that while the King is sitting on the throne of judgment and the books of life and the books of death are open before Him, the Jewish people are reciting joyous

40. *Shibbolei HaLeket* 30.
41. See *Mishna Berura* 131:30.
42. *Gesher HaḤayim* 20:3:4. Although *Avinu Malkeinu* is recited, *Taḥanun* is omitted. *Seliḥot* are recited until the *zekhor raḥamekha* passage, and then the first three verses of the *Shema Koleinu* are recited, at which point the *Seliḥot* are concluded.
43. *Eliya Rabba, Oraḥ Ḥayim* 131:9.
44. *Shibbolei HaLeket* 22.
45. Roke'aḥ 316.

songs of praise,"[46] so too, it would be inappropriate to recite Hallel in the house of a mourner.[47]

What should the comforters do on Rosh Ḥodesh? *Mishna Berura*[48] rules that there is no need to recite Hallel upon returning home from the mourner's house, as the recitation of Hallel on Rosh Ḥodesh is a custom and not an obligation. R. Yechezkel Landau, in his *Noda BiYehuda,* writes that the mourners should leave the room and then return after the *minyan* has completed Hallel.[49] Others express discomfort with this position and suggest that the *minyan* should move to a different room to recite Hallel.[50] Some suggest that one should recite Hallel privately upon returning home.[51]

On Ḥanukka, when the recitation of Hallel is obligatory, some *Aḥaronim* write that the congregation should recite Hallel upon returning home,[52] while others rule that Hallel should be recited in the *beit haavel,* with the mourner.[53]

If Rosh Ḥodesh, Ḥanukka, or other days upon which Hallel is recited coincide with the seventh day of the *shiva,* some suggest that before Hallel, those praying with the mourner should comfort the mourner, thus officially ending the *shiva,* in accordance with the principle: *Miktzat hayom kekhulo.* Then they may recite Hallel together with the mourner. Others disagree with this opinion.

Each community should follow its local custom.

### *Birkat Kohanim*

Ashkenazic communities outside of Israel recite *Birkat Kohanim* only on festivals.[54] In Israel, where *Birkat Kohanim* is recited daily in most communities,

46. Rosh HaShana 32b.
47. Roke'aḥ, ibid.
48. *Mishna Berura* 131:20.
49. *Noda BiYehuda, Mahadura Tinyana, Yoreh De'ah* 215.
50. *Divrei Yatziv, Yoreh De'ah* 241.
51. *Shulḥan Arukh HaRav* 131; see *Gesher HaḤayim* (20:3:6), who cites all of these opinions.
52. *Magen Avraham* 131:10; *Mishna Berura,* ibid., 20.
53. *Shulḥan Arukh HaRav, Oraḥ Ḥayim* 131:5.
54. Rema (*Oraḥ Ḥayim* 128:48) records that the practice in Ashkenazic lands is not to recite *Birkat Kohanim,* except during the Musaf prayer of Yom Tov. He explains that on the festivals, "they are experiencing the happiness of Yom Tov, and it is proper for him to recite the blessing, as opposed to the other days, even on Shabbat, when people are distracted by thoughts of sustenance and loss of work."

there are different customs regarding whether a mourner who is also a Kohen participates in *Birkat Kohanim,* and whether *Birkat Kohanim* is recited in the mourner's house.

*Shibbolei HaLeket*[55] criticizes those who permit a mourner who is a Kohen to recite *Birkat Kohanim,* as "one who rises to bless should be happy." Similarly, the *Mordekhai*[56] writes that a Kohen, during the entire twelve months of mourning following the death of a parent, should leave the sanctuary before the blessing of *Retzei* to avoid reciting *Birkat Kohanim.* R. Yosef Karo[57] records that the custom is not in accordance with their opinions.

*Shulḥan Arukh*[58] rules that during the *shiva,* if the mourner is a Kohen, he should leave the room before the *sheliaḥ tzibbur* reaches *Retzei.* After the *shiva,* however, he may recite *Birkat Kohanim.* Rema records that the custom is that a Kohen does not recite *Birkat Kohanim* during the entire twelve months of mourning for a parent. In practice, in Israel, mourners resume participating in *Birkat Kohanim* after *shiva,* while outside of Israel, where, in Ashkenazic communities, *Birkat Kohanim* is recited only on festivals, there are different customs.[59]

In most communities, *Birkat Kohanim* is not recited in the house of the mourner during the seven days of mourning, by any Kohanim. There are different customs regarding whether *Elokeinu VeElokei Avoteinu* should be recited.[60] In Jerusalem, and in Sephardic communities,[61] *Birkat Kohanim* is often recited in the house of the mourner.

At the end of the morning and evening prayers (in *Nusaḥ Sepharad* it is at the end of the morning and afternoon prayers), it is customary to recite

---

R. Yisrael of Shklov (1770–1839), writes (*Pe'at HaShulḥan, Hilkhot Eretz Yisrael* 2:16) that the custom in Jerusalem is to recite *Birkat Kohanim* daily, and he attributes this position to his teacher, Gra, many of whose students emigrated to Israel in the late eighteenth century. R. Yechiel Michel Tukachinsky, in his *Ir HaKodesh VeHaMikdash* (3:25:6), concurs with the above, but adds that the Ashkenazic communities of the Galilee are not accustomed to recite *Birkat Kohanim* daily; rather, they recite it during Musaf of Shabbat and Yom Tov. Many Sephardic communities outside of Israel recite *Birkat Kohanim* daily.

55. *Shibbolei HaLeket, Hilkhot Semaḥot* 22–23.
56. *Mordekhai,* Megilla 817.
57. *Beit Yosef, Oraḥ Ḥayim* 128.
58. *Shulḥan Arukh, Oraḥ Ḥayim* 128:43.
59. See *Piskei Teshuvot* 128:87.
60. See *Eliya Rabba, Oraḥ Ḥayim* 559:13; *Mishna Berura* 121:6; see also *Ḥayei Adam* 27:25.
61. *Yalkut Yosef* 29:8.

Psalms 49, *Lamenatze'aḥ Livnei Koraḥ Mizmor*. On days of the year when *Taḥanun* is omitted, Psalms 16, *Mikhtam LeDavid,* is recited instead of Psalms 49. *Mishnayot* are often studied after the *tefillot,* especially after Minḥa.

# *Chapter 9*

# The Laws of the Thirty-Day Mourning Period [*Sheloshim*]

The Talmud teaches that some mourning practices, including the prohibition of cutting one's hair and attending festive gatherings, are observed for thirty days after the burial. What is the nature of the thirty-day mourning period? What is its status relative to the seven-day period of mourning?[1]

Ostensibly, the thirty-day mourning period may simply be an extension of *shiva*, similar in nature but less intense. The mourning practices of *sheloshim* may reflect the mourner's inner sorrow during a period of healing, as he prepares to return to his daily routine. Alternatively, unlike the seven days of mourning, which are characterized by mourning practices that express inner sadness and sorrow [*avelut shebalev*], during the thirty-day period the mourner refrains from activities that bring joy. Indeed, R. Soloveitchik[2] explains:

> The *avelut* of *sheloshim* differs from *avelut* of *shiva*. Regarding the *avelut* of *shiva*, the *kiyum* of *avelut* is in the heart, which has no place during

1. See R. Aharon Lichtenstein, *Minḥat Aviv*, pp. 311–19.
2. *Shiurim LeZekher Abba Mari*, vol. 2, p. 192.

> festivals. Regarding the *avelut* of *sheloshim*, however, there is no formal *kiyum* of *avelut*. Rather, only prohibitions involving the five forbidden activities apply, but this entails only prohibitions, without any formal observance. Therefore, all those matters that do not undermine the honor and enjoyment of the festival apply; and once it applies, we can count even the [days of the] festival toward the thirty days.

R. Soloveitchik employs this distinction to explain why *simḥat Yom Tov* is incompatible with the *avelut* of *shiva*, and therefore the *shiva* is delayed or even canceled by Yom Tov, while the *avelut* of *sheloshim* is not affected.

Different sources for the thirty-day mourning period may reflect these different understandings. On the one hand, some sources describe the thirty days of mourning as a period of crying [*bekhi*]. For example, Rambam[3] writes:

> According to rabbinic law, a mourner should observe some mourning practices for thirty days. From where did the sages draw support for the period of *sheloshim*? The Torah states: "And she shall lament her father and mother a month of days" (Deut. 21:13); by inference, a mourner suffers for thirty days.

Similarly, the mishna[4] derives the thirty-day mourning period from the death of Moses: "The children of Israel wept for Moses in the plains of Moab thirty days" (Deut. 34:8). These sources portray the *sheloshim* as a period of weeping.

On the other hand, the Talmud[5] cites a different source for the thirty-day period of mourning.[6]

> From where do we derive the thirty-day period of mourning? It is derived by means of a verbal analogy between one instance of the word *pera*, and a different instance of the word *pera*, stated with regard to a Nazirite. Here [in the instructions given to Aaron not to mourn the

3. Rambam, *Hilkhot Avel* 6:1.
4. Semaḥot 7:9.
5. Mo'ed Katan 19b.
6. Raavad (*Hilkhot Avel* 6:1) insists that this is the source for the laws of *sheloshim*.

> deaths of his sons], it is written: "Let the hair of your heads not grow loose [*tifra'u*]" (Lev. 10:6), which indicates that ordinary mourners are required to grow their hair long. And there, with regard to a Nazirite, it is written: "He shall let the hair of his head grow long [*pera*]" (Num. 6:5). Just as there, in the case of the Nazirite, he must grow his hair for thirty days, so too here, a mourner must grow his hair for thirty days.

This source does not address an inner experience; rather, it calls for a mode of conduct.[7]

These approaches highlight and reflect the different ways in which mourners may experience these additional three weeks of mourning.

Rambam[8] enumerates the prohibitions observed during this period:

> These are the practices prohibited for a mourner for the entire thirty-day period: It is prohibited for him to cut his hair, to wear freshly ironed clothing, to marry, to enter a celebration of friends, and to go on a business trip to another city – five matters in all.

In this chapter, we will discuss these prohibitions, as well as other customs observed during the *sheloshim*. We dedicate a separate chapter, chapter 11, to the question of marriage and attending celebrations during the post-*shiva* periods of mourning.

## CUTTING HAIR AND NAILS DURING *SHELOSHIM*

Is there a difference between the prohibition to cut one's hair during *shiva* and the prohibition to cut one's hair during *sheloshim*?

Rambam writes that "the sages instituted that a mourner observes some practices of mourning all thirty days ... These are the practices prohibited for a mourner for the entire thirty-day period: It is prohibited for him to cut his hair," implying that the prohibition is fundamentally identical – haircuts are prohibited for thirty days.[9] Some authorities, however, distinguish between the *shiva* and *sheloshim*; during the thirty-

7. See also Y. Mo'ed Katan 3:5.
8. Rambam, ibid., 6:2.
9. R. Lichtenstein (ibid.) notes that Rambam permits the "removal of hair" [*netilat se'ar*] for women during the *sheloshim* period. This distinction needs clarification.

day mourning period a man may trim his mustache if it interferes with his eating.[10]

These *Rishonim* may disagree whether, fundamentally, the prohibition of cutting one's hair during *sheloshim* differs from the prohibition during *shiva*. While Rambam apparently views them as one thirty-day prohibition, other authorities hold that while during the *shiva* this prohibition is designed to cause discomfort, during the *sheloshim*, it denies the mourner a pleasure.

In practice, *Shulḥan Arukh*[11] permits trimming one's mustache if it interferes with eating.

Furthermore, *Shulḥan Arukh*, based upon some *Rishonim*, writes that a woman may trim her hair immediately after the *shiva*; this is the custom in Sephardic communities.[12] Rema disagrees and rules that a woman may not cut her hair after *shiva*.[13] It is customary in Ashkenazic communities not to distinguish between men and women regarding haircuts, except that a woman may trim the hair around her hair covering after the *shiva* in the interest of modesty.[14]

Some *Aḥaronim* write that one who must appear before a government official to represent the community,[15] or one who may incur financial loss,[16] may cut his hair during the *sheloshim* period. Furthermore, a groom [*ḥatan*][17] who is permitted to marry during *sheloshim* may cut his hair.[18]

As discussed previously, *Shulḥan Arukh*[19] rules that although one may not cut one's nails for thirty days with a nail clipper, one may remove

---

10. Ramban (*Torat HaAdam, Inyan HaAvelut, BeTisporet Keitzad*) cites the view of the *Geonim*.
11. *Shulḥan Arukh, Yoreh De'ah* 391:1, 5.
12. Based upon a *baraita* (Semaḥot 7:11), Rif (Mo'ed Katan 14b) and Rambam (*Hilkhot Avel* 6:3) rule that a woman may cut her hair after *shiva*. *Shulḥan Arukh* (ibid., 5) rules accordingly.
13. Rema, ibid.; see also *Darkhei Moshe*.
14. *Baḥ*, ibid.; see also Shakh, ibid., 3; *Ḥokhmat Adam* 165:28.
15. See *Sefer Kol Bo al Avelut*, p. 353; *Gesher HaḤayim* 21:11:5.
16. See *Divrei Aharon, Yoreh De'ah* 44.
17. See *Eliya Rabba* 132:4.
18. The *Aḥaronim* debate whether the father of a newborn baby may cut his hair in honor of the *Brit Mila*; see *Pitḥei Teshuva* 390:1; *Eliya Rabba* 551:10; *Shevut Yaakov* 3:94.
19. *Shulḥan Arukh, Yoreh De'ah* 390:7.

them in an alternative manner, e.g., with his hands or teeth, even during *shiva.*[20] If one's nails are particularly long one may cut them before Shabbat.[21]

**FRESHLY LAUNDERED AND NEW CLOTHING**

The prohibition of laundering [*kibus*] during the seven days of mourning was discussed previously. The mourner may not launder, nor may he wear freshly laundered clothing, during the seven days of mourning.[22]

The *Rishonim* debate whether the prohibition of wearing laundered clothing continues throughout the entire *sheloshim* period. Some *Rishonim*[23] insist that laundering is prohibited only for the first week. Others[24] maintain that this prohibition lasts for the entire thirty-day mourning period. Furthermore, some[25] insist that it is customary to observe this stringent position and to have others wear the mourner's clean clothing before he wears them. Many question the validity of the custom not to launder for the entire *sheloshim.*[26]

*Shulḥan Arukh*[27] prohibits laundering only during the week of *shiva.* Rema, however, records that it is customary not to wear laundered clothing for the entire month unless another person wears the mourner's garment for "an hour" before he wears it.[28]

---

20. The *Aḥaronim* discuss whether a woman who is preparing for the *mikveh* during *sheloshim* should ask a non-Jewish woman (*Shulḥan Arukh,* ibid.), or even a Jewish woman (Rema, ibid.), to cut her nails with a scissors, or whether she may cut them herself (see *Taz,* ibid., 3; *Ḥokhmat Adam* 165:30).
21. *Gesher HaḤayim* 21:11:9.
22. It was noted previously that *Laḥmei Toda* (cited in *Pitḥei Teshuva* 399:2) rules that just as washing and anointing are prohibited only for pleasure, so too, wearing laundered clothing for pleasure is prohibited; however, if one's clothing becomes stained or dirty, one may change into a laundered garment. *Penei Barukh* (18:4) writes that one may even wash the shirt, without soap, in order to remove the dirt. When mourning for a parent, one must rend the replacement shirt as well.
23. Rambam, *Hilkhot Avel* 5:1; Ramban, *Torat HaAdam, Inyan HaAvelut, BeTikhboset Keitzad.*
24. See, for example, Riva, cited in Tosafot, Mo'ed Katan 23a, s.v. *kol.* Rivash (67) also attests to this custom.
25. See *Semak* 97; *Mordekhai,* Mo'ed Katan 905.
26. *Beit Yosef* (*Yoreh De'ah* 389) describes this as "a custom without a reason." *Darkhei Moshe* (ibid.) notes that even Riva would not have prohibited wearing clothing laundered in the manner that we launder our clothes, after the *shiva.*
27. *Shulḥan Arukh, Yoreh De'ah* 389:1.
28. Shakh (389:4) explains that Rema means "for only a short time."

Despite the ruling of Rema, the custom is not to insist upon wearing pre-worn clothing during the *sheloshim*. *Arukh HaShulḥan*[29] writes that today "it is not the custom for others to wear a mourner's shirt, as many people are disgusted by [the notion of] wearing a shirt worn by others, and in addition, regarding shirts one can be lenient even according to Riva, as [wearing laundered shirts] is not for enjoyment, but rather because it is not possible to wear a shirt that was worn, due to perspiration." One should preferably avoid wearing freshly dry-cleaned clothing, e.g., suits and dress pants. If necessary, they should be worn by another person, or placed on the ground for a short time to neutralize their "freshness."[30]

A mourner should not buy or wear new clothing during the thirty days of mourning.[31] Rema[32] records that it is customary to refrain from wearing new clothing for the entire twelve months one mourns for a parent. One may buy and wear undergarments and clothes that are not worn for one's dignity [*kavod*].[33]

## GREETING [*SHE'ELAT SHALOM*]

As discussed previously, the Talmud[34] enumerates the times during which the mourner and others should not exchange greetings. The Gemara teaches that the mourner should not extend a greeting to others until after the *shiva*, but may respond, if greeted, after the first three days. Others should refrain from greeting the mourner for the entire period of mourning, i.e., twelve months for a parent and thirty days for other relatives.

In practice, Rema[35] records that it is not customary to observe this prohibition after the *sheloshim*, for those mourning for their parents. During *sheloshim*, however, one should refrain from greeting mourners.[36] Previously,

29. *Arukh HaShulḥan, Yoreh De'ah* 389:6.
30. See *MeOlam VeAd Olam* 33:41.
31. *Shulḥan Arukh, Yoreh De'ah* 389:5.
32. Ibid., 3. *Be'er HaGola* (17) writes that one may wear a new garment after another person has worn it for two or three days.
33. *Penei Barukh* (18:11) cites R. Shlomo Zalman Auerbach and R. Eliezer Waldenberg.
34. Mo'ed Katan 21b.
35. Rema, *Yoreh De'ah* 385:1.
36. The *Aḥaronim* discuss whether all greetings, even "Good morning," are prohibited (see *Gesher HaḤayim* 21:7:5), or only the word *shalom* (see *Be'er Heitev, Yoreh De'ah* 385:2). Some point out that it is customary to be lenient regarding this matter (see Ritva, Mo'ed Katan 21b).

it was discussed whether all greetings, or only those that include the word *shalom*, or the name of God, are prohibited. Obviously, one should make certain that his behavior will not be misunderstood, and that it will not offend the mourner or lead to the desecration of God's name.

Finally, as mentioned above, Rema[37] writes that one should refrain from sending the mourner gifts during the entire period of mourning, as sending gifts is similar to *she'elat shalom*. He also rules that one should not send *mishlo'aḥ manot* on Purim during the entire period of mourning.[38] One may, however, send *mishlo'aḥ manot* to the mourner's spouse, or to his entire family. One may also send *mishlo'aḥ manot* to a mourner as an expression of respect, such as to a rabbi or to one's parent.[39]

## *SHINUI MAKOM*: CHANGING ONE'S SEAT IN SYNAGOGUE

The Talmud[40] teaches that during the first week of mourning, the mourner does not leave his house, and during the second week, he does not sit in his "usual place." In this context, Rema[41] relates that "it is customary [for mourners] not to sit in their regular places for thirty days, and [for one mourning his father or mother,] for twelve months." Rema adds that "[although] this custom has no basis, it should not be changed, and each place should act according to its custom."[42] Despite Rema's assertion that this custom "has no basis," the *Aharonim*[43] offer numerous explanations, which reflect different understandings of the mourning experience.

Some suggest that leaving one's usual seat is a form of self-imposed exile [*galut*], similar to the cities of refuge [*arei miklat*], and this act expresses the mourner's sense of guilt over the death of his close relative. Others explain that the mourner, fearful of sharing the bad fortune of the deceased, changes his place in the hope of achieving better fortune.[44] Changing one's seat may also be a component of the mourner's withdrawal from social

37. Ibid., 385:3; see Maharil 31:1.
38. Rema, *Oraḥ Ḥayim* 696:7.
39. See *Piskei Teshuvot* 696:10.
40. Mo'ed Katan 2a.
41. Rema, *Yoreh De'ah* 393:2.
42. Interestingly, *Ḥokhmat Adam* (167) insists that the mourner should also change his seat at home, although he acknowledges that this is not the custom.
43. *Nitei Gavriel* (2:12:1, 20) records the reasons cited below.
44. See Taanit 24b.

gatherings, as one who refrains from participating in a *ḥaburat mitzva* is considered to be "estranged from Heaven."[45]

Some suggest that changing one's place in synagogue arouses feelings of sadness and grief among the congregants. Similarly, the Talmud[46] teaches:

> When a sage dies, his study hall ceases [its regular study as a sign of mourning over him]. When the president of the court dies, all the study halls in his city cease [their regular study], and everyone enters the synagogue and changes their places [there as a sign of mourning over him]. Those who ordinarily sit in the north should sit in the south, and those who ordinarily sit in the south should sit in the north.

By changing their places in the study hall, the students express the fact that they have not forgotten their teacher or his Torah. Here too, the mourner changes his place to lead the community to grieve with the mourner.

Similarly, changing one's place in the synagogue may afford his neighbors the opportunity to fulfill the mitzva of *niḥum avelim*. Indeed, *Pirkei DeRabbi Eliezer*[47] teaches:

> Solomon saw that the quality of performing acts of loving-kindness was great before the Omnipresent. When he built the Temple he erected two gates, one for the bridegrooms, and the other for the mourners and the ostracized. On Shabbatot the Israelites went and sat between those two gates; and they knew that anyone who entered through the gate of the bridegrooms was a bridegroom, and they said to him: May He who dwells in this House cause you to rejoice with sons and daughters. If one entered through the gate of the mourners with his upper lip covered, then they knew that he was a mourner, and they would say to him: May He who dwells in this House comfort you… When the Temple was destroyed, the sages instituted that the bridegrooms and mourners should go to the synagogues and to the houses of study. The men of the place see the bridegroom and rejoice with him, and they see the mourner and sit with him on the earth, so that all the Israelites may fulfill their obligation of loving-kindness.

45. See Pesaḥim 113b.
46. Mo'ed Katan 22b.
47. *Pirkei DeRabbi Eliezer* 17.

The practice of changing one's place in the synagogue may be intended to achieve the same goal – "so that all the Israelites may fulfill their obligation of loving-kindness."

Does the mourner change his place in the synagogue on Shabbat as well? R. Yosef Karo[48] rules that a mourner should not change his place in synagogue on Shabbat, as that would be considered to be an act of public mourning. *Nimukei Yosef*[49] disagrees, and Rema rules that it is customary to change one's place on Shabbat as well.[50] This question is a subject of dispute among the *Aḥaronim* as well.[51] *Gesher HaḤayim*[52] suggests, as a compromise, that during the thirty-day mourning period the mourner should change his seat; afterward, for those mourning the loss of a parent, there is no need to change one's seat. Furthermore, he concludes that one who does not change his seat on Shabbat after the *shiva* "has not lost anything."

A rabbi, or another with an assigned seat or pew, as well as one who will pray with greater fervor [*kavana*] in his usual location, need not change his place in synagogue during the mourning period.[53]

* * *

As we discussed previously, we apply the halakhic principle: "The legal status of part of the day is like that of the entire day" [*miktzat hayom kekhulo*], on the thirtieth day, and one mourning for a relative other than his parent may cut his hair or shave any time after sunrise on the thirtieth day.[54] If the thirtieth day falls out on Shabbat, the mourner may not cut his hair on Friday.[55]

---

48. See *Beit Yosef, Yoreh De'ah* 393; *Shulḥan Arukh,* ibid., 3.
49. *Nimukei Yosef,* Bava Batra 49b.
50. Rema, *Yoreh De'ah* 393:4; see also Shakh 7.
51. While some cite Arizal as opposing this custom, *Birkei Yosef,* as well as Gra (11), maintains that one should change one's seat even on Shabbat. R. Moshe Feinstein (*Iggerot Moshe, Yoreh De'ah* 1:257) records that this is indeed the custom, although he relates that his father did not change his place when he was a mourner.
52. *Gesher HaḤayim* 22:3
53. *Nitei Gavriel,* chap. 12.
54. *Shulḥan Arukh, Yoreh De'ah* 395:1; Shakh 1.
55. See *Dagul Merevava* 400:2.

*Chapter 10*

# The Laws of the Twelve-Month Mourning Period [*Yud-Bet Ḥodesh*]

The Talmud teaches that in addition to the seven- and thirty-day mourning periods, a child observes certain mourning practices for the entire twelve-month period after the death of his parent. Indeed, the Gemara relates that "the deceased is not forgotten from one's heart until twelve months have passed."[1] Some of these practices appear in the Talmud, such as refraining from having one's hair cut and refraining from attending festive gatherings, while others are customs.

Maharam of Rothenburg, in his *Hilkhot Semaḥot*,[2] explains that the mourning practices of the twelve months in some way atone for the sins of the deceased.

> The reason for the decree of the twelve-month [mourning period] is that we learned that "The judgment of the wicked [*resha'im*]

1. Berakhot 58b.
2. *Hilkhot Semaḥot* 50.

> lasts twelve months" (Eduyot 2:10); therefore, for the entire twelve months his son says: I am atonement for his resting place [*hareinu kapparat mishkavo*] (see Kiddushin 31b).

Although it is customary to stop reciting the Mourner's Kaddish after eleven months, as it would be disrespectful to act as though one's parent was wicked, the prohibitions in effect after the end of *sheloshim* last for the entire twelve-month period.

Some *Aḥaronim* suggest that these mourning practices are an expression of respect for the mourner's parent, i.e., a fulfillment of *kibbud av va'em.*[3]

---

3. See Shakh, *Yoreh De'ah* 344:9; *Kitzur Shulḥan Arukh* 216:3. R. Yosef Blau, in his eulogy for R. Yosef Dov Soloveitchik ("*Hesped* for the Rav," in *Memories of a Giant: Eulogies in Memory of Rabbi Dr. Joseph B. Soloveitchik zt"l* [Urim, 2003]), writes: "During 5727 (1966–1967), the Rav lost his mother, brother and wife within a few months... During his *shiva* for his wife, I would go back and forth between the Rav's house and the school, bringing students to be *menaḥem* the Rav. One afternoon, I arrived when Rav Yitzchak Hutner, Rosh Yeshiva of Yeshivas Rabbeinu Chaim Berlin, and Rav Mordechai Pinchas Teitz, Rav of Elizabeth, New Jersey, and dean of its Jewish Educational Center, were there. The Rav said to them that he found it difficult to comprehend that after completing the *sheloshim* for his mother, who lived into her late eighties, he remained obligated to mourn until the completion of twelve months... Sharpening his question, he contrasted the loss by a parent of a child, a devastating tragedy – in which mourning ends with *sheloshim* – with a child's loss of a parent, which is natural, and yet halakha required him to mourn for *yud-bet ḥodesh*, twelve months.

   "Rav Hutner answered that the passing of a parent also represents a loss in the chain that extends back to Mount Sinai. Rav Teitz gave two explanations: The mitzva of *kibbud av va'em*, honoring one's parents, continues even after their passing and creates the additional time of mourning. In addition, father and mother are the only halakhic relationships that cannot be duplicated.

   "The Rav then gave his answer, which reflected a remarkable psychological insight. It is precisely the fact that the parent, a generation older, normally passes away before the child that creates an additional need for mourning. Over the years, the relationship of dependency that the child has to the parent reduces and, if the parent lives a long life, may even reverse itself. The sense of loss is diminished by the infirmity of the aged parent. In order to force the child to reflect back on his total relationship with his parent, including his early years, and acknowledge the enormity of the debt owed to both father and mother, halakha requires this extended period of mourning. When a parent loses a child, there is no need for halakha to tell him to mourn. It is a natural response. Rather, what is needed is a process that ends, enabling one to go beyond mourning, return to functioning, and tend to the other family members."

Indeed, some write that if the parent explicitly ordered the child to refrain from observing the mourning practices of the *yud-bet ḥodesh,* he may heed this command.[4]

As will be explained, during the twelve-month mourning period, the mourner does not cut his hair or attend festive meals, and in general, he restricts his participation in joyful activities. In addition, he recites the Mourner's Kaddish (and if possible, leads the prayer service), and refrains from purchasing and wearing new, elegant garments. Some mourners also refrain from participating in other festive rites, such as the *Hoshanot* on Sukkot and dancing with the Torah on Simḥat Torah.

In this chapter, we will summarize the laws of mourning that apply during the *yud-bet ḥodesh.* As mentioned previously, a separate chapter, chapter 11, is dedicated to the question of marriage and attending celebrations during the post-*shiva* periods of mourning.

## HAIRCUTS [*TISPORET*]

The Talmud[5] teaches that the prohibition of cutting one's hair [*tisporet*] extends beyond *sheloshim* when mourning a parent.

> With regard to all deceased relatives except for parents, one may cut his hair after thirty days. In the case of one's father or mother, one may not cut his hair until his colleagues rebuke him for his hair being too long.

The Gemara permits cutting one's hair after "his colleagues rebuke him" for his hair being too long. This rebuking is known as *ge'ara.*

The *Rishonim* appear to understand this practice in different ways. Some maintain that the Talmud refers to the mourner's physical state; the mourner is supposed to continue his state of unkemptness until it is no longer socially tolerated. Others appear to understand that by not cutting his hair the mourner withdraws from society, turning inward while mourning his loss. He must be summoned back to normative societal behavior,

---

R. Blau recalled that years later, the Rav added that "parents, in different ways, are teachers of their children as well as physical parents, and thus there is a double *avelut.*"

4. Shakh, ibid.
5. Mo'ed Katan 22b.

either by his colleagues, or due to an upcoming festival.[6] Interestingly, the Yerushalmi[7] appears to incorporate both of these ideas, teaching that a mourner may not cut his hair until "he lets his hair grow, or until he is rebuked by his colleagues."

Although technically if a mourner is rebuked immediately after the *sheloshim* he may cut his hair,[8] several *Rishonim* establish a minimum period after which a mourner may cut his hair even without being rebuked. Rema rules in accordance with those *Rishonim*[9] who maintain that a mourner should not get a haircut until at least three months have passed.[10] R. Moshe Feinstein[11] explains that one should wait twice the customary interval between haircuts. Therefore, if the mourner generally cuts his hair once a month, he waits two months before cutting his hair. Clearly, this interval is much shorter for beards; a person who is clean-shaven may shave immediately at the conclusion of the thirty days of mourning.

The *Aḥaronim* discuss whether the prohibition of cutting one's hair continues throughout the entire twelve-month period, and all subsequent haircuts are permitted only after the mourner is rebuked or the prescribed interval has passed, or whether the restriction lasts only until the first haircut. R. Moshe Feinstein[12] rules that each time, the mourner may cut his hair or shave his beard only after the period of *ge'ara* has passed. R. Akiva Eiger[13] maintains that after the mourner's first haircut, with regard to all subsequent haircuts the mourner is not required to wait for an interval to pass. Although some rule stringently, the custom is in accordance with the lenient opinion.

---

6. Some *Rishonim* (*Hagahot Maimoniyot, Hilkhot Avel* 10:5; *Semag,* cited by *Tur, Yoreh De'ah* 399) maintain that once the initial thirty days of mourning have passed, a mourner may cut his hair before a festival. Others, including Rosh (Mo'ed Katan 3:42), Rambam (*Hilkhot Avel* 10:5), Ramban (*Torah HaAdam, Inyan HaAvelut, BeTisporet Keitzad*), and *Shulḥan Arukh* (*Yoreh De'ah* 399:2), disagree.
7. Y. Mo'ed Katan 3:8; see Rambam, *Hilkhot Avel* 6:3.
8. See R. Akiva Eiger, *Yoreh De'ah* 399:4.
9. See, for example, Maharil 22.
10. Maharam Schick (*Yoreh De'ah* 371) explains that Rema refers to three months since the person's last haircut. He notes that others apparently disagree. Indeed, *Gesher HaḤayim* (21:11:2) writes that some are strict and count three months from the beginning of the mourning period.
11. *Iggerot Moshe, Yoreh De'ah* 3:156.
12. *Iggerot Moshe,* ibid.
13. R. Akiva Eiger, ibid.

## WEARING NEW GARMENTS

Rema[14] writes that it is customary to refrain from wearing new garments during the entire twelve months of mourning. This custom does not apply to undergarments or to standard daily garments; only "important" garments, e.g., a suit or jacket, are included in this custom.[15]

The twelve-month mourning period is observed for a full twelve months, from the day of the burial, even during a leap year. Although the principle that the legal status of part of a day is like that of an entire day [*miktzat hayom kekhulo*] applies to the seventh and thirtieth days, it does not apply to the final day of the twelve-month mourning period, as we have discussed.

14. Rema, *Yoreh De'ah* 389:3.
15. See *Arukh HaShulḥan, Yoreh De'ah* 389:11. Regarding these garments, he cites *Be'er HaGola* (393), who mentions that if necessary, one may wear new garments after someone else has worn them for two or three days.

*Chapter 11*

# *Simḥa*, Marriage, and Attending *Semaḥot* and Social Gatherings after *Shiva*

## REJOICING [*SIMḤA*]

The Talmud, in several places, cautions a mourner to refrain from excessive *simḥa* during the entire mourning period. R. Mordekhai Yoffe, in his commentary to *Shulḥan Arukh*,[1] explains:

> It is obvious that since he is called a "mourner" he must refrain from *simḥa* for the entire thirty days, as *simḥa* is the opposite of mourning, and these are antithetical to each other; therefore, it would be inappropriate to engage in joyful activity, as he is supposed to be mourning.

In this context, it is clear why the Yerushalmi[2] prohibits joining a caravan of merchants, as the atmosphere among the merchants was especially social and festive.[3] Similarly, while it is permitted to travel for business purposes, a mourner should refrain from recreational outings and vacations.

---

1. *Levush, Yoreh De'ah* 391.
2. Y. Mo'ed Katan 3:10.
3. See *Shulḥan Arukh, Yoreh De'ah* 380:25; see also *Arukh HaShulḥan*, ibid., 33.

He may, however, take a family vacation, or travel for medical reasons, or to rest. In other words, the mourner should avoid public, overtly festive activities, and choose a quieter form of recreation, if necessary, during the mourning period.

Due to the general prohibition of *simḥa*, many authorities prohibit listening to live music.[4] R. Moshe Schick (1807–1879) explains that music is prohibited only when one plays, or listens, for enjoyment (*simḥa*); therefore, one who teaches music, or one who plays music for his livelihood, may continue to play to prevent financial loss.[5] Some prohibit listening to recorded music as well.[6] R. Yehoshua Ehrenberg (1905–1976), in his *Devar Yehoshua*,[7] insists that there is no inherent prohibition of listening to music, live or recorded, and rules that only music that moves one to dance is prohibited. R. Yosef Dov Soloveitchik also rules that one should refrain only from listening to music that may prompt one to dance.[8] Listening to music while driving, to remain awake, as well as hearing background music, is certainly not problematic. The mourner's family need not refrain from listening to music during the mourning period, although they should be considerate regarding the type of music they play and the volume at which they play it.

Finally, some *Aḥaronim* raise other ramifications of this broad prohibition of *simḥa*. For example, some write that it is customary not to recite the blessing over the moon [*Kiddush Levana*], which is supposed to be recited in a festive mood, during the week of mourning, unless it will be too late to recite the blessing after *shiva*.[9] Others write that if the mourner recites Havdala, he omits the *pesukei simḥa* that precede the Havdala blessings.[10]

4. See also Rema (*Yoreh De'ah* 391:2), who prohibits being present at a wedding while there are *mizmutei ḥatan vekhala*, festive wedding music.
5. Maharam Schick, *Yoreh De'ah* 366; see also *Arukh HaShulḥan*, ibid., 391:14.
6. R. Moshe Feinstein, cited in *Yesodei Semachos*, p. 108.
7. *Devar Yehoshua* 3:63.
8. Cited by R. Maurice Lamm, *The Jewish Way in Death and Mourning*, pp. 174–75.
9. See *Pitḥei Teshuva* 391:1; he concludes that the mourner should certainly not recite *Birkat HaLevana* during the first three days of mourning, and should refrain from reciting the blessing until the tenth night of the month.
10. *Pitḥei Teshuva*, ibid.

## MARRIAGE

The Talmud[11] teaches that "during the entire thirty-day period of mourning, it is prohibited to marry."[12] Some *Rishonim*[13] explain that one may not get married even if the wedding is not accompanied by a festive meal, which is certainly prohibited during the thirty-day mourning period.

In addition to the prohibition to marry during the thirty-day period of mourning, the Talmud[14] teaches that after one's wife passes away, the prohibition to marry lasts beyond the thirty days of mourning.

> If one's wife died, it is prohibited to marry another wife until three festivals pass since her death. R. Yehuda says: Until the first and second festivals have passed, he is prohibited from marrying; before the third festival, however, he is permitted to do so.

The *Rishonim* disagree as to whether the halakha is in accordance with the first opinion,[15] which requires the mourner to wait until three festivals have passed, or the second opinion.[16] *Shulḥan Arukh*[17] rules that the mourner must wait until three festivals have passed.

What is the reason for this added stringency? Rosh[18] explains that waiting until three festivals have passed "is not an additional layer of mourning, but rather it is to ensure that his first [wife] will be forgotten and [her memory will] fade from his mind when he is with the second [wife]."

Which festive days are characterized as festivals? Some[19] suggest that Rosh HaShana and Yom Kippur may have the status of festivals in this regard, just as they do with regard to abrogating *shiva* or *sheloshim*. Most

---

11. Mo'ed Katan 23a.
12. The *Rishonim* disagree whether this prohibition includes *kiddushin* as well (Rosh, Mo'ed Katan 3:48), or just *nisuin* (Rambam, *Hilkhot Avel* 6:5). Nowadays, as *kiddushin* and *nisuin* are performed together at the marriage ceremony, there is no practical difference. A mourner may certainly be engaged to be married during the thirty-day mourning period (*Baḥ* 392:2, cited by Shakh 392:1).
13. See, for example, Rosh, Mo'ed Katan 3:48; see also *Shulḥan Arukh, Yoreh De'ah* 393:1.
14. Ibid.
15. See, for example, Rambam, *Hilkhot Avel* 6:5; *Hagahot Maimoniyot.*
16. See, for example, Ramban, *Torat HaAdam, Inyan HaAvelut, BeSimḥa Keitzad*; Rosh, ibid.
17. *Shulḥan Arukh, Yoreh De'ah* 392:2.
18. Rosh, Mo'ed Katan 3:48.
19. *Taz* (392:2) cites *Sefer HaAguda* (Germany, fourteenth century).

*Rishonim* explain that they do not have the status of festivals in this regard, as the determining factor is not the number of festivals that have elapsed; rather, it is experiencing the *simḥat Yom Tov* of three festivals that enables the widower to remarry.[20] This is the conclusion of *Shulḥan Arukh*.[21] *Gesher HaḤayim*[22] rules that Shemini Atzeret may count as an independent festival in this regard.

The Talmud[23] relates to situations where it would be permitted to marry before three festivals have passed.

> If he does not have children, he is permitted to marry another wife immediately due to the obligation to fulfill the mitzva: Be fruitful and multiply. Similarly, if his wife died and left young children, he is permitted to marry another wife immediately, so that she might take care of them. There was an incident when the wife of Yosef the Priest died, and he said to her sister at the cemetery [immediately after the funeral]: Go and care for your sister's children. But even though [he married her immediately], he did not engage in sexual relations with her for a long time afterward. [The Gemara asks:] What is the meaning of the term: A long time? R. Pappa said: After thirty days.

The Talmud permits a man who has not yet fulfilled the commandment to procreate, or who has young children who require care, to marry shortly after his wife's death. Also, the Yerushalmi[24] rules that the mourner may even marry due to the fact that he has no one to care for him.

Accordingly, *Shulḥan Arukh* rules that one who has not yet fulfilled the commandment of *peru urvu* may marry, and engage in relations with his bride, after the seven-day mourning period.[25] One who has small children or

20. Rosh, ibid.; Ramban, ibid.
21. *Pitḥei Teshuva* (392:1) cites *Dagul Merevava*, who suggests that Shemini Atzeret counts as one of the three festivals. R. Akiva Eiger, cited by his son-in-law R. Moshe Sofer (Ḥatam Sofer 2:350), disagrees. They do, however, permit a widower to remarry if twelve months have passed, even if three festivals have not (i.e., if one's wife passed away on Ḥol HaMo'ed Pesaḥ, he may remarry during II Adar).
22. *Gesher HaḤayim* 21:9:3.
23. Ibid.
24. Y. Yevamot 4:11.
25. *Shulḥan Arukh, Yoreh De'ah* 392:3.

who marries someone to care for him may be wed after the *shiva* but may not engage in relations until after the thirty-day mourning period.[26] Similarly, as discussed previously, if a close relative passed away shortly before one's wedding, one first observes *shiva*, and may marry immediately thereafter.[27]

Regarding the allowance for one to remarry shortly after his wife's death because he has no one to care for him, Rema[28] rules that this applies even to one who is wealthy and able to hire servants to see to his needs. In addition, he records the widespread custom of remarrying before three festivals have passed. The *Aḥaronim* offer additional reasons for this practice.[29]

The *Rishonim* write that although technically, a woman whose husband died may remarry after the thirty-day period of mourning,[30] she must wait three months, as if she were to become pregnant, the identity of the father would be uncertain.[31] Some record that it is customary for a woman to wait until a year has passed before remarrying.[32] The decision of whether to remarry during the year following the death of one's husband or wife should take into account the sensitivities of one's children, who are still in mourning for their parent.

One for whom it is permitted to marry during *sheloshim*, or during the twelve-month period of mourning, may hold and participate in the customary wedding festivities.

### ATTENDING SOCIAL GATHERINGS AND *SEMAḤOT*

One of the defining characteristics, as well as one of the most challenging post-*shiva* mourning practices, is the obligation to refrain from participating

26. Rema, ibid., 3.
27. *Shulḥan Arukh, Yoreh De'ah* 342.
28. Rema, *Yoreh De'ah* 392:2; see Also *Terumat HaDeshen* 3. *Pitḥei Teshuva* cites *Beit Leḥem Yehuda*, who insists that everyone agrees that one should not remarry until two festivals have passed.
29. *Pitḥei Teshuva* (3–4) cites *Shevut Yaakov* (2:100), who suggests that, in order to prevent sexual relations from occurring outside of marriage, it is customary not to object to those who wish to remarry before three festivals have passed. *Dagul Merevava* expresses the concern that since today *eirusin* and *nisuin* are performed together, if the widower is not allowed to remarry, someone else may precede him and marry the woman.
30. *Mordekhai*, Mo'ed Katan 936; see also *Baḥ* 392:4, cited by Shakh (2). *Pitḥei Teshuva* concludes that it is preferable for one who is especially devoted to observing halakha [*baal nefesh*] to wait until three festivals have passed.
31. See Yevamot 41a.
32. See *Taz* 392:3.

in social gatherings and festive celebrations. On the one hand, the mourner often does not wish to socialize or celebrate, and may also feel a sense of duty to the deceased to resist excessive socializing and festivities. On the other hand, the mourner may feel pressure, and at times even an obligation, to attend and even participate in the *semaḥot* of close friends and relatives.

R. Gavriel Zinner,[33] the author of the halakhic work *Nitei Gavriel*, describes the difficulty in forming clear and consistent halakhic rulings regarding this prohibition. He writes:

> This topic is extremely complex as there are differences of opinion among the halakhic decisors regarding each and every case, so much so that one halakhic authority may occasionally rule differently... and the truth is that these matters depend upon [the decisor's] judgment, and upon the situation and the place.

He continues to describe the complexity of these questions.

> And furthermore there is no agreement among the rabbis,[34] as some believe that we should not search for leniencies regarding that which the rabbis taught, "that a mourner should not enter a place where a joyous celebration is taking place"; rather [this law] should be observed according to its literal meaning. And others maintain that due to the honor of the family and love for one's friends, and to prevent strife, we should be lenient, of course in accordance with the conclusions of the halakhic authorities, and as we see, later halakhic authorities were inclined to be lenient.

Despite the difficulty expressed above, we will attempt to outline the basic halakhic principles and demonstrate the range of opinions and customs,

---

33. *Nitei Gavriel, Hilkhot Avelut*, vol. 2, pp. 9–10. *Gesher HaḤayim* (21:8:1) also notes the difficulty in arriving at clear halakhic conclusions as the rabbis discuss these questions in numerous places.

34. Interestingly, he attributes this confusion, in part, to the lack of halakhic tradition in this area: "The difficulty in [the laws of] *avelut* is that we do not have [the benefit of learning from] the service of Torah scholars [*shimush talmidei ḥakhamim*], as the rabbis and Torah scholars do not involve themselves in these matters."

enabling the mourner to navigate this difficult period of mourning. Of course, the mourner should discuss these matters with his or her halakhic authority.

## Prohibited Gatherings and the Definition of *Simḥa* Participation: Talmud and *Rishonim*

A mourner may not participate in certain gatherings during the thirty-day and twelve-month periods of mourning. There is much confusion, however, regarding the scope and details of this prohibition. In this section, we will discuss which gatherings and what type of participation are prohibited, and whether there are special leniencies in cases of celebrations of close family members.

The Talmud[35] cites the basic prohibition of entering a "place where a joyous celebration is taking place [*beit hasimḥa*]" during the mourning period.

> With regard to all other deceased relatives, he may enter a place where a joyous celebration is taking place after thirty days; in the case of his father or mother, he may enter such a place only after twelve months.

The Gemara continues and prohibits a mourner from attending a social gathering, or a *simḥat mere'ut*. The Gemara explains that there are really two types of social gatherings, an *arisuta* and a *puranuta*. When friends take turns hosting a gathering [*puranuta*], the mourner may "repay" his obligation immediately after the conclusion of *shiva*. However, he may not initiate, host, or enter another social gathering [*arisuta*], until after the thirty-day or twelve-month period of mourning.[36]

The Talmud does not explicitly relate to other types of gatherings, and it is therefore unclear whether other festivities, such as weddings, are also prohibited. Other sources, however, do mention other types of celebrations. For example, the Yerushalmi[37] rules that a mourner may attend a *ḥaburat mitzva* or *kiddush haḥodesh*.[38] *Rishonim* question whether these sources disagree with the Talmud Bavli.

35. Mo'ed Katan 22b.
36. See Rambam, *Hilkhot Avel* 6:6.
37. Y. Mo'ed Katan 3:8.
38. See also Semaḥot 9:15, where it is ruled that one may enter a *beit hamishteh* if the

On the one hand, some *Rishonim* assume that the Bavli prohibits only social gatherings, while festive gatherings for the sake of a mitzva [*seudat mitzva*] are permitted. This appears to be the view of numerous medieval Ashkenazic authorities,[39] as well as Rambam.[40]

On the other hand, the majority of *Rishonim* prohibit participating in a *simḥat mitzva*, described by the Gemara as *beit hasimḥa*, although they do permit attending certain gatherings, depending on the circumstances. For example, Raavad[41] explains that although a mourner may not attend a wedding or any other festive gathering, he may participate in the wedding of orphans after the thirty-day mourning period, if his absence is liable to cause the wedding to be canceled. *Nimukei Yosef*[42] adds that one may attend a *seudat mitzva* that is not especially joyful, e.g., a *Brit Mila*, which causes the child to suffer pain. These *Rishonim* maintain that fundamentally, all social and festive gatherings are prohibited, although extenuating circumstances, or a defined ritual purpose, may permit participation in a particular gathering.

In addition, these *Rishonim* attempt to define what type of participation is prohibited. Some *Rishonim*, including R. Yehuda b. Barzillai (Albargeloni)[43] suggest that a mourner may attend the ceremony, but not participate in the meal, as it is the festive meal that is prohibited. Ramban[44] and Rosh[45] disagree and rule that one may not even enter a *beit hasimḥa*. Interestingly, Raavan[46] permits a mourner to hear the wedding blessings only after thirty days.[47]

We will now discuss the practical application of these discussions.

---

purpose is for the sake of Heaven [*leshem Shamayim*].

39. See R. Yosef HaLevi, cited by Rosh (Yevamot 4:27) and *Teshuvot Maimoni* (*Shofetim*, n. 19). This opinion is shared by a number of *Baalei Tosafot*; see Rosh (Mo'ed Katan 3:48; Yevamot 4:27).
40. See Rambam, *Hilkhot Avel* 5:20, 6:7. Radbaz (ibid., 6:7) notes that it appears that Rambam does not prohibit gatherings that are not social [*mere'ut*].
41. See Rosh, Mo'ed Katan 3:42. Ramban (*Torat HaAdam, Inyan HaAvelut, BeSimḥa Keitzad*) prohibits participation even in a wedding of orphans, although he permits participating in a group that is partaking of the meat of an offering, and he also permits observing the sanctification of the new moon.
42. *Nimukei Yosef*, Mo'ed Katan 14a, s.v. *bein kakh*.
43. Cited by Ramban, ibid.; see *Tur* 391; *Beit Yosef*.
44. Ramban, ibid.
45. Rosh, Mo'ed Katan 3:42.
46. Raavan, Mo'ed Katan.
47. Cited by *Hagahot Maimoniyot, Hilkhot Avel* 6:7.

## Social Gatherings [*Simḥat Mere'ut*]

As stated above, the Talmud prohibits participating in *simḥat mere'ut*. Rema[48] writes that "it is customary not to eat any meals out of one's house" during the mourning period. It is not clear how literally one should understand the words of Rema. Some avoid all social engagements during the mourning period, in their own homes, and certainly in the homes of others. Others seek a more nuanced understanding. Some suggest a quantitative approach according to which the mourner should avoid socializing with more than a handful of people. Others explain that the tone and nature of the gathering determine whether the mourner's participation is permitted. It appears that quantity and quality both play a role; therefore, while attending a charity dinner, a conference, or an awards ceremony, and avoiding music and dancing there, may be permitted, a mourner should refrain from going out with friends for dinner when this is accompanied by a recreational activity. As R. Maurice Lamm writes, "fellowship is fine, but festivities are not appropriate."[49]

There are different customs regarding whether during this period of mourning one may invite guests, or be hosted by others, for Shabbat meals.[50] Regarding meals during the week, and for those who are stringent regarding Shabbat meals, it is important to note the distinction between *hakhnasat orḥim*, i.e., inviting those in need of a meal or companionship, hosting one's students or teachers, or even business meetings, and hosting purely for social reasons.

Some relate that Sephardim refrain from attending only festive meals [*seudat simḥa*], not social meals. Indeed, R. Chaim Yosef David Azulai (1724–1806), known as Ḥida, records that "it is well known that we [Sephardim] are not accustomed to observe the ruling of Rema that one should not eat any meal [out of his house during the period of mourning]; rather, as long as the meal is not somewhat festive [*seudat simḥa*], the mourner sits and eats with them."[51]

48. Rema, *Yoreh De'ah* 391:2.
49. R. Maurice Lamm, *The Jewish Way in Death and Mourning*, p. 181.
50. *Shemirat Shabbat KeHilkhata* (65:64) maintains that this prohibition applies on Shabbat as well. See R. Reuven Margoliot (*Ḥiddushim UBiurim* 23), who mentions participation in a communal *seuda shelishit*. R. Yaakov Emden (*She'elat Yaavetz* 2:180) permits inviting guests on Shabbat. *Gesher HaḤayim* (21:8:12) and *Penei Barukh* (20:15) add that one mourning a parent should wait until after the thirty-day mourning period.
51. *Birkei Yosef*, *Yoreh De'ah* 391:2.

## Attending Weddings

*Shulḥan Arukh*[52] rules explicitly in accordance with those who prohibit participating in the festive wedding meal. However, he cites a disagreement regarding whether the mourner may attend the ceremony and hear the blessings without attending the meal, or whether, if necessary, he may only hear the blessings while standing outside. Rema explains that this dispute relates to a wedding held in the place where the festive meal is eaten; however, one may certainly attend a wedding ceremony that takes place in a synagogue, where there is no festive meal, after the seven days of mourning, or, according to another view, with which he concurs, after the thirty days of mourning.[53] In addition, Rema adds another important qualification: It is improper to be present in the wedding hall while festive wedding music [*mizmutei ḥatan vekhala*] is being played.[54]

On this basis, although a mourner after *sheloshim* for a parent, and after *shiva* for another relative, should not attend the wedding reception, he may attend the ceremony itself. The decision whether or not to attend the ceremony should be based on several factors, including the state of mind of the mourner and his relationship to the *ḥatan* and *kalla*.

In certain circumstances, the mourner may participate in the wedding ceremony and even the festive wedding meal. For example, Rema writes that the mourner, after the thirty-day mourning period, may escort the *ḥatan* or *kalla* to the *ḥuppa* and recite the wedding blessings. Some *Aḥaronim* rule that one who is mourning for a relative other than a parent may escort the *ḥatan* or *kalla* immediately after *shiva*.[55] A parent, or even grandparent, may escort the *ḥatan* or *kalla* even during their seven-day period of mourning, as we will see.

---

52. *Shulḥan Arukh, Yoreh De'ah* 391:1–2.

53. He adds that in some communities mourners refrain from attending wedding ceremonies for the entire twelve-month period of mourning.

54. *Devar Yehoshua*, cited above, insists that *mizmutei ḥatan vekhala* refers to music that leads people to dance and rejoice with the *ḥatan* and *kalla*, and not to instrumental music to which the *ḥatan* and *kalla* walk to the *ḥuppa*.

55. *Taz* (4) cites R. Yoel Sirkis (*Baḥ*), who maintains that one mourning for a relative other than a parent may participate after the *shiva*. Although Shakh (3, 5) disagrees, several *Aḥaronim*, including *Noda BiYehuda* (*Mahadura Kama, Yoreh De'ah* 100), concur. *Gesher HaḤayim* (21:8:4) writes that a brother or sister may escort the *ḥatan* or *kalla* to the *ḥuppa* immediately after the seven-day mourning period for a parent.

As for the festive meal, many *Aḥaronim* permit the parents, grandparents, and even siblings of the *ḥatan* and *kalla* to participate in the festive meal during the period of mourning. Some cite Rema,[56] who permits a mourner to participate in the festive meal celebrating the marriage of orphans, as support for this view. Rema permits eating at the festive wedding meal after the thirty days of mourning if the mourner's absence may cause the wedding to be canceled. *Arukh HaShulḥan*[57] explains that even if his absence will cause distress to the bride and groom, the mourner may participate in the wedding. The *Aḥaronim* disagree as to whether Rema referred only to those mourning their parents, as in this case those mourning other relatives may participate in the wedding immediately after the *shiva*, or whether even in this case all mourners should refrain from participating in the wedding meal until after the *sheloshim*.[58]

Similarly, R. Shmuel di Medina (1506–1580), known as Maharashdam,[59] permits a mourner, after the *sheloshim*, to participate in and to eat at his brother's wedding. He argues that since the mourner's absence may cause the bride and groom anguish, he is exempt from the laws of mourning and may attend the wedding, participate in the festive meal, and dance with the bride or groom. Some *Aḥaronim* adopt this ruling, including R. David Zvi Hoffmann,[60] R. Yechiel Michel Epstein,[61] and R. Yechiel Michel Tukachinsky.[62] *Arukh HaShulḥan* adds that one may rely upon those *Rishonim*, cited above, who maintain that a mourner may attend any *seudat mitzva*. He adds that even grandparents who

56. Rema (*Yoreh De'ah* 391:1) rules in accordance with the opinion of Raavad, cited above.
57. *Arukh HaShulḥan, Yoreh De'ah* 391:5.
58. *Taz* (4; see also *Baḥ*) explains that only one mourning a parent should be strict until the end of the thirty-day mourning period. Shakh (3) disagrees and insists that all mourners should refrain from attending even this type of wedding until after the conclusion of the *sheloshim*. R. Yechezkel Landau (*Noda BiYehuda, Mahadura Kama, Yoreh De'ah* 100) rules in accordance with the opinion of *Taz*.
59. Maharashdam, *Yoreh De'ah* 202. He explains that the Talmud (Sukka 25b) acknowledges the anguish one feels when another person is upset due to his absence. The Gemara exempts those who accompany a groom throughout the wedding and the seven festive days [*sheva berakhot*] from the mitzva of *sukka* due to the anguish they experience knowing that their absence causes the groom to be upset. These people are considered to be "suffering" [*mitzta'er*], and are therefore exempt from the *sukka*.
60. *Melamed LeHo'il, Yoreh De'ah* 143.
61. *Arukh HaShulḥan, Yoreh De'ah* 391:9.
62. *Gesher HaḤayim* 21:8:11.

are in mourning may participate in the weddings of their grandchildren.[63] The mourner should seek to minimize his participation, focusing on rejoicing with the *ḥatan* and *kalla,* while not forgetting that he is in mourning.

In this context, we should note that R. Moshe Feinstein[64] permits a parent to attend a child's wedding even during the *shiva,* and explains that it is extremely painful for a parent not to attend the wedding of his child and that this is of greater concern even than financial loss. He adds, however, that the mourner should not eat at a special table or dais designated for the couple and their parents, and it is possible that he should be strict and not even sit and eat at one specific table. He concludes that the mourner should not sit "*derekh kavod ugedula*" (in an honorable manner), although there is no reason for the parent not to eat at all.[65]

At times, other relatives, or even close friends of the *ḥatan* or *kalla,* may feel that their presence at the wedding, or other celebrations, is absolutely necessary. Rema cites a dispute among the *Rishonim* regarding whether a mourner may serve as a waiter at the meal, and then eat the meal with the other waiters.[66] He concludes that while the mourner should not even eat with the other waiters, "if he (the mourner) wishes, he may serve there, and eat food that they send with him when he returns home." Although many object to this practice, some record that it is customary for mourners to serve as waiters, and to eat separately, so that they may be present at the meal, while not being distracted from their mourning.[67] Even those who rely upon this leniency should not eat with the guests, or dance at the wedding.

The status of *sheva berakhot* is the same as that of weddings in this regard.

---

63. *Arukh HaShulḥan* 391:10.

64. *Iggerot Moshe, Yoreh De'ah* 2:169 (see also *Gilyon Maharsha, Yoreh De'ah* 392:3). R. Moshe Feinstein (cited in *Yesodei Semachos*) also permits a female mourner to put on makeup for the wedding.

65. *Iggerot Moshe, Oraḥ Ḥayim* 4:40:16.

66. See *Or Zarua, Hilkhot Avelut* 447, cited in *Hagahot Asheri,* Mo'ed Katan 3:44; *Semak* 114.

67. *Gesher HaḤayim* (21:8:11) writes that only relatives of the *ḥatan* or *kalla* should serve as waiters at the wedding. Furthermore, he writes that a brother or sister of the *ḥatan* or *kalla* may rely upon this leniency even immediately after the seven-day mourning period for a parent. *Nitei Gavriel* (vol. 2, chap. 20) extends this leniency to all mourners.

## *Brit Mila, Pidyon HaBen,* Bar or Bat Mitzva, and *Ḥanukkat HaBayit*

As mentioned above, some *Rishonim* rule that a mourner may participate in a *seudat mitzva* that is less joyous than a wedding, e.g., a *Brit Mila* or *Pidyon HaBen*. Rema[68] cites this opinion:

> However, a mourner may attend a *seudat mitzva* that is not joyous, e.g., *Pidyon HaBen* or the meal for a *Brit Mila,* and he may eat there, even during *shiva,* provided he does not leave his house [during the *shiva*]. Some prohibit [participating in] a *Brit Mila.*

Rema concludes, however:

> It is customary not to eat at any festive meal for the entire twelve months if it is held outside of his home. Inside his home, he may partake in the meal of the *Brit Mila,* and all the more so other meals that are not considered [particularly] festive.

Rema permits a mourner to attend a *Brit Mila* and a *Pidyon HaBen,* but adds that is customary not to participate in any festive meal [*seuda*] outside of the mourner's home.

Some *Aḥaronim*[69] permit one mourning for a parent, after the thirty-day mourning period, to participate in the festive meal celebrating the completion of a tractate of the Talmud [*siyum*]. Some insist that only if the mourner himself finished the tractate, he may partake of the meal.[70] Others, based on the custom cited by Rema, insist that the mourner may not participate in any festive meal.[71] Similarly, some authorities indicate that a mourner may participate in the festive meal celebrating a bar mitzva.[72] Most *Aḥaronim,* however, disagree, following the custom cited by Rema of refraining from participating

---

68. See also *Gesher HaḤayim* 1:21:5. R. Ovadia Yosef (*Ḥazon Ovadia,* vol. 2, p. 351) permits a mourner to eat at the *seudat mitzva* at a *Brit Mila, Pidyon HaBen,* and bar mitzva, provided there is no instrumental music.
69. See Shakh, *Yoreh De'ah* 246:27.
70. *Beit Leḥem Yehuda, Yoreh De'ah* 391.
71. *Ḥokhmat Adam* 166:2.
72. See *Dagul Merevava* (*Yoreh De'ah* 391), who suggests that according to R. Shlomo Luria (*Yam Shel Shlomo* 37), the status of a bar mitzva is like that of a *siyum*. *Beit Leḥem Yehuda* (ibid.) concurs.

in any festive meal during the period of mourning. Some suggest that although a *ḥanukkat habayit* may also be considered to be a *seudat mitzva,*[73] a mourner should refrain from participating in the meal.

A parent, sibling, or grandparent may participate in a child's bar mitzva or bat mitzva.[74] Other family members, or even close friends, who feel that their presence at a bar mitzva celebration is crucial, should not partake of the festive meal or participate in the dancing.

A discussion was cited above regarding whether the mourner should limit his social interactions, including inviting guests and being hosted, on Shabbat. The question arises: May a mourner participate in a *seudat mitzva* on Shabbat? Some rule that a mourner should not attend a *shalom zakhar,*[75] or the festive meal after a *Brit Mila,* on Shabbat, as the halakha with regard to Shabbat is no more lenient than the halakha with regard to during the week. Others permit the mourner, after the *shiva,* to attend a *shalom zakhar,* the festive meal after a *Brit Mila,* or even *sheva berakhot,* on Shabbat.[76] Similarly, although some maintain that one may attend a communal Kiddush, others rule that the mourner should refrain from attending events like this for the duration of the *avelut.*

To summarize, during the twelve-month mourning period, a mourner may not participate in festive, social gatherings [*simḥat mere'ut*].[77] Also, a mourner may not participate in a wedding celebration and partake of the meal, but he may stand outside and hear the blessings, provided there is no festive wedding music [*mizmutei ḥatan vekhala*], and preferably only after the thirty-day mourning period, for one mourning a parent. However, he may attend a *seudat mitzva,* e.g., a *Brit Mila,* a festive meal on the occasion of finishing a tractate of the Talmud, or a bar or bat mitzva, provided there is no instrumental music. Rema adds that although one may attend a *seudat mitzva,* e.g., a *Brit Mila* or *Pidyon HaBen,* it is customary not to eat at such events for the entire twelve-month mourning period. *Gesher HaḤayim*[78] also rules that a mourner may attend these events, but that he should not participate in the meal. In extenuating circumstances, a parent, grandparent, close relative, or important acquaintance may attend and even participate in a family *simḥa,* as detailed above.

73. See *Beit Leḥem Yehuda,* ibid.; see also *Iggerot Moshe, Yoreh De'ah* 3:161.
74. See *Sefer Kol Bo al Avelut,* p. 360.
75. See *Pitḥei Teshuva* 391:4.
76. See *Sefer Kol Bo al Avelut,* p. 361.
77. It is not clear whether this type of meal exists today.
78. *Gesher HaḤayim* 21:8:5.

# *Chapter 12*

# *Avelut* on Shabbat, Yom Tov, and Other Holidays

The Talmud teaches that Shabbat does not terminate the mourning period; rather, the mourner observes only certain aspects of *avelut,* and resumes full mourning immediately after Shabbat. Regarding Yom Tov, not only are the laws of mourning not observed, but if the burial occurs before the beginning of the festival, *shiva,* and sometimes *sheloshim,* is canceled. If the burial occurs during Ḥol HaMo'ed, one observes the seven days of mourning after the festival. In addition to Shabbat and Yom Tov, *Rishonim* discuss whether *avelut* clashes with the minor holidays, Ḥanukka and Purim.

In this chapter, we will discuss the nature and details of these scenarios.

## *AVELUT* ON SHABBAT AND YOM TOV

The Mishna[1] teaches that "Shabbat counts as one of the days of mourning, and it does not interrupt." In other words, the seven-day mourning period continues through Shabbat. Why is the seven-day period of mourning abrogated by a festival, but not by Shabbat?

1. Mo'ed Katan 19a.

On the one hand, the Yerushalmi[2] notes that although public rites of mourning are observed neither on Shabbat nor on Yom Tov, private expressions of mourning are observed on both;[3] therefore, there should be no difference between Shabbat and Yom Tov. The Yerushalmi concludes, however, that "it is possible to maintain seven [days of mourning] without a festival but it is impossible for there to be seven [days of mourning] without Shabbat." In other words, the difference between Shabbat and Yom Tov is a technical, not a fundamental, difference.

On the other hand, some *Rishonim* note fundamental differences between Shabbat and Yom Tov. They explain that the private expressions of mourning observed on Shabbat are sufficient to enable Shabbat to be counted among the seven days of mourning, but since there are no mourning rites in effect during a festival (see below), it cannot be counted among the seven days; therefore, the festivals interrupt and abrogate *shiva*.[4] Others point to the fundamentally different nature of these days. On Yom Tov there is a mitzva to rejoice [*simḥat Yom Tov*], while Shabbat is characterized as a day of enjoyment [*oneg*].[5] Mourning is antithetical to the *simḥa* of Yom Tov, and therefore, the festival abrogates the *shiva*.[6]

## *AVELUT* ON SHABBAT

The laws of *avelut* are in effect for the entire Erev Shabbat. The *Aḥaronim* criticize the practice of getting up from *shiva* at midday on Erev Shabbat.[7] One may stop sitting *shiva* and begin preparing for Shabbat at *Minḥa ketana* (two and a half halakhic hours before sunset).[8] Some write that one should not get up from sitting *shiva* until *pelag haMinḥa*, i.e., one and a quarter hal-

2. Y. Mo'ed Katan 3:5.
3. As mentioned below, the *Rishonim* debate this very point, whether private manifestations of mourning, e.g., refraining from marital relations, are observed on Yom Tov.
4. See Rambam, Commentary on the Mishna, Mo'ed Katan 3:5; R. Yonatan of Lunel, Mo'ed Katan 19a.
5. Is. 58:13.
6. Rav Aḥai Gaon, *She'iltot, Parashat Ḥayei Sara* 16; *Behag, Hilkhot Avel*; Tosafot, Mo'ed Katan 23a, s.v. *man*; see also Me'iri 19a. R. Soloveitchik discusses this approach in great depth in "*BeInyan Avelut*," in *Shiurim LeZekher Abba Mari*, vol. 2.
7. *Pitḥei Teshuva, Yoreh De'ah* 400:1; see also *Arukh HaShulḥan, Yoreh De'ah* 400:5.
8. See Mo'ed Katan 27a.

akhic hours before sunset. One should not bathe in the manner permitted,[9] or change his clothes, until just before the onset of Shabbat.

There is an ancient custom that the mourner enters the synagogue before Maariv, and the congregation consoles him with the traditional greeting: May God comfort you among the other mourners of Zion and Jerusalem [*HaMakom yenaḥem etkhem*, etc.].[10] This practice is most likely based on a beautiful passage that appears in *Pirkei DeRabbi Eliezer*:[11]

> Solomon saw that the quality of performing acts of loving-kindness was great before the Omnipresent. When he built the Temple he erected two gates, one for the bridegrooms, and the other for the mourners and the ostracized. On Shabbatot the Israelites went and sat between those two gates; and they knew that anyone who entered through the gate of the bridegrooms was a bridegroom, and they said to him: May He who dwells in this House cause you to rejoice with sons and daughters. If one entered through the gate of the mourners with his upper lip covered, then they knew that he was a mourner, and they would say to him: May He who dwells in this House comfort you…
>
> When the Temple was destroyed, the sages instituted that the bridegrooms and mourners should go to the synagogues and to the houses of study. The men of the place see the bridegroom and rejoice with him, and they see the mourner and sit with him on the earth, so that all the Israelites may fulfill their obligation of loving-kindness.

It is customary for the mourner to enter the synagogue before the congregation recites the psalm: *Mizmor Shir LeYom HaShabbat*, at which point the congregation accepts the Shabbat.[12]

---

9. R. Gavriel Goldman (*MeOlam VeAd Olam*, p. 172) writes that a mourner may wash his face, arms, and legs before Shabbat. In addition, he notes that a mourner who is especially sensitive [*istenis*], as well as one who has perspired, may bathe quickly in lukewarm water, to remove perspiration, and for *kevod haberiot*.
10. *Be'er HaGola, Yoreh De'ah* 393.
11. *Pirkei DeRabbi Eliezer* 17.
12. Some *Aḥaronim* question this practice. First, it is possible that the congregation accepts Shabbat with the recitation of *Lekha Dodi*. In addition, nowadays, it is usually dark by the time the congregation recites *Mizmor Shir* (see *Shemirat Shabbat*

Which aspects of *avelut* are observed on Shabbat? The Talmud[13] teaches that on Shabbat the mourner uncovers his head (i.e., *atifat harosh* is not observed), reverses his rent garment, and lifts the bed (i.e., *kefiyat hamita* is not observed). However, inconspicuous mourning practices [*devarim shebetzina*], e.g., refraining from bathing and from sexual relations, are observed. In practice, as *Shulḥan Arukh*[14] rules, one should refrain from sexual relations and from bathing, but one should also refrain from public expressions of mourning. The mourner is permitted to wear leather shoes.

Regarding the study of Torah, while some *Rishonim* permit studying Torah on Shabbat, most authorities, including Rabbeinu Tam, Maharam of Rothenburg, and Rosh, as well as the *Shulḥan Arukh*,[15] maintain that *Talmud Torah* is also considered to be an inconspicuous form of mourning and is prohibited. Similarly, a mourner may not read the Torah or be called to the Torah, unless he is the only Kohen.[16] *Pitḥei Te-shuva*[17] cites *Aḥaronim* who permit the mourner to be called to the Torah on occasions where he would ordinarily receive an *aliya*, for example, on a *yahrzeit*, on his son's *Brit Mila*, etc. The *Rishonim* disagree whether reviewing the weekly Torah portion [*shenayim mikra ve'eḥad targum*] is also prohibited. *Shulḥan Arukh* rules that one may review the weekly Torah reading on Shabbat.[18]

The *Aḥaronim* discuss whether the mourner may wear Shabbat clothing, or whether he wears unrent weekday garments. R. David b. Solomon ibn Zimra, known as Radbaz, maintains that just as one wears Shabbat clothing on the Shabbat before Tisha B'Av, so too, the mourner should wear Shabbat

*KeHilkhata* 65, n. 94) and therefore, it is preferable to greet the mourner immediately before reciting *Kabbalat Shabbat*.

13. See Mo'ed Katan 24b.
14. *Shulḥan Arukh, Yoreh De'ah* 400:1.
15. Ibid.
16. Rema, ibid.
17. *Pitḥei Teshuva, Yoreh De'ah* 400:1.
18. The *Aḥaronim* discuss whether one may review the portion with Rashi as well; see *Arukh HaShulḥan* (*Yoreh De'ah* 400:6), who permits doing so, while R. Ovadia Yosef (*Yabia Omer, Yoreh De'ah* 4:31; see also *Birkei Yosef, Yoreh De'ah* 400:4) rules that one may review the *parasha* only with Targum Onkelos.

clothing on the Shabbat during the week of mourning.[19] Although Rema[20] disagrees and writes that for the entire month, one should not wear Shabbat clothing, nowadays, it is customary to wear Shabbat clothing. However, one should change into Shabbat clothing just before Shabbat.

The Talmud[21] teaches that it is permitted to comfort mourners on Shabbat.

> And Beit Hillel permits [comforting mourners on Shabbat] ... And R. Ḥanina said: It was only with great difficulty that the sages permitted to comfort the mourners and visit the ill on Shabbat.

The *Rishonim* explain that although the rabbis feared that a mourner might become overcome by pain and grief,[22] *niḥum avelim* is still permitted. The *Aḥaronim,* however, criticize those who avoid visiting the mourner during the week and postpone *niḥum avelim* until Shabbat.[23] There are different customs regarding whether one may recite: May God comfort you among the other mourners of Zion and Jerusalem [*HaMakom yenaḥem etkhem,* etc.], or: It is Shabbat and prohibited to comfort, but consolation is soon to come [*Shabbat hi milenaḥem uneḥama kerova lavo*].[24] Some report that in Ashkenazic communities it is customary to refrain from visiting the house of a mourner to engage in *niḥum avelim* on Shabbat in the manner that one would during the week.[25]

It is preferable to recite the Saturday-night prayers in the mourner's house. Immediately after Shabbat, the mourner removes his leather shoes.[26] He must also remove his Shabbat clothing and don his mourning clothing, including the rent garment. It is preferable to wait until the

19. Radbaz, Responsa 2:693; see also *Magen Avraham* 262:2; *Maase Rav, Hilkhot Tisha B'Av* 197.
20. Rema, *Yoreh De'ah* 389:3. *Arukh HaShulḥan* (*Yoreh De'ah* 400:5) concurs, and attests that it is customary to refrain from wearing Shabbat clothing during *shiva* (although during the remaining Shabbatot of the *sheloshim* one may wear Shabbat clothing).
21. Shabbat 12a.
22. See Rashi, ibid.; Ran 5a.
23. See *Magen Avraham,* ibid.
24. See *Mishna Berura* 287:3.
25. *Gesher HaḤayim* 20:5:2.
26. Some remove their shoes before Maariv, either after reciting *Barukh HaMavdil* or after *Barekhu,* and some wait until after the conclusion of Maariv. A woman who does not recite Maariv removes her shoes after reciting *Barukh HaMavdil,* or after Havdala.

conclusion of the seven days of mourning to recite *Kiddush Levana*. If it will then be too late to recite *Kiddush Levana*, i.e., after half the monthly lunar cycle has passed (after the fifteenth night of the month),[27] the mourner should recite the blessing of *Kiddush Levana* alone, without the traditional additions typically recited.[28] Some write that a mourner who recites Havdala should omit the introductory verses recited before Havdala, and begin with the blessings.[29]

Although there is no prohibition, it is customary for a mourner not to serve as the *sheliaḥ tzibbur* on Shabbat.[30]

## *AVELUT* ON YOM TOV AND ḤOL HAMO'ED

### Burial before Yom Tov

As mentioned above, the Talmud[31] teaches that if a close relative is buried even one hour before a festival, the festival abrogates the seven-day mourning period. The mishna cites a dispute regarding which festive days abrogate the seven-day mourning period.

> R. Eliezer says: From the time that the Temple was destroyed, Shavuot is like Shabbat. Rabban Gamliel says: Even Rosh HaShana and Yom Kippur are considered like the Pilgrimage Festivals. And the Rabbis say: The halakha is neither in accordance with the statement of Rabban Gamliel nor in accordance with the statement of the Rabbis. Rather, with regard to mourning, Shavuot is treated like the other Pilgrimage Festivals, whereas Rosh HaShana and Yom Kippur are treated like Shabbat.

In practice, Pesaḥ, Shavuot, and Sukkot, as well as Rosh HaShana and Yom Kippur, all abrogate the seven days of mourning.[32]

---

27. *Shulḥan Arukh, Oraḥ Ḥayim* 426:3.
28. See *Gesher HaḤayim* 21:13:8.
29. *Pitḥei Teshuva, Yoreh De'ah* 391:1.
30. *Shulḥan Arukh, Yoreh De'ah* 376:4.
31. Mo'ed Katan 19a.
32. R. Aḥai Gaon (*She'iltot, Parashat Ḥayei Sara* 15) explains that Rabban Gamliel, who rules: Rosh HaShana and Yom Kippur are considered like the Pilgrimage Festivals, maintains that the mitzva of *simḥat Yom Tov* applies on these days as well. R. Aḥai Gaon clearly understands that it is the mitzva to rejoice that abrogates *shiva*.

On Erev Yom Tov before these days, the mourner observes the *shiva* until late in the day, as close to nightfall as possible. He preferably recites the Minḥa prayer, after which he may bathe and even launder his garments.[33] On Erev Yom Kippur it is permitted to bathe even before Minḥa, and the mourner may attend the Minḥa service and eat the *seuda mafseket* sitting on a chair.[34] Some rule that on the day before Pesaḥ, mourning ceases at midday; since the *korban pesaḥ* was offered on the fourteenth of Nissan beginning at noon, that time has the status of a quasi-festival.[35]

The festival does not abrogate the thirty-day mourning period; therefore, during the intermediate days of a festival [Ḥol HaMo'ed], one observes the mourning rites of *sheloshim*. In addition to not cutting one's hair or laundering one's garments, as these are already prohibited on Ḥol HaMo'ed, the mourner may not cut his nails and should refrain from attending and participating in festive social gatherings [*simḥat mere'ut*].[36]

How many days of *sheloshim* does the mourner observe after the festival? Since the festival abrogates the seven-day period of mourning, it is as though seven days of the *sheloshim* have already passed. Therefore, if the deceased was buried on one of the six days before Pesaḥ, that period counts as seven days of mourning, and Pesaḥ counts as an additional seven days, or eight outside of Israel, leaving sixteen days, or fifteen outside of Israel, for the mourner to observe after the festival.[37] Similarly, if the burial occurred on any of the six days before Shavuot, that period counts as seven days of mourning, and the festival counts as seven days, or eight outside of Israel, so the mourner observes another sixteen days of *sheloshim*, or fifteen outside of Israel.[38] If the burial occurs on any of the six days before Sukkot, the first day of Sukkot cancels the *shiva* and the days before the festival count

33. Rema 399:5; see also *Mishna Berura* 548:42.
34. See *Pitḥei Teshuva, Yoreh De'ah* 389:1.
35. *Ḥokhmat Adam* 169:3.
36. *Shulḥan Arukh, Yoreh De'ah* 399:1.
37. *Shulḥan Arukh, Yoreh De'ah* 399:7.
38. The Talmud (Mo'ed Katan 24b) teaches that if one failed to bring the festival offering on Shavuot itself, he may bring it during the six days following the festival, and just as the offerings of the Festival of Pesaḥ have redress for all seven days, as Pesaḥ is seven days long, so too, the offerings of the Festival of Shavuot have redress for seven days, during the week following Shavuot. From this we learn that the halakhic status of Shavuot is like that of a seven-day festival for all halakhic purposes, including the laws of mourning; see *Shulḥan Arukh, Yoreh De'ah* 8.

as seven days, the festival counts as seven days, and Shemini Atzeret, whose status is that of a separate festival, counts as an additional seven days, totaling twenty-one days, or twenty-two days outside of Israel, leaving nine days, or eight outside of Israel.[39]

The Talmud teaches that not only do the festivals [*regalim*], during which one is obligated to bring a special burnt offering of appearance, count as seven days, but the same is true with regard to Rosh HaShana and Yom Kippur, which are in certain respects equated to festivals. They too count as seven days of the *sheloshim*.[40] Therefore, if the burial occurred before Rosh HaShana, the days before Rosh HaShana count as seven days, and Rosh HaShana counts as an additional seven days. The *Rishonim* debate whether in that case Yom Kippur abrogates the remaining days of *sheloshim*. The *Shulḥan Arukh*[41] rules that just as one who began observing *shiva* seven days before Yom Kippur, on the third of Tishrei, may cut his hair before Yom Kippur, as Yom Kippur cancels the *sheloshim* (see below), so too, in a case where Rosh HaShana abrogated the *shiva*. If the burial occurs on or after the fourth of Tishrei, six days before Yom Kippur, Yom Kippur abrogates the *shiva*, and the first day of Sukkot abrogates the *sheloshim*. In that case, the mourner may cut his hair before Sukkot.[42]

The mishna teaches that if the burial occurs eight days before the festival, the festival abrogates the thirty-day mourning period. The Talmud[43] adds that even if the burial occurred seven days before the festival, the principle of *miktzat hayom kekhulo* means that the *shiva* ends on the morning of the seventh day, the afternoon counts as the eighth day, and the festival abrogates the remaining days of mourning.

If the eighth day after the burial coincides with a Shabbat that immediately precedes a festival, when haircutting and laundry are prohibited, one may launder his garments and cut his hair on Erev Shabbat. However, if the seventh day coincides with such a Shabbat, the mourner may not cut his hair on Friday; however, he may cut his hair during Ḥol HaMo'ed, because he was unable to do so before the festival.[44]

---

39. Mo'ed Katan, ibid.; *Shulḥan Arukh, Yoreh De'ah* 11.
40. Mo'ed Katan, ibid.
41. Mo'ed Katan, ibid.; *Shulḥan Arukh, Yoreh De'ah* 399:9.
42. *Shulḥan Arukh* (*Yoreh De'ah* 399:10) rules in accordance with Rosh, that consecutive festivals abrogate both *shiva* and *sheloshim*.
43. Mo'ed Katan 19a–b.
44. See *Shulḥan Arukh, Oraḥ Ḥayim* 548:8; see also *Mishna Berura* 38.

Although there is no prohibition, it is customary for a mourner not to serve as the *sheliaḥ tzibbur* on Yom Tov.[45]

### Burial on Ḥol HaMo'ed

If the deceased is buried on Ḥol HaMo'ed, the *shiva* begins after Yom Tov. Outside of Israel, the *shiva* begins after Yom Tov Sheni, the eighth day of Pesaḥ, or Simḥat Torah, but Yom Tov Sheni counts as the first day of *shiva*, and therefore, only six additional days are observed after Yom Tov Sheni.[46] Inconspicuous mourning practices [*devarim shebetzina*] are in effect on Ḥol HaMo'ed; the mourner may not engage in sexual relations or bathe for pleasure in hot water. It is customary to permit Torah study during Ḥol HaMo'ed, although the mourner should not be called to the Torah for an *aliya*.[47] He may bathe as usual before the last day of Yom Tov.[48]

In this case the thirty-day period of mourning is calculated from the burial.[49] The *Aḥaronim* discuss whether Shemini Atzeret, which the Talmud considers to be an independent festival with regard to certain laws,[50] and which as mentioned above counts as seven days toward the *sheloshim* in a case where the burial took place before Sukkot, would count in this case too as an additional seven days. Although some suggest that when the burial is on Ḥol HaMo'ed, Shemini Atzeret should count as seven days,[51] most *Aḥaronim* rule that Shemini Atzeret counts as only one day.[52]

## ROSH HASHANA AND YOM KIPPUR [*YAMIM NORA'IM*]

Although the mourner serves as the *sheliaḥ tzibbur* on weekdays whenever possible, he may not lead the services on Rosh HaShana and Yom Kippur,

45. *Shulḥan Arukh, Yoreh De'ah* 376:4.
46. *Shulḥan Arukh, Oraḥ Ḥayim* 548:1; *Mishna Berura* 6.
47. *Mishna Berura*, ibid., 16.
48. *Derisha, Yoreh De'ah* 389:1.
49. Mo'ed Katan 24a; *Shulḥan Arukh, Yoreh De'ah* 399:2.
50. Sukka 47a.
51. See Maharshal 5; *Masat Binyamin* 71.
52. See *Beit Yosef, Yoreh De'ah* 399; *Taz* 4; Shakh 7; *Magen Avraham, Oraḥ Ḥayim* 548:1. More recently, this is also the ruling of the *Mishna Berura* (ibid., 4), and R. Moshe Feinstein (*Iggerot Moshe, Yoreh De'ah* 1:256). R. Ovadia Yosef (*Ḥazon Ovadia*, vol. 3, pp. 117–18) rules likewise; *Gesher HaḤayim* (23:2:12) and *Penei Barukh* (29:13) rule that in extenuating circumstances one may rely upon the minority view and count Shemini Atzeret as seven days.

unless there is no one else better qualified to do so. Similarly, some write that he should not sound the shofar during the period of mourning.[53]

There are different views regarding whether a mourner may wear the white outer garment [*kittel*] worn by some on Rosh HaShana and Yom Kippur and at the Pesaḥ Seder. This may relate to the dispute whether the purpose of wearing the *kittel* is to emulate the angels, or to subdue and humble a person's heart.[54]

## SUKKOT

*Beit Yosef*[55] cites *Kol Bo*, who relates that the custom in Narbonne was that the mourner did not circle the *bima* with his lulav [*Hoshanot*]. Although *Beit Yosef* rejects this practice, R. Moshe Isserles, in his *Darkhei Moshe*, and later in his comments to the *Shulḥan Arukh*,[56] cites this custom.

Why should the mourner refrain from participating in the *Hoshanot*? Some suggest that circling the *bima* is similar to circling the altar in the Temple, which a mourner may not do.[57] Others reject this explanation.[58] *Taz* writes that just as a mourner does not serve as the *sheliaḥ tzibbur*, so too, he does not circle the *bima* during the *hakafot*. Many *Aḥaronim* also reject this explanation.

R. Yechiel Michel Tukachinsky, in his *Gesher HaḤayim*,[59] concludes that the *Hoshanot* are a manifestation of rejoicing [*simḥa*], from which a mourner must refrain. He notes that even this understanding poses numerous difficulties, as the laws of mourning are not observed on festivals. Some suggest that the mourner may participate in the *Hoshanot* on the first day of Yom Tov, and on Ḥol HaMo'ed.[60] One should follow the local custom.

---

53. See *Mateh Efraim* 585:7.
54. See Rema, *Oraḥ Ḥayim* 610; *Taz* 2. *Eliya Rabba* (ibid.) explains that a mourner does not wear a *kittel*; *Mateh Efraim* disagrees.
55. Beit Yosef, *Oraḥ Ḥayim* 600.
56. Rema, *Oraḥ Ḥayim* 660:2.
57. *Baḥ, Oraḥ Ḥayim* 660:2. He cites the Talmud (Sukka 44a; see also Tosafot, s.v. *Kohanim*), which cites R. Yoḥanan, who rules that Kohanim who are blemished [*baalei mum*] or who grow their hair long [*peruei rosh*] do not circle the altar. It is extrapolated from here that mourners, who also let their hair grow long, do not participate in *Hoshanot*, which symbolize the circling of the altar in the Temple.
58. See *Taz*, ibid., 2; see also *Iggerot Moshe, Yoreh De'ah* 4:61.
59. *Gesher HaḤayim* 2:17:5.
60. See *Kaf HaḤayim* 660:18.

In most communities, mourners stand on the *bima* and hold *sifrei Torah* during the *Hoshanot*, to avoid publicly displaying their state of mourning.

On Simḥat Torah, mourners generally refrain from the festive dancing during the *hakafot*. The rabbi, and other individuals whose failure to participate would constitute a public display of mourning, may participate in the *hakafot*.[61] Some rule that the mourner may hold the *sefer Torah* and circle the *bima*.[62] In Sephardic communities, after the *shiva* has ended, the mourner participates fully in the Simḥat Torah festivities.[63]

### *AVELUT* ON PURIM

The Talmud discusses the conflict between *avelut* and Shabbat and Yom Tov. The Gemara[64] presents the conflicting legal values:

> If it is a mourning period that had already begun at the outset of the festival, the positive mitzva of rejoicing on the festival, which is incumbent upon the community, comes and overrides the positive mitzva of the individual, i.e., mourning. And if the mourning period began only now, i.e., the deceased died during the festival, the positive mitzva of the individual does not come and override the positive mitzva of the community.

According to the Talmud's reasoning, i.e., that the positive mitzva of rejoicing on the festival, which is incumbent upon the community, comes and overrides the positive mitzva of the individual, *avelut* must certainly be observed on Ḥanukka and Purim.

However, although it is only a holiday by rabbinic law, Purim is also described as a day of *simḥa*.[65]

---

61. See *Minḥat Yitzḥak* 6:62.
62. See *Gesher HaḤayim* 23:3:7; see also ibid., 2:17:4:2.
63. R. Eliezer Melamed, in his *Peninei Halakha* (*Hilkhot Sukka*, chap. 7, n. 4), suggests that in congregations comprised of Ashkenazim and Sephardim, one who wishes to rely upon the Sephardic practice may do so. In addition, he cites his father, who rules that since the mourning practices of the twelve months are an expression of respect for one's parents, if one estimates that his parents would not wish him to refrain from the Simḥat Torah festivities, he may participate in the *hakafot*.
64. Mo'ed Katan 14b.
65. Est. 9:19–22.

> Therefore, the unwalled Jews, who live in the unwalled cities, observe the fourteenth day of the month Adar as a day of joy [*simḥa*], banqueting, and a holiday, and of sending portions one to another. Mordecai wrote these matters, and he sent scrolls to all the Jews who were in all the provinces of King Ahasuerus, near and far, to establish for them to observe the fourteenth day of the month Adar, and the fifteenth day of it, in each and every year...To observe them as days of banquet and joy [*simḥa*], and of sending portions one to another, and gifts to the indigent.

The nature of this *simḥa* is subject to much discussion, and the question whether or not *avelut* is observed on Purim may shed light on the nature of this *simḥa*.

On the one hand, Rambam[66] rules that all aspects of *avelut* are observed on Ḥanukka and Purim. On the other hand, R. Aḥai Gaon, cited by the *Tur*,[67] maintains that since Purim is called a day of *simḥa*, like Yom Tov, if the burial takes place before Purim, Purim abrogates the seven-day mourning period. Rosh, and his teacher Maharam of Rothenburg,[68] disagree with R. Aḥai Gaon, but rule that one does not observe mourning customs on Purim; Purim is like Shabbat regarding *avelut*.

The position of the *Shulḥan Arukh* is unclear.[69] Rema rules in accordance with Rosh, that one does not observe *avelut* on Purim, or on the next day, Shushan Purim, except for *devarim shebetzina*. After Purim, however, the *shiva* continues. Many recent *Aḥaronim* adopt this position as well.[70]

This debate may reflect different approaches to why Yom Tov cancels

---

66. Rambam, *Hilkhot Avel* 11:3; see Rabbeinu Gershom, cited by the *Hagahot Maimoniyot* (3), who concurs.
67. See *Tur, Oraḥ Ḥayim* 696. Our text of the *She'iltot* (67) appears to be different.
68. See Rosh, Mo'ed Katan 3:85.
69. In *Yoreh De'ah* (401:7), he rules in accordance with the opinion of Rosh, but in *Oraḥ Ḥayim* (696:4), he cites the opinion of Rambam. Some suggest that the *Shulḥan Arukh* distinguishes between a case where the relative died and was buried on Purim, in which case mourning is observed, and a case where the deceased was buried before Purim, in which case only private expressions of mourning are observed on Purim (*Derisha*; see Shakh 4). Others attribute this contradiction to a scribal error; the second passage really says that "all *private* matters of *avelut* are observed on Purim" (see *Be'er Heitev, Yoreh De'ah* 401:2). R. Ovadia Yosef (*Ḥazon Ovadia*, vol. 3, p. 122) asserts that the *Shulḥan Arukh* changed his mind and his ruling in *Yoreh De'ah* reflects his revised opinion.
70. See *Mishna Berura* 696:12; *Gesher HaḤayim* 23:3:9; *Ḥazon Ovadia*, ibid. Shakh (4)

*avelut*, and to the nature of *simḥat Purim*. Regarding Yom Tov, we can point to three different expressions of *simḥat Yom Tov*: Eating a festive meal consisting of either peace offerings of rejoicing [*shalmei simḥa*] or meat and wine [*basar veyayin*]; personal joy [*simḥa shebalev*]; and the joy of sharing one's good fortune with those less fortunate (see Deut. 16:14 and Rambam, *Hilkhot Yom Tov* 6:18). Ostensibly, the second type of *simḥa*, *simḥa shebalev*, conflicts with *avelut*.

What is the nature of the *simḥa* observed on Purim? R. Aḥai Gaon apparently believes that on Purim one experiences an inner, personal joy, which in turn abrogates *avelut*. Others disagree and maintain that the *simḥa* of Purim is of an external nature, manifest through the *seudat Purim*, and this may be powerful enough to override, but not abrogate, *avelut*. Alternatively, the *simḥa* of Purim is of the third variety, the joy of sharing with others. Indeed, Rambam[71] writes:

> It is preferable for a person to be generous with his gifts to the poor rather than to be lavish in his preparation of the Purim feast or in sending portions to his friends, as there is no greater and more glorious joy than to cause the hearts of the poor, the orphans, the widows, and the converts to rejoice. One who brings joy to the hearts of these unfortunate individuals is similar to the Divine Presence, as it is stated: "To revive the spirit of the humble and to revive the heart of the downtrodden" (Is. 57:15).

Rambam apparently maintains that *simḥat Purim* is manifest primarily through *matanot la'evyonim* and sharing one's meal with others, which do not in any way conflict with the essential experience of mourning.

In practice, public expressions of mourning are not practiced on Purim, or on Shushan Purim. However, the mourner observes *devarim shebetzina*, and refrains from bathing and marital relations. The mourner is obligated to hear the reading of Megillat Esther at night, and again during the day, to give *mishlo'aḥ manot* and *matanot la'evyonim*, and to eat a *seudat Purim*. The mourner may wear standard garments, as well as leather shoes, but should keep any festive behavior to a minimum. If the deceased is buried

---

cites Maharshal and *Baḥ*, who write that the custom is in accordance with the ruling of Rambam.

71. *Hilkhot Megilla* 2:17

on Purim, the mourner should rend his garment and then change into unrent garments. He should eat the *seudat havraa* upon returning home, although some write that he should not eat hard-boiled eggs in that *seuda*, an indication that full-fledged mourning is not observed on Purim.

*Chapter 13*

# The Mourner's Kaddish [*Kaddish Yatom*] and Leading the Prayer Service

### KADDISH: BACKGROUND

Although the earliest version of the Kaddish prayer appears in the ninth-century Siddur of R. Amram Gaon, the Talmud and midrashim refer to the recitation of Kaddish, and more specifically, to the congregation's response: May His great name be blessed forever and for all eternity [*yehe shemeh rabba*, etc.], in numerous places.[1] For example, R. Yosei relates:[2]

> I was once walking along the road when I entered the ruins of an old, abandoned building among the ruins of Jerusalem in order to pray. I noticed that Elijah, of blessed memory, came and guarded the entrance for me and waited at the entrance until I finished my prayer. When I finished praying… Elijah said to me: What voice did you hear in that ruin? I responded: I heard a heavenly voice, cooing like a dove and saying: Woe to the children, due to whose sins I destroyed My house, burned My Temple, and exiled them among

1. Sifri, Deut. 306.
2. Berakhot 3b.

> the nations. And Elijah said to me: By your life and by your head, not only did that voice cry out in that moment, but it cries out three times each and every day. Moreover, any time that God's greatness is evoked, such as when Israel enters synagogues and study halls and answers [in the Kaddish prayer], *yehe shemeh rabba*, the Holy One, Blessed be He, shakes His head and says: Happy is the king who is thus praised in his house.

Similarly, the Talmud[3] relates:

> R. Yehoshua b. Levi said that anyone who answers, wholeheartedly, with all his might: *Amen, yehe shemeh rabba*, his judgment is torn, as it is stated: "When punishments are annulled in Israel, when the people volunteered, bless the Lord" (Judges 5:2).

The Targum Yerushalmi,[4] in a variation of a story that appears in the Talmud,[5] attributes this statement to Jacob, in response to hearing his sons declare: "Hear Israel [the Lord is our God the Lord is one]."

Elsewhere, rabbinic sources also mention the special Kaddish recited after the study of the Talmud or Aggada.[6]

> On what basis does the world endure? On the *kedusha desidra* and on *yehe shemeh rabba*... recited after the [public study of] Aggada.

Similarly, the Midrash[7] relates:

> When the Jews gather in their houses of study to hear Aggada from a sage, after which they respond: *Yehe shemeh rabba*... God rejoices and is elevated in His world. He then says to His ministering angels: Come see this nation I created and how they praise Me. [The angels] then dress Him in glory and splendor.

---

3. Shabbat 119b; see also Berakhot 21b, 57a.
4. Targum Yerushalmi, Gen. 49:2.
5. Pesaḥim 56a.
6. Sota 49a; See also Soferim 19:9.
7. *Yalkut Shimoni*, Prov. 952.

Finally, the special Kaddish recited at a funeral is mentioned in geonic sources.[8]

## MOURNER'S KADDISH [*KADDISH YATOM*]

Mourner's Kaddish is not mentioned in the Talmud, geonic literature,[9] or the early Spanish *Rishonim*, e.g., Rambam and Ramban. R. Elazar of Worms (1176–1238), author of Roke'aḥ, writes: "The orphan recites Kaddish."[10] He attributes this practice to the following story, which appears in various forms and in the works of other *Rishonim*, including his disciple, R. Yitzchak of Vienna, the *Or Zarua*,[11] as well as the *Maḥzor Vitry*.[12]

> An incident that occurred to R. Akiva as he was walking on the road adjacent to a cemetery: R. Akiva noticed a man in the cemetery who appeared to be unclothed and his body black as coal. He was carrying a large bundle of thorns on his head. It seemed to R. Akiva that the man was alive and that he was galloping like a horse. R. Akiva commanded the man to stop and the man stopped. R. Akiva then asked him: Why are you doing such hard work?...The man said: I am deceased. They send me each day to chop wood. R. Akiva said: What was your occupation in the world from which you came? The man said to him: I was a tax collector. I would favor the rich and kill the poor. R. Akiva said: Have you not heard from your supervisors a remedy for you? The man said: Please do not detain me any longer, lest my tormentors get angry at me; there is no remedy for this man. I heard them say: If this poor man had a son who could stand in the congregation and recite: *Barekhu et Hashem hamevorakh,* and they would respond after him: *Barukh Hashem hamevorakh leolam va'ed,* or if he recites: *Yitgadel,* and they respond after him: *Yehe shemeh rabba mevorakh,* this man would be freed of his punishment. But when I died I did not leave a son in this world. But I left a pregnant wife.

8. *Teshuvot R. Natronai Gaon* (ed. Brody), *Yoreh De'ah* 284; see also *Siddur R. Saadia Gaon*, pp. 358–59.
9. See, however, Soferim 19:9.
10. *Peirushei Siddur HaTefilla LaRoke'aḥ*, vol. 2, p. 602.
11. *Or Zarua* 2:50.
12. *Maḥzor Vitry* 144.

> I do not know, if she gave birth to a son, who would teach him, as I have no one in the world who loves me.
>
> At that moment, R. Akiva accepted upon himself to search for the man's wife and to discover whether she had given birth to a son in order to teach him Torah and have him stand before the congregation. R. Akiva said to him: What is your name? He said to him: Akiva. And your wife's name? Shoshniva. And the name of your city? Ludkiya. R. Akiva was greatly pained but he went and asked about him. He came to that place and asked about him. They said to him: May the bones of that wicked one rot... He asked about the son. They said: He was uncircumcised; we did not even engage in the mitzva of *mila*. R. Akiva took him and circumcised him and he sat him before him but the boy would not receive the Torah. It was only after he fasted for forty days that a divine voice emerged and said to him: Go and teach him. He went and taught him Torah and *Keriat Shema* and the eighteen blessings and *Birkat HaMazon*, and he stood him before the congregation and he recited: *Barekhu et Hashem hamevorakh* and the congregation responded: *Barukh Hashem hamevorakh leolam va'ed*, until: *Amen yehe shemeh rabba*. At that moment, the deceased man was freed from his punishment. He appeared to R. Akiva in a dream and said to him: May it be His will that your mind find peace in *Gan Eden* as you rescued me from the judgment of Gehinnom.

Based on this story, the custom developed that the one to lead services on Motza'ei Shabbat was someone whose father or mother had died, providing the mourner with the opportunity to recite *Barekhu* and Kaddish.

R. Yitzchak of Vienna, cited above, concludes:

> Our custom in Bohemia and the custom in the Rhineland as well is that on Shabbat after the congregation recites *Ein KeElokeinu*, the orphan stands and recites Kaddish, but in France I saw that they are not insistent with regard to who recites Kaddish, whether it is a child who lost a parent, or a child who has both parents. But our custom is more appropriate due to the story of R. Akiva.

This story appears in earlier sources as well, including the *Eliyahu Zuta,*[13] although there the story is related regarding R. Yoḥanan b. Zakkai, and does not specifically mention reciting Kaddish. Later medieval sources cite this custom, and mention that the mourner should recite Kaddish for twelve months, read the *haftara* on Shabbat, and lead the prayers at the conclusion of Shabbat.[14]

It appears that this Kaddish was initially instituted for minors who were not eligible to lead the service.[15] R. Moshe b. Avraham of Przemysl (d. 1606), in his *Mateh Moshe,*[16] describes why adult mourners began to say Kaddish.

> The practice of mourners reciting Kaddish during the mourning period was instituted due to minors, and later due to adults incapable of leading the services. That is why the Kaddish became known as the orphan's Kaddish [*Kaddish Yatom*].

Although *Shulḥan Arukh* does not mention this Kaddish, Rema writes:[17]

> Reciting Kaddish for a parent appears in the *midrashot*; therefore, it is customary to recite the final Kaddish for one's father and mother for twelve months, and it is customary to read the *haftara,* and to lead the Saturday-evening service, as that is the time when souls return to Gehinnom, and when a child prays and sanctifies [God's name] publicly he redeems his father and mother from Gehinnom.

Elsewhere he rules:[18]

> *Kaddish Yatom* is said after *Aleinu*. Even if there are no orphans in the congregation, another person who does not have a father or mother should recite it, and even one with both a father and a mother may recite [Kaddish] if his parents do not mind.

---

13. *Eliyahu Zuta* 17; see also *Zohar Ḥadash, Parashat Aḥarei Mot.*
14. See for example, *Orḥot Ḥayim, Hilkhot Avel.*
15. See *Siddur Rashi* 216; see also *Maḥzor Vitry* 93, 101.
16. *Mateh Moshe* 213.
17. Rema, *Yoreh De'ah* 376:4.
18. Rema, *Oraḥ Ḥayim* 132:2; see also Maharil 28.

By the late Middle Ages, it appears that *Kaddish Yatom* became an integral part of the mourning process.

## HOW MANY PEOPLE RECITE EACH KADDISH

The original custom was that even if there were many mourners praying in the congregation, only one would recite the *Kaddish Yatom*. In fact, several *Aḥaronim* formulated principles to determine which mourner takes precedence [*kedima*] over which others.[19] This practice, however, led to dispute, communal strife, and at times, even violence.[20]

R. Yaakov Emden (1697–1776) relates that the custom in Sephardic communities was for all the mourners to recite Kaddish in unison.[21] In his Siddur, he writes that he did not bother discussing the laws of precedence [*kedima*] in reciting Kaddish, which were relevant only in communities where one person would recite each Kaddish, because he preferred the Sephardic custom. He does not appear, however, to have instituted this practice. R. Moshe Sofer, in deference to the prevalent Ashkenazic custom, strongly disagrees with R. Emden.[22]

Interestingly, R. Menachem Mendel Steinhardt, an eighteenth-century German rabbi, and one of the three members of the consistory, the body governing Jewish congregations, of Westphalia, published a small pamphlet called *Divrei Iggeret* (ed. W. Heidenheim, Rödelheim, 1812), which justified ritual innovations introduced by the Jewish consistory at Cassel, attempting to prove that they corresponded to Jewish law. Alongside the numerous ordinances, including lifting the ban on *kitniyot* on Pesaḥ and abolishing the practice of *Hoshanot* and *ḥibut arava*, R. Steinhardt endorses, and provides halakhic support for, a previous call to permit all mourners to recite the

19. See, for example, *Magen Avraham* 132:2.
20. R. Yechiel Michel Tukachinsky, in his *Gesher HaḤayim* 30:10:13, relates: "And this sickness that I have seen, that there are some mourners who fight and cause great strife in the synagogue, for the Kaddish! Isn't the entire purpose of the Kaddish to compensate for the sin of the desecration of God's name, and to sanctify the heavenly name, and ultimately, through their actions they, God forbid, add to the desecration of His name."
21. See, for example, R. Yaakov Ḥagiz, *Halakhot Ketanot* (2:48). See also *Ben Ish Ḥai* (*Shana Rishona, Vayigash* 16), who relates that in Baghdad the entire community would (mistakenly) recite the Kaddish after *Barekhu*.
22. Ḥatam Sofer, *Oraḥ Ḥayim* 159.

Kaddish in unison. He cites the rulings of R. Yaakov Emden, as well as that of R. Yaakov Ḥagiz, a seventeenth-century Sephardic scholar, in support of his position. R. Avraham Hirsch Eisenstadt (1812–1868) cites this position in his *Pitḥei Teshuva*.[23] Although it is unlikely that the *Pitḥei Teshuva*, or the numerous *Aḥaronim* who cite this view,[24] knew who this German rabbi was, the *Divrei Iggeret* became the primary source for this relatively new practice.

The original practice, according to which only one mourner recited Kaddish, was observed into the nineteenth century, as R. Yaakov Ettlinger, a halakhic authority and leader of German Orthodox Jewry, was consulted regarding a congregation whose rabbi sought to allow all the mourners to recite Kaddish in unison to prevent communal strife. R. Ettlinger responded:[25]

> I am curious as to how this rabbi called for changing the custom of the Jewish people, which has been practiced in all of the lands of Germany and Poland for more than three hundred years, regarding the recitation of the Mourner's Kaddish by each and every mourner, following in the footsteps of the Reformers of our time, who have instituted changes in the prayers, and they established this practice as well.

It is possible that another incident led to this new practice taking root in Ashkenazic communities. In 1831, what later became known as the Asiatic cholera pandemic reached the Jewish communities of Northern Europe. R. Akiva Eiger, a halakhic authority and leader in the early nineteenth century, records that there were apparently too many mourners who wished to recite Kaddish. He writes:[26]

> In the month of Av, 5591 (1831), when, due to our great sins, the cholera plague spread, and there were many mourners who wished to recite Kaddish, I established that the mourners may recite

23. *Pitḥei Teshuva, Yoreh De'ah* 376:6.
24. See *Kitzur Shulḥan Arukh* 26:18; *Taamei HaMinhagim UMekor HaDinim*, p. 457; *Sefer Kol Bo al Avelut*, p. 371; *Penei Barukh*, pp. 368–69; *Nitei Gavriel, Hilkhot Avelut*, p. 346, etc.
25. *Binyan Tziyon* 122.
26. *Pesakim VeTakanot Rabbi Akiva Eiger* (Jerusalem, 1971), pp. 63–64.

> Kaddish together, for an entire year, and at the end of that year, on Rosh Ḥodesh Av, 5592 (1832), when, God willing, the plague will end, I established that they should no longer recite Kaddish together, except for the one Kaddish recited after the morning prayer, but not the other *Kaddishim*.

It appears that this ordinance may have facilitated the spread of the custom of many mourners reciting Kaddish together, as R. Akiva Eiger's son, R. Shlomo Eiger, wrote[27]:

> I already protested that which began in numerous synagogues that all of the mourners recite Kaddish together…it is clear to me that that which my father ruled, that they should all recite Kaddish together, wasn't because he agreed with this practice, but rather because he permitted violating this minor prohibition because of the psychological need of the people [*tzorekh hahamonim*] during the cholera outbreak.

Although the cholera pandemic passed, the practice of permitting mourners to recite Kaddish in unison continued to spread across Europe.

Those who opposed this practice raised several concerns. First, the Talmud[28] teaches: "Two voices cannot be heard simultaneously" [*trei kali lo mishtama'i*]. How then is it possible for the congregation to hear the Kaddish, and properly respond? Second, according to some, the benefit provided by reciting Kaddish is that it elicits the response of the congregation: *Yehe shemeh rabba*, but when several people recite Kaddish together, it is unlikely that the congregation will respond to all of them. The *Aḥaronim* provide possible justifications for this practice, including the suggestion that reciting Kaddish is considered to be dear; therefore, even when several people recite it in unison each voice is heard. In addition, it is possible that there is no obligation to hear the Kaddish, as indicated in the Talmud.[29]

27. R. Binyamin Shlomo Hamburger, in his *HaYeshiva HaRama BeFiorda* (Machon Moreshet Ashkenaz, 2010), discusses this issue, and cites a previously unpublished manuscript of R. Shlomo Eiger (vol. 2, p. 455, n. 115).
28. Rosh HaShana 27a.
29. See Sukka 51b, which relates that in the large synagogue in Alexandria, they would wave flags in order to indicate when the congregation should answer Amen. *Beit Yosef*

With the exception of those who assiduously adhere to German customs, it is customary in almost all congregations for all mourners to recite Kaddish together. Some insist that they all stand together at a central location.[30] It is proper for the mourners to recite Kaddish at the same pace, i.e., in unison.

### IS IT PERMITTED FOR WOMEN TO RECITE THE MOURNER'S KADDISH?

First discussed over three hundred years ago, this question has been raised again in recent years, as many women have expressed interest in reciting Kaddish during their year of mourning. While a woman does not serve as the *sheliaḥ tzibbur*, is it permitted for her to recite Kaddish with the other mourners?[31]

This question was first raised in the seventeenth century by R. Yair Chaim Bacharach (1638–1701). R. Bacharach, in his *Ḥavot Ya'ir*,[32] relates a person's request that, following his death, ten men would study Torah in his home, and that his daughter would recite Kaddish at the conclusion of the Torah study. R. Bacharach notes that the congregation's scholars, in Amsterdam, did not object. R. Bacharach writes that legally, it is not prohibited to do this, as women, too, are obligated to sanctify God's name. By reciting Kaddish in the presence of ten men, she sanctifies God's name and brings benefit and comfort to the soul of the departed. He concludes, however, that one should oppose this practice, as it is contrary to Jewish custom. He concludes: "We should be concerned that [by condoning this practice] the authority [*ko'aḥ*] of the customs of the Jewish people, which also have the status of Torah, will be weakened, and each person will construct an

---

(*Oraḥ Ḥayim* 56) and *Magen Avraham* (*Oraḥ Ḥayim* 56:9) appear to disagree, implying that it is crucial to hear the entire Kaddish.

30. *Teshuvot VeHanhagot, Oraḥ Ḥayim* 11:42.

31. Some *Aḥaronim* note that if the women's section [*ezrat nashim*] is located in a different room, or separated by a full wall [*meḥitza*], then the women might not be considered to be in the same prayer space [*reshut*] as the men, and may certainly not recite Kaddish (*Minḥat Yitzḥak* 4:10; *She'erit Yosef* 2:60; *Yaḥel Yisrael* 84); see R. Yehuda Herzl Henkin's *Benei Banim* (2:7), which claims that those who permit women to recite Kaddish are clearly referring to a sanctuary where the *meḥitzot* do not reach the ceiling. In addition, although some identify *kol isha* as the primary obstacle, that does not seem to be a concern; see, for example, Megilla 23a and *Yeḥave Daat* 4:15.

32. *Ḥavot Ya'ir* 222.

altar for himself, based on his own rationale, and the words of the rabbis will become a laughingstock." A slightly younger contemporary, R. Yaakov Reischer (1661–1733),[33] addresses a similar question and permits a daughter not yet bat mitzva to recite Kaddish for her father at a *minyan* convened in her home, but not in the synagogue.[34]

Interestingly, years later, R. Eleazer Fleckeles (1754–1826),[35] a student of R. Yechezkel Landau, recorded that the custom of the congregations of Prague was to assemble in the morning in the vestibule of the synagogue to recite psalms. After the conclusion of the recitation of the psalms, the young orphan girls, aged five or six, would recite Kaddish. He emphasized that this practice should not be performed in the synagogue sanctuary, as it is inappropriate for women to enter the synagogue at all when men are praying there.

The question of women reciting Kaddish arose more frequently at the end of the nineteenth century and during the twentieth century. Numerous halakhic authorities[36] prohibited women from reciting Kaddish. The popular halakhic compendium, *Penei Barukh*,[37] summarizes that approach.

> There are those who say that a daughter can recite Kaddish in a *minyan* in her home, but all the authorities dispute that, and write that she may not recite Kaddish, even in her home, and even if her father commanded her to do so. And if she wishes to fulfill her father's wishes or to benefit him, she should ensure that she attend all of the services in the synagogue, and make certain to answer Amen in response to those reciting Kaddish. That will serve her purpose no less than reciting Kaddish.

However, some authorities permit women in general, and daughters in particular, to recite Kaddish. R. Eliezer Zalman Grayevsky (1843–1899), in his

---

33. *Shevut Yaakov* 2:93; see also *Be'er Heitev* 135:5.

34. R. Ephraim Zalman Margolis, in his *Mateh Efraim* (*Dinei Kaddish Yatom* 8; *Elef LeMagen* 9), and R. Chaim Chizkiyah Medini, in his *Sedei Ḥemed* (vol. 4, *Maarekhet Avelut* 170), disagree.

35. *Teshuva MeAhava, Oraḥ Ḥayim* 2:229:10.

36. *Torah Temima* 27; *Minḥat Yitzḥak* 4:30; *Tzitz Eliezer* 14:7; *Yalkut Yosef*, vol. 7, 23:11(9); *Mishpetei Uziel, Tinyana, Oraḥ Ḥayim* 13, and see also 23 and *Piskei Uziel* 3.

37. *Penei Barukh* 34:20.

book *Kaddish LeAlam*, goes to great lengths to establish and prove the view that a daughter may recite Kaddish and that this benefits her father and mother.

> It makes no difference whether the orphan is a son or a daughter… a woman may also recite Kaddish to redeem the soul of the deceased and elevate it… and therefore women, too, may recite Kaddish for their father.

R. Grayevsky assumes that where a man is survived only by a daughter, it is preferable that she recite Kaddish herself rather than pay a stranger to recite it on her behalf. R. Yechiel Michel Tukachinsky,[38] referring to a young girl, attests: "Many places permit her to recite Kaddish in the synagogue." However, he concludes: "In any case, an adult daughter is not permitted to recite Kaddish in the synagogue."

R. Yosef Eliyahu Henkin, one of the great American Torah scholars of the last century, discusses this issue and concludes: "If she also wishes to recite Kaddish before the women while Kaddish is being recited by the men in the synagogue, we are not particular."[39] His grandson, R. Yehuda Herzl Henkin,[40] records that his grandfather permitted an adult woman, too, to recite Kaddish. Elsewhere,[41] he notes that until recently, as described above, it was customary in Ashkenazic communities for only one mourner to recite Kaddish; therefore, he argues, even those who prohibited women from reciting Kaddish might agree that when many people recite Kaddish in unison, as is customary today, Kaddish recited publicly by a woman may no longer be perceived as a violation of custom or of communal standards of modesty. Ostensibly, according to this approach, it would be proper for at least one man to recite Kaddish so that the woman would not be reciting it alone.

Interestingly, R. Yehuda Herzl Henkin records that his grandfather attested: "I recall that in my childhood, a young woman recited Kaddish in the presence of the men in a pious, God-fearing congregation." Similarly, R. Moshe Feinstein[42] writes: "Throughout the generations it was customary

38. *Gesher HaḤayim* 30:8:5.
39. *Pardes* 6 (Adar, 5723).
40. *Benei Banim* 2:7.
41. Ibid., 3:27.
42. *Iggerot Moshe, Oraḥ Ḥayim* 5:12.

that, from time to time, a female mourner would enter the synagogue to recite Kaddish." R. Chanoch Grossberg, in his *Ḥazon LaMo'ed*, writes: "There were some whose custom was that a young daughter would recite Kaddish where there was no son, and that was the custom of my teacher and father-in-law (R. Neta Weiss, the Jerusalem Maggid) *z"l*." More recently, R. Yosef Dov Soloveitchik[43] and his brother R. Ahron Soloveichik[44] ruled that it is permitted for a woman to recite the Mourner's Kaddish alone from the women's section. Similarly, R. Shaul Yisraeli (1909–1995)[45] writes: "If a woman recites Kaddish in an inconspicuous voice in the women's section, it can be permitted, and it does not constitute a weakening of custom."

In conclusion, many authorities prohibited women from reciting Kaddish, and those who permitted recitation of Kaddish did so for a child, or in a private *minyan*. Many of these authorities expressed their deep concern that encouraging women to recite Kaddish could weaken accepted religious standards and communal customs, citing concerns about modesty and reform. However, there is clear evidence of this practice in previous generations, and some authorities permit women who wish to, to express their mourning through the public recitation of Kaddish.

It is the community's responsibility to ensure that all men and women can participate in daily prayers. Communities where it is customary for women to recite the Mourner's Kaddish should ensure that there is always at least one man reciting Kaddish, so that women mourners, and other members of the congregation, will not feel any discomfort. It is customary in many communities for women not to recite Kaddish. It is of paramount importance to avoid communal strife; this question should be handled with the greatest care and sensitivity. Of course, those women who choose not to recite Kaddish, like other mourners, should dedicate the period of mourning to other means of sanctifying God's name, e.g., Torah study, charitable acts, and good deeds, as discussed below.

---

43. See R. Dr. Joel B. Wolowelsky, "Women and Kaddish," *Judaism* 44, no. 3 (1995), pp. 282–90. See also R. Maurice Lamm's *The Jewish Way in Death and Mourning* (p. 160), which relates that R. Soloveitchik reported that women recited Kaddish in Gra's synagogue, the Gaon's *Klaus*.
44. *Od Yisrael Yosef Beni Ḥai* 32.
45. *BeMareh HaBazak* 1:4; see also R. Yaakov Ariel's comments to R. Maurice Lamm, *Darkah shel HaYahadut BeMavet UVeAvelut*, p. 358.

## PRACTICAL ASPECTS OF *KADDISH YATOM*

It is customary for the son of the deceased to recite *Kaddish Yatom*, in accordance with the principle: "The son causes merit for the father" [*bera mezakei abba*] (Sanhedrin 104a). We discussed above whether daughters may also recite the Kaddish, especially when the deceased had no sons. When there are no children to recite Kaddish, it may be recited by a grandchild, son-in-law, or brother. In the unfortunate case where a child dies before a parent, and had no children of his own, the parent may recite Kaddish for the child. As discussed previously, an adopted child may recite Kaddish for his adoptive parents, and a convert may recite Kaddish for his Jewish parents, and even for his non-Jewish parents. Although Kaddish is not typically recited for one's spouse especially if there are children to recite Kaddish, one who wishes to do so may recite Kaddish for a spouse.

Although theoretically, it would be appropriate to recite Kaddish for the entire twelve-month mourning period, Rema records that it is customary to recite Kaddish for only eleven months. He explains that since it is taught: "The judgment of the wicked [*resha'im*] lasts twelve months" (Eduyot 2:10), it would be disrespectful to treat one's parents as *resha'im*.[46] Some mourners continue reciting *Kaddish DeRabbanan* for the entire twelve months, as even one whose parents are alive may theoretically recite this. When reciting Kaddish for someone other than a parent, one recites Kaddish for the entire twelve months.[47]

In certain cases, there may be no one who is able to recite Kaddish for the deceased, or a mourner may be unable to commit to the rigors of thrice-daily attendance at *minyan*. The *Aḥaronim* discuss whether, and under what circumstances, one may pay another to recite Kaddish on his behalf.[48] One should consider whether greater benefit for the deceased may be accrued through charity and Torah study rather than merely appointing another to recite Kaddish.

## REASONS FOR THE *KADDISH YATOM*

Despite the fact that it is a relatively recent custom, i.e., approximately eight hundred years old, *Kaddish Yatom* undoubtedly plays a central role in per-

46. See Rema, *Yoreh De'ah* 376:4.
47. *Gesher HaḤayim* 30:9.
48. See *Beit Yosef, Yoreh De'ah* 403; *Magen Avraham, Oraḥ Ḥayim* 132:2. Some *Aḥaronim* write that it may be preferable to pay another to recite Kaddish rather than to just ask that person.

sonal mourning and communal prayer. What is the reason for the practice of reciting Kaddish? More specifically, what is the relationship between Kaddish and *avelut*?

The *Aḥaronim* offer numerous explanations for this practice. It appears that the recitation of Kaddish is perceived as aiding the deceased and as being spiritually beneficial and religiously uplifting for the mourner.

Some suggest that the recitation of Kaddish fulfills the talmudic principle: The son causes merit for the father [*bera mezakei abba*] (Sanhedrin 104a). The child is an extension of the parent, who is partially responsible, and consequently rewarded, for his good deeds. In that manner, the merit of reciting the Kaddish and publicly sanctifying the name of God greatly benefits the deceased.[49] Similarly, R. Moshe Sofer explains that it is not the recitation of Kaddish that benefits the deceased; rather, it is the response from the congregation: *Amen yehe shemeh rabba,* or: *Barukh Hashem hamevorakh leolam va'ed.*[50]

Others view the recitation of Kaddish as a form of acceptance and justification of God's judgment [*tziduk hadin*]. R. Chaim b. Betzalel (1520–1588), brother of Maharal of Prague, explains that as death in this world is related to sin, and especially to the sin of desecrating God's name, the recitation of Kaddish, which exalts and sanctifies God's name, brings about atonement.[51] In a similar vein, R. Yechiel Michel Tukachinsky, in his *Gesher HaḤayim,*[52] explains that the mourner may be inclined to question God's ways. The Kaddish is an affirmation of his belief in God's ways, "That all of His ways are true and just."

Interestingly, R. Soloveitchik focuses on the message that the mourner proclaims with the recitation of Kaddish:[53]

> The Kaddish marks the beginning of a new phase of courageous and heroic mourning to which the message of salvation is addressed… Through the Kaddish we hurl defiance at death and its fiendish conspiracy against man. When the mourner recites: "Glorified and

49. See *Gesher HaḤayim* 30:4:1.
50. Ḥatam Sofer, *Oraḥ Ḥayim* 1:159.
51. *Sefer HaḤayim* 2:8.
52. *Gesher HaḤayim,* ibid.
53. R. Yosef Dov Soloveitchik, *Out of the Whirlwind,* p. 5.

> sanctified be the Great Name," he declares: No matter how powerful death is, notwithstanding the ugly end of man, however terrifying the grave is, however nonsensical and absurd everything appears, no matter how black one's despair is and how nauseating an affair life is, we declare and profess publicly and solemnly that we are not giving up, that we are not surrendering, that we will carry on the work of our ancestors as though nothing has happened, that we will not be satisfied with less than the full realization of the ultimate goal – the establishment of God's kingdom, the resurrection of the dead, and eternal life for man.

Kaddish does not relate to the deceased, or to the death, but rather to the mourner's emergence from despair and sorrow.

Some *Aḥaronim* emphasize that reciting Kaddish is not the only means of properly commemorating and praying for the soul of the departed. For example, R. Joseph Yospa Hahn (d. 1637), in his *Yosef Ometz,*[54] writes:

> The matter of *Kaddishim* and *Barekhu* and *Lamenatze'aḥ* and *Birkat HaMazon* for mourners is well known, that [the deceased] are raised through [their recitation]... however, this method is only for the *amei haaratzot* (the uneducated). Torah study, however, works seventy times more than any prayer, and through this, one brings the deceased into *Gan Eden.* If the child can produce Torah novellae, then there is no estimating the honor the parent receives in the world above.

In this context, we should note that R. Shlomo Ganzfried (1804–1886), in his *Kitzur Shulḥan Arukh,* writes:[55]

> Though Kaddish and prayers are helpful to the departed, they are not of primary importance. What is most essential is that their children proceed in the path of righteousness and, in that manner, bring merit to their parents... A person should command his children to be scrupulous in the observance of a particular mitzva. Their practice of it will be considered more important than their recitation of Kaddish.

54. *Yosef Ometz,* p. 331.
55. *Kitzur Shulḥan Arukh* 26:22.

While Kaddish is often perceived as the primary form of both commemorating and elevating the soul of the deceased, one should view the entire mourning period as an opportunity to enhance one's faith and commitment to mitzvot, study Torah, and engage in acts of charity and kindness, which are all appropriate and effective means of commemorating the death of a loved one.

## LEADING THE PRAYER SERVICE

It is proper, if possible, for the mourner to serve as the *sheliaḥ tzibbur*, i.e., to lead the prayer service, for the period during which the Kaddish is recited. In fact, as mentioned above, the Mourner's Kaddish was originally instituted for children, who were unable to lead the services, especially *Barekhu*, Kaddish, and *Kedusha*. One who is incapable of leading the entire morning service (Shaḥarit) should lead the last part, from *Ashrei* through the final Kaddish.[56]

Although the laws regulating precedence in reciting Kaddish are no longer relevant, as in most communities all of the mourners recite Kaddish together, they are relevant with regard to leading the prayers. The *Aḥaronim* write that a mourner observing *shiva* takes precedence over all others. A mourner observing *sheloshim* takes precedence over others, except for one observing *shiva*. A mourner reciting Kaddish on the final day of the period of his reciting Kaddish, and a mourner observing *yahrzeit*, take precedence over those observing the twelve-month period of mourning.[57] One should take special care to avoid allowing the right to lead the service to be a source of contention.

It is customary for the mourner not to lead the service on Shabbat or Yom Tov.[58] On Rosh Ḥodesh, the mourner may lead the service until Hallel is recited; a non-mourner leads the congregation in Hallel and Musaf. When there is no one else better qualified to serve as the *sheliaḥ tzibbur*, a mourner may lead the services. This is especially relevant on Rosh HaShana and Yom Kippur.[59] In some communities, the mourner does not lead the services on days when *Lamenatze'aḥ* is omitted, i.e., Rosh Ḥodesh, Ḥanukka, Purim, and Erev Pesaḥ;[60] this custom is especially prevalent among Hasidim.

---

56. Rema, *Yoreh De'ah* 376:4.
57. See, for example, *Biur Halakha* 132.
58. Rema, ibid.
59. See Shakh, *Yoreh De'ah* 376:14.
60. See *Biur Halakha*, ibid.

*Chapter 14*

# The *Yahrzeit*

It is customary to mark the anniversary of the death of a parent each year.[1] This date is commonly known as the *yahrzeit*. One may observe the *yahrzeit* of other close relatives as well. There are many customs associated with this day, including reciting Kaddish, fasting, visiting the grave, lighting a *ner neshama*, leading communal prayers, studying Torah, and engaging in acts of charity and kindness.

The commentaries and halakhic works devoted to the laws of mourning cite various reasons for observing the *yahrzeit*. Some suggest that these customs are designed to benefit the soul of the deceased. Others insist that they are for the sake of the relatives. The *yahrzeit* is certainly an appropriate occasion to remember, express appreciation for, and learn from the qualities and attributes of the deceased. The first *yahrzeit* also marks the end of the twelve-month mourning period and is often accompanied by the *hakamat matzeva*.

1. Rema, *Yoreh De'ah* 376:4.

**CALCULATING THE *YAHRZEIT***

The *yahrzeit* is observed on the anniversary of the death of a parent or of another close relative.[2] Although one may observe the *yahrzeit* of a spouse, if he has remarried, he should be sensitive to the feelings of his new partner.[3]

The *Aḥaronim* discuss when to observe the first *yahrzeit*. As mentioned previously, the twelve-month mourning period ends exactly twelve months after the burial, i.e., the calendrical day *before* the one-year anniversary of the burial. Therefore, if the parent passed away, and was buried on the twentieth of Ḥeshvan, mourning concludes on the nineteenth of Ḥeshvan. If, however, the parent passed away on the nineteenth of Ḥeshvan, and was buried on the twenty-first of Ḥeshvan, mourning concludes on the twentieth of Ḥeshvan.

R. Binyamin Aaron Salnik (Poland, 1550–1620), in his *Masat Binyamin*,[4] rules that the first year, the *yahrzeit* should be observed on the anniversary of the burial. He argues that if the mourner observes the *yahrzeit* on the anniversary of the death, he might mistakenly stop observing the mourning practices of the twelve months prematurely. R. David HaLevi Segal, in his commentary on the *Shulḥan Arukh*, the *Taz*, disagrees, and rules that even the first *yahrzeit* should be observed on the anniversary of the death. While Shakh[5] agrees, he suggests that if the burial occurred three or four days after the death, one should observe the first *yahrzeit* on the anniversary of the burial.[6] Certainly, if the death occurred during a leap year, everyone would agree that the *yahrzeit* is observed on the anniversary of the death, even though the twelve-month mourning practices concluded a month earlier.[7]

---

2. *Shulḥan Arukh, Oraḥ Ḥayim* 568:8. Although Rema (*Yoreh De'ah* 402:12) implies that one who was present at the burial observes that day, i.e., the anniversary of the burial, as the *yahrzeit*, the *Aḥaronim* (see *Taz* 9; Shakh 10) rule that the anniversary of the death is always observed as the *yahrzeit*.
3. *Sefer Kol Bo al Avelut* 5:4:34; see also *Tzitz Eliezer* 8:34.
4. *Masat Binyamin* 84.
5. Ibid.
6. It is not clear whether Shakh refers to two days, i.e., the third day, or three days after the death. See *Penei Barukh* 39:35 and n. 94.
7. *Pitḥei Teshuva* 3.

It is customary and proper to observe the *yahrzeit*, even the first year, on the anniversary of the death, and to be careful to observe the twelve-month mourning practices until the anniversary of the burial.[8]

*Gesher HaḤayim*[9] writes that if the death occurred during twilight, i.e., between sunset and nightfall [*bein hashemashot*], and the mourner is uncertain on which day to observe the *yahrzeit*, the day that just concluded or the day that just began, the *yahrzeit* should be observed on the first day. R. Moshe Feinstein[10] rules that since the person was certainly alive on the first day, the mourner should observe the *yahrzeit* on the second day.

If the date of death is unknown, one should observe the *yahrzeit* on the day of interment. When does one who does not know the date that his parent died observe his *yahrzeit*? R. Moshe b. Avraham of Przemysl, in his *Mateh Moshe*,[11] cites his teacher, Maharshal, who rules that one should simply choose a day and designate it as the *yahrzeit*. R. Yitzchak Weiss,[12] in a responsum dedicated to determining whether those whose parents perished in the Holocaust could arbitrarily choose the days on which to observe *yahrzeit*, writes that one should not choose the same day for his father and mother unless he has reason to believe that they died on the same day.

If the death occurred on one day, but the mourners were in a place where, due to time differences, it was the next day or the previous day, when should the *yahrzeit* be observed? *Gesher HaḤayim* rules that one observes the *yahrzeit* according to the date where the death occurred.[13] In any case, the children of the deceased should not observe different days of *yahrzeit*, especially at the conclusion of the first year of mourning.

The *Aḥaronim* discuss some complicated scenarios.

---

8. See *Mishna Berura* 568:44; *Yalkut Yosef, Avelut* 40:4. *Gesher HaḤayim* (32:8) writes that if the burial was three or four days after the death, many are accustomed to observe the first *yahrzeit* on the anniversary of the burial; see also *Iggerot Moshe, Yoreh De'ah* 3:160.
9. *Gesher HaḤayim* 32:12.
10. *Iggerot Moshe, Yoreh De'ah* 3:159.
11. *Mateh Moshe* 767, cited by *Magen Avraham* (568:20) and *Mishna Berura* (568:42).
12. *Minḥat Yitzḥak* 1:83.
13. *Gesher HaḤayim* 32:14. *Sefer Kol Bo al Avelut* (p. 396) suggests that this may depend upon whether the *yahrzeit* is for the benefit of the deceased or the mourner.

If a parent dies during the month of Adar in a regular year, when does one observe the *yahrzeit* during a leap year? While *Shulḥan Arukh*[14] rules that one observes the *yahrzeit* during the second month, II Adar, Rema notes that it is customary to observe the *yahrzeit* and fast during I Adar.[15] He adds, however, that some are stringent and fast during both months.[16] The custom is not to fast during both months.[17] If a parent dies in II Adar of a leap year, the *yahrzeit* is observed in II Adar in future leap years as well.[18]

If one's parent dies on Rosh Ḥodesh Kislev or Rosh Ḥodesh Tevet, in a year when there is only one day of Rosh Ḥodesh that month, then in future years, when there are two days of Rosh Ḥodesh the *yahrzeit* is observed on the second day of Rosh Ḥodesh, i.e., on the first of Kislev or the first of Tevet. If, however, one's parent dies on the first of two days of Rosh Ḥodesh Kislev, i.e., on the thirtieth of Ḥeshvan, or on the first of two days of Rosh Ḥodesh Tevet, i.e., on the thirtieth of Kislev, there is a debate regarding when the *yahrzeit* should be observed.

Some *Aḥaronim* maintain that the *yahrzeit* should always be observed on the day Rosh Ḥodesh is observed, even in a year where there is only one day of Rosh Ḥodesh, i.e., the first of the month. The day's identity as "Rosh Ḥodesh" determines the day of the *yahrzeit*.[19] Others maintain that the *yahrzeit* date in future years is determined by the date of the first *yahrzeit*. Therefore, if the first *yahrzeit* occurs in a year when there are two days of Rosh Ḥodesh, and is therefore observed on the first day of Rosh Ḥodesh (the last day of the previous month), the *yahrzeit* is forever observed on Rosh Ḥodesh, which, depending on the year, will either be the thirtieth day of the previous month (in years when there are two days of Rosh Ḥodesh), or the first of the next month (in years when there is only one day of Rosh Ḥodesh). If the first *yahrzeit* occurs in a year when there was only one day of Rosh Ḥodesh, the *yahrzeit* is observed on the last day of the previous

---

14. *Shulḥan Arukh, Oraḥ Ḥayim* 568:7; see also Ḥatam Sofer, *Oraḥ Ḥayim* 163.
15. See *Terumat HaDeshen* 294.
16. See Mahari Weil, *Dinin VeHalakhot* 5. *Mishna Berura* (42) writes that it is preferable for one to fast on both days, although if that is too difficult, it is customary to fast during I Adar.
17. See *Gesher HaḤayim* 32:10.
18. Rema, ibid.
19. See *Shaarei Teshuva* 568:16; *Arukh HaShulḥan, Oraḥ Ḥayim* 568:15; *Iggerot Moshe, Yoreh De'ah* 3:159.

month, and in future years the *yahrzeit* is observed on the last day of the month that is not Rosh Ḥodesh. Many *Aḥaronim* appear to accept this view.[20]

## *YAHRZEIT* CUSTOMS

### Mourning on the *Yahrzeit*

R. Yisrael Isserlin[21] writes that although the twelve months of mourning conclude the day before the anniversary of the death and burial (provided that they were on the same day), one observes the mourning practices on the first anniversary of the day of the parent's death as well. He explains that since it is customary to fast and recite Kaddish on the *yahrzeit*, one should also observe the mourning restrictions of the twelve months of mourning.

Rema[22] cites this practice. *Taz*[23] writes that although his father-in-law, *Baḥ*,[24] maintained that this would apply only if the *yahrzeit* occurs immediately after the conclusion of the twelve-month mourning period, it is customary to observe the laws of the twelve-month mourning period every year on the anniversary of a parent's death. Therefore, on the night of the *yahrzeit* one should not get married or participate in a wedding meal.[25] Some limit this stringency to especially festive meals, e.g., a wedding meal, but one may attend a meal in honor of a *Brit Mila*, a *siyum*, or other social gatherings.[26] When there are extenuating circumstances, one may be lenient.

### Fasting

The Talmud[27] mentions the ancient custom of observing the anniversary of a parent's death.

> Which is the vow of prohibition [*issar*] mentioned in the Torah? It is a case where one said: I hereby declare that I will not eat meat

---

20. See *Magen Avraham, Oraḥ Ḥayim* 568:20; *Mishna Berura* 568:42; see also *Gesher HaḤayim* 32:11.
21. *Terumat HaDeshen* 292; see also *Leket Yosher* p. 98.
22. Rema, *Yoreh De'ah* 395:3.
23. Ibid., 3.
24. See also Shakh, ibid., 3.
25. See Rema, ibid., 391:3, 402:12.
26. *Pitḥei Teshuva* 391:8. *Ḥokhmat Adam* (171:11) appears to prohibit a *seudat Brit Mila* as well.
27. Nedarim 12a.

> and I will not drink wine today like the day his father died, or like the day his teacher died.

The Gemara relates that there was a custom not to eat meat or drink wine on the *yahrzeit* of a parent.[28]

A custom to fast on the *yahrzeit* of a parent developed during the Middle Ages. The commentaries disagree as to whether the fast is for the benefit of the mourner or the deceased. R. Yehuda HeChasid (1140–1217), in his *Sefer Ḥasidim*,[29] writes:

> Regarding fasting on the day upon which one's father died, [King] David fasted for Saul (II Sam. 1:12) because he called him "my father" (I Sam. 24:11), and for Jonathan and Abner, because one fasts over the death of an important person… Alternatively, because a father and son are one being and it is appropriate for a child to express sorrow [over the death of their father].

R. Mordekhai Yoffe, in his commentary to the *Shulḥan Arukh*, the *Levush*,[30] suggests that since the day upon which one's father or mother dies is apparently not a fortuitous day [*re'a mazlei*], one should repent on that day. Elsewhere, he writes that the fast is for the benefit of the deceased.[31] The *Kitzur Shulḥan Arukh*[32] writes: "It is a meritorious practice to fast on the anniversary of the death of one's father or mother as an incentive to repent and engage in self-introspection. By doing this one obtains divine grace for one's father and mother in heaven."

Although R. Yosef Colon[33] suggests that if the *yahrzeit* coincides with Shabbat or Yom Tov, the fast is observed the following day, Rema[34] rules that if the *yahrzeit* coincides with a day on which *Taḥanun* is omitted, one does not fast. Furthermore, those actively participating in a *Brit Mila*, i.e.,

28. Elsewhere, the Talmud (Bava Batra 60b) relates that some Jews refrained from eating meat and drinking wine in mourning for the destruction of the Temple.
29. *Sefer Ḥasidim* 231.
30. *Levush, Yoreh De'ah* 402:12.
31. Ibid., *Oraḥ Ḥayim* 785; see also Ḥatam Sofer 1:161.
32. *Kitzur Shulḥan Arukh* 221:1.
33. Cited in *Beit Yosef, Oraḥ Ḥayim* 568.
34. Ibid.

the father, *mohel*, or *sandak*; or in a *Pidyon HaBen*, i.e., the father or Kohen; as well as a bride and groom during the seven festive days following their wedding, should not fast.[35]

Some *Aḥaronim* write that if one fasts on the first *yahrzeit* this practice could attain the legal status of a vow [*neder*], unless he stipulates that he does not wish the practice to be binding in the future.[36] If one is unable to fast one year but does not intend to dissolve the vow, there is no need for a *hatarat nedarim*.[37]

The day before the fast, at Minḥa, one should accept upon himself to fast the next day, as one does for every individual fast [*taanit yaḥid*].[38] One should recite, or at least have in mind: "I intend to fast tomorrow [*hareini betaanit maḥar*]," after reciting the *Shemoneh Esreh* prayer, before or during *Elokai Netzor*.[39] If he forgot to recite this or to have it in mind during the Minḥa prayer, he may do so anytime during the afternoon.[40] If he fasts every year, this acceptance is unnecessary.

*Shulḥan Arukh*[41] cites the custom to fast on a parent's *yahrzeit*, and Rema[42] writes: "It is a mitzva to fast on the day on which one's father or mother died." However, some *Aḥaronim* note that in recent years it has become less common to fast, and those who feel weak do not fast.[43] Some are accustomed to finish the study of a tractate of the Talmud and participate in a *seudat mitzva*, and to engage in acts of kindness.[44] R. Yechiel Michel

35. See *Pitḥei Teshuva* 391:4–5.
36. See Rema, *Yoreh De'ah* 402:12; see also *Kitzur Shulḥan Arukh* 221:1; *Gesher HaḤayim* 32:7. R. Ovadia Yosef writes that the fast becomes a binding vow only after three times (*Yalkut Yosef* 40:17). He adds that while one who cannot fast once, due to being sick, need not perform *hatarat nedarim*, one who wishes to dissolve the vow must perform *hatarat nedarim*; see *Pitḥei Teshuva*, ibid., 8.
37. See *Dagul Merevava, Yoreh De'ah* 214; see also *Yalkut Yosef* 40:18.
38. See Taanit 12a; *Shulḥan Arukh, Oraḥ Ḥayim* 562:5.
39. *Shulḥan Arukh, Oraḥ Ḥayim* 362:5.
40. See *Baḥ*, as cited by *Magen Avraham* (ibid., 12).
41. See *Shulḥan Arukh, Oraḥ Ḥayim* 568:1, 7, and *Yoreh De'ah* 376:4.
42. Rema, *Yoreh De'ah* 376:4, 402:12.
43. See *Minḥat Yitzḥak* 6:135; see also *Nitei Gavriel* 72:1. If the fast will severely hinder one's ability to function, or to work (*Tzeror HaḤayim* 245), or if he is a teacher and will not be able to teach properly (*Ben Ish Ḥai, Shana Sheniya, Parashat Ki Tetzeh* 23), he need not fast. Even then, one should refrain from eating meat and drinking wine (*Yesodei Semachos*, p. 135).
44. See *Piskei Teshuvot* 568:7; see also *Gesher HaḤayim* 32:7.

Epstein, in his *Arukh HaShulḥan*,[45] writes: "One who has difficulty fasting may redeem the fast with money and distribute it to the poor." Indeed, some Hasidim share liquor and cake with the congregation after Shaḥarit, during which blessings are recited and people wish each other, and the son, *leḥayim*.[46] In any case, one should dedicate the *yahrzeit* to introspection and repentance, facilitating the ascent of the soul of the deceased further into *Gan Eden*.

### *Yahrzeit* Candle

As discussed previously, it is customary during *shiva* to light a candle in the place where the deceased passed away, or where the relatives are observing *shiva*.[47] It is also customary to light a candle in memory of the deceased on Yom Kippur eve,[48] and some light one on the last day of Pesaḥ, on Shavuot, and on Shemini Atzeret,[49] i.e., the days on which the *Yizkor* prayer is recited.

In addition, R. Shlomo Luria mentions that it was customary in all the lands of Ashkenaz to light a candle on the anniversary of the day on which one's mother or father died.[50] The *Aḥaronim* provide reasons for this practice. Ostensibly, it is related to the verses: "The soul of man is the candle of the Lord" (Prov. 20:27), and: "For the commandment is a lamp, and the teaching is light" (Prov. 6:23). The soul is likened to a candle, which evokes both God and the Torah. The eternity and sanctity of the soul are a source of comfort for the mourner.

The candle remains lit for more than twenty-four hours. If one does not have a candle or is unable to light one, he should light an electric lamp

---

45. *Arukh HaShulḥan, Yoreh De'ah* 376:13.
46. *Minḥat Yitzḥak* 6:135.
47. *Shibbolei HaLeket, Hilkhot Semaḥot* 21.
48. *Orḥot Ḥayim, Erev Yom HaKippurim* 11; Rema, *Oraḥ Ḥayim* 610:2; see also *Mishna Berura* 610:12.
49. The *Aḥaronim* discuss whether one may light the *ner neshama* on Yom Tov. The *Shulḥan Arukh* (*Oraḥ Ḥayim* 514:5) rules that one should not light a candle on Yom Tov that serves no purpose. See *Biur Halakha* (s.v. *ner shel batala*), who cites the opinion of those who justify lighting a *ner neshama* to honor one's parents. It is preferable to light the candle before Yom Tov.
50. Maharshal 46. R. Luria rules that if one forgot to light the *ner neshama* before Shabbat, one may ask a non-Jew to light it during twilight [*bein hashemashot*]; see *Magen Avraham* 262:6. This custom is also cited in *Minhagei Vermaysa* (Mifal Toras Chachmei Ashkenaz, Machon Yerushalayim, 1992) vol. 2, p. 112.

designated for this purpose.[51] While on Yom Kippur it is customary to light one *ner neshama* for both parents, some suggest that one who observes *yahrzeit* for both parents on one day should kindle two lights.[52]

### Visiting the Cemetery on the *Yahrzeit*

There is an ancient practice of visiting graves, especially the graves of the righteous. For example, the Gemara relates that Calev ben Yefuneh went to pray at the graves of the Patriarchs, in Hebron, during the mission of the spies [*meraglim*].[53] Furthermore, the Talmud relates that one of the sages went to pray at the grave of R. Ḥiyya.[54]

Rema records that some are accustomed to pray at graves on the day before Rosh HaShana.[55] Some explain that a cemetery is the resting place of the righteous and is therefore particularly conducive to prayer.[56] Others explain that the souls of the deceased beseech God on behalf of the Jewish people.[57] The *Aḥaronim* discuss whether praying at the graves of the righteous violates the biblical prohibition of necromancy (Deut. 18:11).[58]

There are authorities who raise numerous objections to this practice. They cite Rambam, who appears to oppose visiting cemeteries. He writes:

---

51. Some *Aḥaronim* (*Yesodei Semachos*, p. 137) write that one may use a movable electric lamp, based upon the ruling of R. Yitzchak Shmelkis (*Beit Yitzḥak, Yoreh De'ah* 1:120:5), who permits using electric lights for Shabbat candles. Some *Aḥaronim* (see, for example, *Mishneh Halakhot* 5:70) maintain that electric lights may not be used.
52. *Sefer Kol Bo al Avelut*, p. 398.
53. Sota 34b.
54. Bava Metzia 85b; see also Taanit 23b.
55. Rema, *Oraḥ Ḥayim* 581:4; *Magen Avraham* 16; see also Rema 559:10.
56. *Mishna Berura* 581:27, citing Maharil, *Hilkhot Taanit*.
57. *Mishna Berura* 559:41.
58. R. Yechiel Michel Tukachinsky addresses this in his *Gesher HaḤayim* (29:9). He first suggests that one prays to God, and wishes that due to the merits of the deceased his prayers will be answered. He adds that one may request that the deceased serve as a righteous advocate [*melitz yosher*]. Some even suggest that one may directly request from the deceased to petition God (*Gesher HaḤayim*, ibid.; *Minḥat Elazar, Oraḥ Ḥayim* 1:68; Maharam Schick, *Oraḥ Ḥayim* 293; see also Sota 34a).

> One marks graves and places a tombstone on the grave. For the righteous, one does not place a tombstone, because their words are their memorial; a person need not visit the graves.[59]

Furthermore, Rambam writes: "A person may not walk within four cubits of a grave with *tefillin* in his hand or a Torah scroll in his arm, and he should not pray there; but at a distance of four cubits, it is permitted."[60] Praying at a gravesite, accordingly, would be inappropriate. To this day halakhic authorities debate whether or not visiting and praying at the graves of the righteous should be encouraged, condoned, or discouraged.

Some visit the graves of their parents at the conclusion of the *shiva, sheloshim*, and the twelve-month mourning period, as well as on subsequent *yahrzeits*. This custom can be traced to the geonic era[61] and is cited by halakhic authorities.[62] Some also visit cemeteries on the days preceding Rosh HaShana, Yom Kippur, and on Tisha B'Av.[63] One should not expend great effort or incur great expense to visit a parent's gravesite.

When visiting a relative's gravesite, if one has not seen Jewish graves for thirty days, the following blessing is recited.[64]

> Praised be the Lord, our God, the Ruler of the Universe, who created you in judgment, who maintained and sustained you in judgment, and brought death upon you in judgment; who knows the deeds of every one of you in judgment, and who will hereafter restore you to life in judgment. Praised be the Lord who will restore life to the dead.

In addition, it is customary to recite several prayers, including seven chapters of Psalms (33, 16, 17, 72, 91, 104, and 130), as well as the passages

---

59. Rambam, *Hilkhot Avel* 4:4; see Radbaz for an alternative explanation.
60. Ibid, 14:13; see also *Shulḥan Arukh, Yoreh De'ah* 367:3.
61. See *Teshuvot R. Natronai Gaon* (ed. Brody), *Yoreh De'ah* 291; see also *Torat HaAdam, Inyan HaHesped.*
62. See Rashi (Yevamot 122a, s.v. *telata*) and *Shulḥan Arukh* (ibid., 344:20) regarding the anniversary of the death of a Torah scholar. R. Yisrael Lipschitz (1782–1860), in his commentary to the Mishna, *Tiferet Yisrael* (Eduyot 2:76), writes: "It is proper to go to the grave of one's parents on the *yahrzeit*." See also *Gesher HaḤayim* 32:5.
63. See Rema, *Oraḥ Ḥayim* 581:4, 605:1, 559:10.
64. *Shulḥan Arukh, Oraḥ Ḥayim* 224:12; *Mishna Berura* 17.

corresponding to the name of the deceased from Psalms 119. The *El Maleh Raḥamim* prayer is recited, and if there is a *minyan,* one concludes with the Mourner's Kaddish.

One does not visit the grave of a close relative on Shabbat or Yom Tov. Similarly, it is customary not to visit the gravesite on Ḥol HaMo'ed or on Purim. There are different customs regarding the days upon which one does not recite *Taḥanun,* e.g., Rosh Ḥodesh, Ḥanukka, Erev Purim, Lag BaOmer, etc.[65] Although many refrain from visiting cemeteries during the month of Nissan, some will visit the grave of a close relative and say the relevant prayers upon conclusion of *shiva, sheloshim,* or the twelve-month period of mourning. In those cases, some omit *El Maleh Raḥamim.*[66]

## *Yahrzeit* in the Synagogue

On the Shabbat before the *yahrzeit,* the son of the deceased should receive an *aliya.*[67] In Ashkenazic communities, he is often called for *maftir,* and reads the *haftara.* Some lead the entire Shabbat service; others lead the Musaf prayer. It is also common for the son to lead the Maariv prayer on Motza'ei Shabbat. One should not serve as a *sheliaḥ tzibbur* on Shabbat, nor even during the week, if he does not know the proper tunes [*nusaḥ*] of the prayers. In some communities, the *El Maleh Raḥamim* prayer is recited at Minḥa.

On the *yahrzeit* itself, it is preferable that the son of the deceased lead the three daily prayers and recite Kaddish at every opportunity.[68] If the Torah is read on the day of the *yahrzeit,* he should be called to the Torah. In some communities, the *El Maleh Raḥamim* prayer is recited. One should avoid traveling before or on the day of the *yahrzeit* if that will prevent him from reciting Kaddish with a *minyan.* In extenuating circumstances, it is customary to ask a relative, or even to hire someone, to recite Kaddish on his behalf; the mourner should also dedicate at least part of the day to Torah study and/or the performance of good deeds.

---

65. See *Penei Barukh* 37:10.
66. There are different customs regarding visiting cemeteries during the month of Nissan. See, for example, *Melamed LeHo'il, Yoreh De'ah* 145; *Gesher HaḤayim* 29:5; *Penei Barukh* 37:11.
67. See *Magen Avraham* 282:18.
68. See Rema, *Yoreh De'ah* 376:4. He writes: "It is customary that on the day on which a person's father or mother died, he recites the Mourner's Kaddish, and if he knows how to lead the prayers, he leads the prayers as a *sheliaḥ tzibbur.*"

*Chapter 15*

# The Monument and Memorial Prayers

### THE GRAVESIDE MONUMENT

There is an ancient tradition of erecting a monument marking the grave. The Torah relates that when Rachel died: "Jacob erected a tombstone [*matzeva*] on her grave" (Gen. 35:20). The tombstone, referred to in the verse as *matzeva,* is also called *tziyun* (II Kings 23:17) and *nefesh* (Shekalim 2:5). The responsibility for erecting a monument, similar to the responsibility to tend to the burial, falls upon the family members.[1]

Some suggest that a monument ensures remembrance. Based upon this rationale, Rambam[2] writes:

> One marks graves and places a tombstone on the grave. For the righteous, one does not place a tombstone, because their words are their memorial; a person need not visit the graves.

1. See Rosh, Responsa 13:19; see also his commentary to Sanhedrin 6:2. R. Moshe Feinstein (*Iggerot Moshe,* ibid.) writes that one's children are obligated to erect a tombstone even if they were not left an inheritance.
2. *Hilkhot Avel* 4:4. See *Iggerot Moshe* (*Yoreh De'ah* 4:57) regarding the mitzva of erecting a monument in general, and the prevalent custom of marking the graves of great rabbis and *tzaddikim.*

Others explain that a tombstone is an expression of honor [*kavod*] for the deceased.[3] In addition, the grave is marked so that Kohanim can avoid passing over a grave and thereby becoming impure.[4]

There are different customs regarding the appropriate time to erect a tombstone. Some write that one should erect the stone immediately after the conclusion of *shiva*.[5] Some wait until after *sheloshim*,[6] while others wait until the conclusion of the twelve-month mourning period.[7] In America it is customary to wait twelve months before erecting a tombstone.

There is no standard formula to be recited at an unveiling. Often, several psalms (1, 15, 23, 90, 91, 103, and 121; and 16 on days when *Taḥanun* is not recited) are recited. *El Maleh Raḥamim*, Mourner's Kaddish (when there is a *minyan*), and eulogies often follow. One who has not visited a cemetery in over thirty days recites the special blessing.

## MEMORIAL PRAYERS

### *AV HARAḤAMIM* AND *EL MALEH RAḤAMIM*

Throughout the Middle Ages, many prayers were composed to commemorate communal and personal tragedies. Three of these prayers remain central to Ashkenazic liturgy: *Av HaRaḥamim*, *El Maleh Raḥamim*, and *Yizkor*.

*Av HaRaḥamim* was most likely composed after the First Crusade (1096), and first appears in a prayer book from the late thirteenth century. *Av HaRaḥamim* emphasizes the martyrs who were killed sanctifying God's name. There are a variety of customs regarding the recitation of *Av HaRaḥamim*; in most communities, it is recited every Shabbat, except on days of the year when *Taḥanun* would be omitted. Likewise, it is not recited

---

3. Rashba, Responsa 1:375.
4. The Talmud (Mo'ed Katan 5a) cites numerous sources for the obligation to mark graves:

   > R. Shimon b. Pazi said: Where is there an allusion in the Torah to the marking of graves? The verse states: "And one who sees the bone of a man will build a marker near it" (Ezek. 39:15)... R. Abbahu said: From here: "[And the leper]... shall cry: Impure, impure" (Lev. 13:45). This verse teaches that impurity cries out to the passerby and tells him: Remove yourself... Abaye said: "You shall not place an obstacle before the blind" (Lev. 19:14). R. Pappa said: "And He will say: Pave, pave, clear the way, remove the obstruction from the way of My people" (Is. 57:14).

5. See *Gesher HaḤayim* 28:2; *Sefer Kol Bo al Avelut*, p. 379.
6. *Nitei Gavriel* (68:1) cites sources for all of the prevalent customs.
7. *Beit Leḥem Yehuda* and R. Akiva Eiger, *Yoreh De'ah* 376.

on the Shabbat before Rosh Ḥodesh (*Shabbat Mevarekhim*). However, *Av HaRaḥamim* is said on each Shabbat during *Sefirat HaOmer*, the period between Pesaḥ and Shavuot, during which the Crusades occurred.

The *sheliaḥ tzibbur* recites *El Maleh Raḥamim*, a request that God welcome and protect the soul of the deceased.

> God, full of mercy, who dwells on high, grant fitting rest on the wings of the Divine Presence, in the heights of the holy and the pure, who shine like the radiance of heaven, to the soul of _____ son/daughter of _____ because I will give charity for the memory of his soul. Therefore, the Master of mercy will shelter him in the shadow of His wings forever, and bind his soul in the bond of life. The Lord is his heritage; and he will rest in peace on his resting place, and let us say: Amen.

*El Maleh Raḥamim* is first mentioned by R. Aaron Berekhiah of Modena, in his *Maavar Yabok* (1626), and appears in R. Yaakov Emden's *Siddur Beit Yaakov* (p. 268). Versions of this prayer were also composed to commemorate the Chmielnicki massacres of 1648–49, especially after the twentieth of Sivan was designated as a day of fasting and prayer. Nowadays, *El Maleh Raḥamim* is recited at the funeral, at memorial services, on the Shabbat before a *yahrzeit* (after the Torah Reading during Minḥa), and in the *Yizkor* prayers.

### YIZKOR

It is customary to recite another memorial prayer, *Yizkor*, on Yom Kippur, the last day of Pesaḥ, Shemini Atzeret, and Shavuot. Although *Yizkor* is only a custom, R. Betzalel Stern, in his *BeTzel HaḤokhma*,[8] writes:

> Remembering the Souls (*Yizkor*) is considered to be great and holy in the eyes of the people, and many are more meticulous with [*Yizkor*] than with the most severe mitzvot of the Torah. Honestly, it is appropriate to reinforce this custom, as it is a means of internalizing belief in reward and punishment and the eternity of the soul, and it also inspires people to repent.

What is the origin, and the nature, of this prayer?

8. *BeTzel HaḤokhma* 4:121.

There is an ancient tradition that prayer and charity atone for sins of the deceased.[9] There are expressions of this tradition in the Talmud[10] and in numerous midrashim. For example, the Sifri,[11] in discussing the beheaded calf [*egla arufa*], brought to atone for an unsolved murder, teaches:

> The Priests recite: "Atone for Your people of Israel, O Lord, [whom You have redeemed]" (Deut. 21:8). When it says: Atone for Your people, the reference is to those who are alive; [when it says:] Whom You have redeemed, the reference is to those who are dead.

*Beit Yosef*[12] quotes R. Shneur, who attributes the custom to pray for the deceased and give charity on their behalf to this midrash.

The *Midrash Tanḥuma*[13] cites this Sifri, and teaches that in addition to mentioning the deceased on Shabbat,

> Similarly, it is customary to remember the dead on Yom Kippur and to pledge a specific amount of *tzedaka* in their memory, as we learned in Sifri: "Atone for Your people of Israel" – these are the living; "whom You have redeemed" – these are the deceased. From here, we derive that the living redeem the dead. Could it be that once they have died, *tzedaka* will not help them? No, because the verse instructs us explicitly: Whom You have redeemed, from which it is derived that when a specific amount of money is pledged in their memory, they are taken from Gehinnom and raised as an arrow shot from a bow.

---

9. The earliest source is found in the Book of Maccabees (II Macc. 12:56–60). In response to discovering a sin committed by those killed in battle, the Jewish people "gave themselves to prayer, begging that the sin committed might be completely forgiven." In addition, Judah Maccabee "took a collection from [the soldiers] individually, amounting to nearly two thousand drachmas, and sent it to Jerusalem to have a sin offering sacrificed, an action altogether fine and noble, prompted by his belief in the resurrection... he had this expiatory sacrifice offered for the dead, so that they might be released from their sin."
10. Makkot 11a; Ḥagiga 15b; Sota 10b; see also Tosafot, s.v. *de'atei*.
11. Sifri, *Parashat Shofetim* 210.
12. Beit Yosef, *Oraḥ Ḥayim* 284. R. Avigdor, cited by *Beit Yosef*, does not accept R. Shneur's conclusion regarding charity.
13. *Midrash Tanḥuma, Parashat Haazinu.*

The *Tanḥuma* relates that it is customary to pledge *tzedaka* on Yom Kippur. Indeed, the original custom was to pledge *tzedaka* only on Yom Kippur. This pledge appears in numerous sources.[14] For example, R. Elazar of Worms, in Roke'aḥ,[15] relates that this was the custom on Yom Kippur, and asks:

> And how is it beneficial to the deceased that the living give charity on his behalf? Rather, God examines the hearts of the living and the deceased, and if this dead person, in his lifetime, would have given charity...Then it is somewhat beneficial as the living can attempt to lighten the judgment of the deceased.

Similarly, the *Mordekhai*[16] bases the custom to pledge charity on Yom Kippur on the Sifri cited above.

*Shulḥan Arukh*[17] writes: "It is customary to pledge *tzedaka* on Yom Kippur for the sake of the deceased." Rema adds: "We petition on behalf of the deceased, as the deceased also attain atonement." In his commentary to the *Tur, Darkhei Moshe,* Rema cites Mahari Weil, who explains that Yom Kippur is called *Yom Kippurim,* in plural, as both the living and deceased are forgiven.[18] He cites an additional reason to remember the deceased: remembering those who passed away breaks the spirit and humbles a person's heart, which is, of course, appropriate on Yom Kippur.[19]

Although the original custom did not include the other festivals, R. Mordekhai Yoffe, a younger contemporary of Rema, records the custom of reciting *Yizkor,* in which one pledges to give *tzedaka* in memory of the deceased, on festivals as well. He writes:[20]

> And [the reason] we petition for the deceased on the last day of Pesaḥ is because we want to give charity, as we read [in the Torah] *Parashat*

14. *Siddur Rashi* (214) reflects the original custom: [It is customary] to commit to give charity on behalf of the deceased in all of Ashkenaz only on that day (i.e., Yom Kippur). See also *Maḥzor Vitry* 355.
15. Roke'aḥ 217.
16. *Mordekhai,* Yoma 727.
17. *Shulḥan Arukh, Oraḥ Ḥayim* 621:6.
18. *Darkhei Moshe, Oraḥ Ḥayim* 621; Mahari Weil 191.
19. *Kol Bo* 70.
20. *Levush, Oraḥ Ḥayim* 490:9; see also 284:7, 621:6.

> *Kol HaBekhor*, in which it is written: "Each man according to the gift of his hand [*ish kematnat yado*]" (Deut. 16:17). And since we are already committed to give *tzedaka*, it is customary to give it as a memorial for the deceased, so that God should remember them, and as a result He also remembers us for good, and that is why we mention the deceased on all of the festivals upon which we read *Kol HaBekhor*.

In other words, while the purpose of reciting *Yizkor* on Yom Kippur is to ask forgiveness for the deceased, on Yom Tov, *Yizkor* is an outgrowth of the desire to commit to giving charity on Yom Tov.

While some question whether the recitation of *Yizkor* conflicts with the mitzva to rejoice on the festivals,[21] in fact, *Yizkor* might be a fulfillment of *simḥat Yom Tov*. The Torah teaches:

> You shall rejoice before the Lord your God, you and your son and your daughter... and the orphan and the widow who are in your midst. You shall remember that you were a slave in Egypt, and you shall observe and you shall perform these statutes. (Deut. 16:11–12)

Rejoicing with the less fortunate is an integral part of *simḥat Yom Tov*. Indeed, Rambam[22] writes:

> When one eats and drinks [in celebration of a holiday], he is obligated to feed the convert, the orphan, and the widow, with the miserable poor. However, one who locks the gates of his courtyard and eats and drinks, he, and his children, and his wife, and does not feed the poor and the embittered, that is not with the joy of a mitzva; rather, it is the rejoicing of his belly.

Pledging to give *tzedaka* is a fulfillment of the true nature and deepest meaning of *simḥat Yom Tov*, sharing and rejoicing with others. In that context, we

21. See, for example, *Peri Megadim, Eshel Avraham* 547:1.
22. Rambam, *Hilkhot Yom Tov* 6:18. See also *Hilkhot Megilla* (2:17), where he writes, "As there is no greater and more glorious joy than to cause the hearts of the poor, the orphans, the widows, and the converts to rejoice. One who brings joy to the hearts of these unfortunate individuals is similar to the Divine Presence, as it is stated (Is. 57:15): 'To revive the spirit of the humble and to revive the heart of the downtrodden.'"

pray for the souls of the deceased and hope that in keeping with the talmudic saying: The son causes merit for the father [*bera mezakei abba*] (Sanhedrin 104a), the merit of the child's charitable actions benefits the deceased.

It is important to emphasize that the original and central component of *Yizkor* is the pledge to give *tzedaka*, and therefore, even if one stipulates, by adding the disclaimer *beli neder*, that the pledge should not have the status of a vow, one should make certain to give *tzedaka* the next day.

### Reciting *Yizkor* during the First Year of Mourning

Many have the custom not to recite *Yizkor* during the first year of mourning. R. Shlomo Ganzfried, in his *Kitzur Shulḥan Arukh*,[23] writes that it is customary for a mourner, during the first year, to leave the sanctuary and refrain from reciting *Yizkor*. *Sefer Kerem Shlomo*[24] cites two reasons for this practice. First, he suggests that since the deceased are themselves judged during the first year, they are unable to serve as righteous advocates [*melitzei yosher*] for their relatives. Second, he raises a concern that during the first year, when the loss is relatively recent, the mourner will be overcome with grief, which may distract others.

Many *Aḥaronim* insist that it is proper to recite *Yizkor* even during the first year of mourning.[25]

### Leaving the Sanctuary for *Yizkor*

In many congregations, it is customary for those whose close relatives are alive to leave the sanctuary during the recitation of *Yizkor*.

R. Efraim Zalman Margolis (1762–1828), in his *Shaarei Efraim*,[26] suggests that this may be due to *ayin hara*; standing alongside those reciting *Yizkor* draws attention to one's living parents (see Yevamot 106a).

On a more technical level, R. Margolis adds that this practice may be rooted in another interesting halakha. *Behag*[27] derives from a passage in the

23. *Kitzur Shulḥan Arukh* 133:21.
24. *Sefer Kerem Shlomo* 668.
25. See *Duda'ei Sadeh* 85; *Divrei Torah* 1:29; *BeTzel HaḤokhma* 4:121; *Iggerot Moshe, Yoreh De'ah* 4:61. See also *Gesher HaḤayim* (31:7), who writes: "It is obvious that even within the first year one remembers the deceased There were those who were hesitant… [but] they have already concluded [*nimnu vegameru*] that this custom has no reason or basis, and they actually have a greater need for prayer during the first year."
26. *Shaarei Efraim, Pitḥei She'arim* 1:32.
27. Cited in Rosh, Berakhot 3:14.

Talmud (Berakhot 20b) that if one enters a synagogue as the congregation is reciting *Shema,* he recites the first verse with them. *Shulḥan Arukh*[28] cites this passage in his ruling and explains that one recites that verse in order to avoid creating the impression that he does not wish to accept upon himself the yoke of Heaven. He adds that even if one finds the congregation reciting *divrei Taḥanunim* or *pesukim,* one should join them provided that he is at a place in his own prayers where it is permitted to interrupt. Some extend this to other central prayers as well.[29] R. Margolis asserts that it is inappropriate for part of the congregation to sit in silence while the rest of the congregation is reciting a specific prayer.

Some[30] raise a concern that a person who is not reciting *Yizkor* may become grief-stricken. While a person who is reciting *Yizkor* is permitted to feel sadness, similar to one who is troubled by a disturbing dream, who may fast even on Shabbat,[31] one who is not reciting *Yizkor* should not place himself in a situation that may lead to sadness and even crying on Yom Tov.

Others explain that those not reciting *Yizkor* may disturb those attempting to concentrate on the *Yizkor* prayer. Even if they do nothing that is overtly disruptive, their mere presence may be distracting.

In recent years many have noted that the phenomenon of people leaving before *Yizkor* is itself disruptive. In addition, there are *Yizkor* prayers that all congregants should recite, including prayers said for victims of the Holocaust, for Israeli soldiers killed in action, and for Jews martyred during terrorist attacks, as well as the aforementioned *Av HaRaḥamim.* Each community should determine whether or not to encourage those who are not reciting *Yizkor* to leave the sanctuary.[32]

Finally, *Yizkor* may be recited at home when circumstances prevent one from reciting it with a *minyan.*

---

28. *Shulḥan Arukh, Oraḥ Ḥayim* 65:2.
29. See *Magen Avraham,* ibid., 3; *Arukh HaShulḥan* 65:6.
30. *Minhagei Beit Yaakov* 125.
31. See *Shulḥan Arukh, Oraḥ Ḥayim* 288.
32. R. Eliezer Waldenberg, in his *Tzitz Eliezer* (12:39), writes: "God forbid that we should attempt to change these customs."

# Index

*The fonts used in this book are from the Arno family*

*Maggid Books*
*The best of contemporary Jewish thought from*
*Koren Publishers Jerusalem Ltd*